DUCIT AMOR PATRIÆ

Phillips

BENJAMIN DWIGHT PHILLIPS

MILDRED WELSHIMER PHILLIPS

B. D. PHILLIPS

LIFE AND LETTERS

By

JAMES DeFOREST MURCH

Memorial Edition

PUBLISHED PRIVATELY

MEMORIAL EDITION, DECEMBER 1969

Printed by
The Standard Printing Co., Inc.
Louisville, Kentucky, U.S.A.

Contents

33934

iii

Illustrations

Greystone Fireplace with Phillips Coat-of-Arms
Pipe Organ in Living Hall
Domestic Scenes of B. D. and Mildred Phillips taken at Butler
Phillips Pack Train Ready to Leave on Hunting Trip
Sheep Camp 500 Feet Below Timberline
Ram's Heads—Trophies of Wyoming Hunt
B. D. Phillips with Buck Antelope He Killed

Foreword

The two greatest blessings of my life have been to be the daughter of P. H. Welshimer and the wife of B. D. Phillips. To perpetuate their memories and the noble principles for which they stood is now my highest privilege and purpose.

I feel I can best perpetuate the memory of Mr. Phillips by sending forth this book. He was always so modest and so humble that the public never fully appreciated his success in the business world and his part in the development of the Restoration Movement which seeks to restore primitive Christianity. Here his life and work receive their due.

Because of his close friendship, deep understanding, and great appreciation of Mr. Phillips, I have asked Dr. James DeForest Murch to be the author of this volume.

Through this book I hope there will not only come a better appreciation of B. D. Phillips the man, but also an inspiration to young men seeking higher attainment in business and in the Christian ministry.

MILDRED WELSHIMER PHILLIPS

Author's Preface

It was a great privilege to know B. D. Phillips.

I first met him in 1923 when we were launching the Cincinnati Bible Institute (later merged with McGarvey Bible College to form Cincinnati Bible Seminary). I had heard of his concern for Christian education and for the perpetuity of the Restoration Movement and I felt he would be interested. In the midst of apostasy and educational declension we had undertaken a modest effort to train for the Christian ministry a new generation of young men who would be loyal to "the faith once for all delivered" and wholly committed to "the restoration of the New Testament Church in doctrine, ordinances, and life." When I arrived in Butler, Mr. Phillips took time from a busy day's schedule to see me and to hear my plea. He was particularly pleased to know we were patterning the new school after the old "Phillips Bible Institute" of Canton, Ohio (page 40). He gladdened my heart with a contribution of $2,500 for the young Institute.

As I grew to know him better I was increasingly amazed at the depth, the breadth, and the greatness of the man. One had to dig to find that greatness, for he himself was so humble and modest that the words power, authority, dignity, honor, wealth, and station seemed somehow out of place in thinking of him. He had a form of greatness which "dies and makes no sign." Lord Lytton said it of a man he knew, and it fits B. D. Phillips like a glove—

> That man is great, and he alone,
> Who serves a greatness not his own,
> For neither praise nor pelf:
> Content to know and be unknown:
> Whole in himself.

Mr. Phillips came to true greatness because he felt that his life was the beneficiary of a great family heritage and of the Christian faith that was theirs, and that it was a stewardship to be held in sacred trust and used for the benefit of mankind. He believed that what God gave him he must give to others. He sought first the approbation of God, then of his own conscience; after that, he was willing to abide by the opinion of his fellowman whatever that might be.

Mr. Phillips was known among his neighbors simply as "a good business man." To him business was the salt of life. He loved to work and he was busy early and late improving the time. His successes brought him immense satisfaction. He sought little more save in his family and in his religion. Public acclaim for any of his achievements or contributions was the least of his desires.

It often happens that such men are not widely known. That is why Mr. Phillips deserves a good biographer—a better one than I. However, I esteem it a high honor and privilege to have been chosen by the family for the task of telling his life story. They have all been most helpful and cooperative in giving me access to his personal papers and in sharing with me the memories and the intimate experiences of their lives. I trust that I may be able in some small way to extend the usefulness of this great man's example to many who were never fortunate enough to know him well. I pray this book may be something of a "gospel" that may be instructive, useful, and helpful to others; teaching high commitment, and high thinking, and inspiring energetic action in the great concerns to which B. D. Phillips gave his "last full measure of devotion."

JAMES DeFOREST MURCH

I

A Noble Family Heritage

B ENJAMIN DWIGHT PHILLIPS came of a noble and distinguished heritage. His family records reveal a genealogy*
reaching back in tradition to the twelfth century in England.

From *Dugdales Chronicles* it appears that the family had docu-
mented its beginnings with Thomas Phylyps, who was the Chief
Builder and Supervisor of Buildings in the Town and Marches of
Calais. The record further says:

> *Thomas Phylyps* had by his wife, the daughter of ———— Smith de Com.
> Somers, four sons, 1. *John*, whose descendants were of Corf. in Com. Dors;
> 2. *Thomas*, father to Sir Thomas Phillips, knighted at Whitehall, 23 July,
> 1603, who was created to the Dignity of a Baronet; 3. *Richard*; 4. *Edward*,
> who being brought up in the Study of Law, arrived at such a reputation
> therein, that he was elected one of the Serjeants at Law in the 45 Eliz. and
> on the 18th of May, 1 Jac. 1 made the King's Serjeant. Also, he was
> knighted at Whitehall, 23 July, 1603, before the Coronation of the King,
> and having serv'd in several Parliaments, was chosen speaker of the House
> of Commons in the first Parliament call'd, wherein he sate as one of the
> Knights for Somersetshire; after which he was constituted Master of the
> Rolls. . . .

---

*The author hereby acknowledges the painstaking work of Thomas W. Phillips,
Jr., in assembling and publishing the genealogical information which appears in
this chapter.

1

The first American ancestor of B. D. Phillips was the Rev. George Phillips, "the founder of the Congregational Church in America." The Rev. George Phillips was the son of Christopher Phillips, of Rainham, district of Gallow, county of Norfolk, England, and Wendell Phillips is authority for the statement that this family could be traced back to the twelfth century in England. Rev. George Phillips was born in 1593, and very early in life he gave indications of deep piety and love of learning. On April 20, 1610, at the age of seventeen, he entered Gonville and Caius College, Cambridge, where he became distinguished for his remarkable scholarship, being especially proficient in theological studies. He was graduated B.A. 1613, and M.A. 1617. After leaving the university he was settled in the ministry at Boxford, Suffolk County, but his strong attachment to the principles of the old Nonconformists soon brought him into difficulty, and, as the storm of persecution grew darker and more threatening, he decided to cast his lot with the Puritans who were about to depart for the New World. On April 12, 1630, he, with his wife, daughter of Richard Sergent, and their two children, Samuel and Elizabeth, embarked for America on the "Arbella" as fellow-passengers with Governor Winthrop, Sir Richard Saltonstall, and other assistants of the Massachusetts Company, arriving at Salem on June 12, 1630, where his wife very soon died. The Rev. George proceeded up the Charles River, and with others founded the settlement called Watertown, and was the greatly respected and beloved minister of the Watertown Church for fourteen years, until the time of his death, July 1, 1644. He was independent and conscientious in forming and maintaining his opinions and was renowned for his learning in the original languages of the Scriptures and in theological doctrines. His hearers counted him "The Irrefragable Doctor," and the historian says he was "mighty in the Scriptures and very diligent to search out the mind of Christ therein contained." He entertained more enlightened views of civil and religious liberty, or had a more just appreciation of it, than that which prevailed among the other planters of Massachusetts Bay, and had repeated theological controversies in which he was characterized by candor and Christian urbanity.

This great, good, and gifted man lived during the formative period of our history, was the earliest advocate of the Congregational order and discipline in which he was, says Hubbard, "deeply

2

versed and very skillful," and, with his ruling elder, Mr. Richard Browne, stood almost unaided and alone until the arrival of Mr. John Cotton in firmly maintaining what was, and still is, the Congregationalism of New England. He took a leading part in, and oftentimes an advanced position on civic affairs, and was upon one occasion put in jail by Governor Winthrop for advocating a plan of government which afterwards became what is known as Representative Government; that is, a form of government where the official is nominated and elected, not directly by the populace, but by their representatives, and this country is indebted more to him than to any other one man for our form of Representative Government. The tendency today to do away entirely with the form of Representative Government advocated by Rev. George Phillips and substitute therefor both nominations and elections of all officers by the direct vote of the populace is fraught with grave perils, for it opens the way for mob rule, making it possible for the demagogue to first rule, then ruin this Republic, and bring upon it the common fate of all the Republics of history.

Rev. George Phillips and his numerous progeny have had a remarkable influence on the religious, educational, and political developments of our country, for from him descended a long line of ministers, educators, philanthropists, judges, counselors, statesmen, soldiers, and the highest type of businessmen—"a sterling race, temperate, just, and high-minded."

Samuel, the eldest son of Reverend George, was also a minister and officiated repeatedly at the great public ceremonies which put in requisition the abilities of the first men in the New England colonies. Descendants of Rev. Samuel Phillips include his grandson, Rev. Samuel Phillips (born at Salem, 1689; died at Andover, 1771), who was pastor of the Andover Church without intermission from the date of his ordination, October 17, 1711, to the day of his death, June 5, 1771, an unbroken ministry at one church for almost sixty years, and who left more published discourses and tracts than any of his predecessors or contemporaries; Hon. Samuel and Judge Samuel Phillips, father and son, founders of Phillips Academy, Andover, Massachusetts; Hon. John Phillips, who joined with his brother and nephew in founding Phillips Academy, was the sole founder of Phillips Exeter Academy, Exeter, New Hampshire, and through his bequests was instrumental in the founding of Andover Theological Seminary; Lieutenant-Governor

William Phillips, of Boston, of whom it was said at the time of his death, in 1827, that "no man of wealth lived and died in this country who has, in proportion to his ability, done so much for the cause of charity"; Wendell Phillips, the great orator of the Abolitionist cause; and Phillips Brooks, the distinguished bishop of the Episcopal Church and renowned lecturer and writer. In the halls of the Andover and Exeter Academies and in Memorial Hall at Harvard may be seen upon the walls the portraits of various men and women of this family, every one of whom belongs among the untitled nobility of New England representing the best element of life there, not always that which dwells in the brightest glare of publicity but that which directs and shapes the current of public opinion.

As before stated, the first wife of Rev. George Phillips died at Salem very soon after landing. His second wife was Elizabeth Weldon, and their children were: Zerobabel, born at Watertown, Massachusetts, April 6, 1632, died at Southampton, Long Island, subsequent to 1689; Jonathan, born November 16, 1633, a magistrate of Watertown, lived on the homestead with his mother, died 1704, leaving numerous children; Theophilus, born May 28, 1636, lived at Watertown, and had more than a dozen children; Annabel, buried April 11, 1638, aged four months; Ephraim, born and died June, 1641; Obadiah, buried April 5, 164- ; Abigail, birth not recorded, married October 8, 1666, James Barnard, no children.

It will thus be seen that there were four sons surviving the Rev. George Phillips; namely, Samuel, Zerobabel, Jonathan, and Theophilus. Some of Samuel's descendants have been mentioned above. Jonathan's line is fully accounted for in local histories of Massachusetts, and the family history of Theophilus is recorded in a book written in 1885 by Albert M. Phillips, one of his descendants.

Zerobabel Phillips, above mentioned, the eldest son of Rev. George Phillips and Elizabeth Weldon Phillips, was born in 1632, and when sixteen years of age, four years after his father's death, moved to Southampton, Long Island, where he died subsequent to 1689. He was married three times; the name of his first wife is unknown, as there are no marriage records of Southampton extant of that time, but by this marriage he had a son Theophilus.

Zerobabel was the progenitor of the Maidenhead (New Jersey) Phillips family. The old town book of Maidenhead shows that

4

this family was more numerous than any other family in Maidenhead from its settlement down as far as the book runs. At one period Maidenhead was entitled to three freeholders, and the book shows on one occasion that all three of these freeholders were members of this family. This family has from generation to generation contained men of notable physical development, of independent and conscientious inclination in forming and maintaining their opinions, of great will power, and of exceptional tenacity of purpose.

The Maidenhead Phillips family enjoys the distinction of having the best military record of any family in the State of New Jersey. In the Colonial period this branch of the family was represented by Maj. Philip Phillips and Theophilus Phillips, and in the Revolutionary War by Capt. John Phillips, Col. Joseph Phillips, Capt. Philip Phillips, Capt. and Maj. Henry Phillips, in whose regiment were Edmund, Andrew, and Lott Phillips, Capt. Jonathan Phillips, Adj. Elias Phillips, Capt. and Maj. John Phillips, Samuel, Asher, and Ralph Phillips, Samuel and Asher being younger brothers of the three last-named officers. While many members of the Maidenhead branch of the Phillips family reside in New Jersey, some are located in various other sections of the country—in Pittsburgh, Pennsylvania, and other localities in western Pennsylvania, in the State of Ohio, in the West, and in the South.

Theophilus Phillips, above mentioned, son of Zerobabel Phillips, was born in Southampton, Long Island, in 1653, and died at Newtown, Long Island. He married in 1671 Ann, daughter of Ralph Hunt, a descendant of Thomas Hunt, a colonel in Cromwell's army, and had several children.

Theophilus Phillips, son of Theophilus and Ann Hunt Phillips, was born at Newtown, Long Island, May 15, 1672, died at Maidenhead, New Jersey, in 1709. (Maidenhead, both village and township, was changed to Lawrenceville and Lawrence, respectively, by an Act of the Legislature, Jan. 24, 1816.) In the year 1694 Theophilus Phillips and his cousin Ralph Hunt jointly purchased land at Maidenhead (the richest agricultural section of New Jersey), and were the founders of Maidenhead. Quickly following them came their kinsfolk Philip Phillips, younger brother of Theophilus Phillips, and Samuel and Edward Hunt, brothers of Ralph Hunt. In 1697 the settlers had become sufficiently numer-

5

ous to form a new township, and by 1698 religious worship was maintained. The children of Theophilus and his wife Frances were Theophilus, John, William, Joseph, Philip, Francis, and three daughters.

Judge Theophilus, son of Theophilus and Frances Phillips, was born in Maidenhead about 1695, and died there in 1762. He was Burgess of Trenton under King George's charter and judge of the Hunterdon County courts from 1723 to 1749. His first wife was Elizabeth Betts and his second wife was her sister, Abigail Betts. The Betts family were from Newtown, Long Island, and were very prominent in the early history of that region. His children were John, William, Richard, Joseph, Frances (married Edmund Bainbridge) and Keziah (married Capt. John Moore).

Capt. John Phillips, eldest son of Judge Theophilus and Elizabeth Betts Phillips, was born at Maidenhead, New Jersey, about 1721. He was an officer in the Continental line and captain of the First Regiment, Hunterdon County Militia, Revolutionary War, and was guide to Washington at the battle of Trenton. This regiment was in the brigade of General Dickinson and participated in the battles of Trenton, Assanpink, Princeton, Germantown, Springfield, and Monmouth. In 1760 he married Abigail Tindall, and their children were Thomas, Joseph, John, Theophilus, and William.

Thomas Phillips, eldest son of Capt. John and Abigail Tindall Phillips, was born at Maidenhead on a three-hundred-acre homestead, deeded February 3, 1752, to his father and uncle by their father, which homestead is still owned by a member of the Phillips family. The wife of Thomas Phillips was Catherine Phillips, who was not related to the "Maidenhead Phillips family," but was descended from Joseph Phillips, a Welshman, who with his wife and family came to Maidenhead about the year 1736, where he shortly afterwards died. Thomas Phillips and his wife moved to Hopewell, Hunterdon County, New Jersey. Their children were William, John, Elijah, Ephraim, Enoch, and Sarah (who married Joseph Moore).

Ephraim Phillips, born September 20, 1795, died December 20, 1835, fourth son of Thomas and Catherine (Phillips) Phillips, married Ann Newton of Philadelphia, Pennsylvania, who was born May 11, 1797, and died June 14, 1867. Ann Newton's parents were Ferdinand (born in England) and Ann Maria Tar-

6

pine Newton (born in Philadelphia, Pennsylvania). Ann Newton had three brothers and one sister, as follows: Joseph, Ebenezer, Isaac, and Sarah. In 1818 Ephraim, with his wife, Ann Newton Phillips, and their babe, Catherine, moved from New Jersey to western Beaver County, now Lawrence County, Pennsylvania, where he erected a fulling-mill and sawmill. Ten years later the family moved to a farm of one hundred acres near Mt. Jackson, a few miles north of Enon, where, in 1835, Ephraim Phillips died, survived by his widow and eight children, as follows: Catherine, born May 30, 1817; Isaac N., born July 19, 1820; Sarah M., born February 28, 1822; Ephraim, born February 23, 1824; John, born January 6, 1826; Mary Ann, born October 6, 1830; Charles M., born January 1, 1833, and Thomas W., who was born February 23, 1835, and died at New Castle, Pennsylvania, July 21, 1912, being in his seventy-eighth year. In 1862 he married Clarinda, daughter of David W. and Nancy Rebecca Arter Hardman. She died in 1866, leaving two sons, Herbert C. (1864-1912) and Norman A. (1865-1903). In 1870 he married Pamphila, a younger sister of his first wife, from which union there were three sons and one daughter: Victor K. (1872-1901), Thomas W. (1874-1956), Clarinda Grace (1877-), wife of Charles H. Johnson, and Benjamin Dwight (1885-1968).

Thomas W., son of Ephraim and Ann Newton Phillips, was a babe only ten months old at the time of his father's death. Both his father and mother were intensely, though sanely, religious, and early became identified with the great Restoration Movement, inaugurated about the year 1809 by Thomas and Alexander Campbell, which has changed the course of religious thought and has given the world a broader, fuller, and more rational conception of the word of God. His mother was a woman of exceptionally forceful character, who, holding the strictest ideas of honesty, taught her children that it was wrong to take even a pin that did not belong to them. Her homely virtues and the philosophical manner in which she faced problems and perplexities made an indelible impression upon her son Thomas. With eight children to raise on a farm encumbered by debt, Mrs. Phillips had a heavy burden to carry for many years, and under such circumstances her boys could not obtain the educational advantages that even under slightly more favorable circumstances would have been theirs.

The aptitude and desire for learning, however, was part of their inheritance, and Thomas supplemented the little education he could obtain at the district schools and from his older brothers, by earnest independent study. It is often the case that where a boy is driven to seek learning under great difficulty by the force of his own desire that he acquires a broader and more thorough knowledge than if fortune had made it possible for him to meander more or less aimlessly through a specific college curriculum. Thomas Phillips was, even in his teens, exceptionally well read in history, biography, and scientific literature, was the leading debater in the Mt. Jackson literary society, and had acquired a reputation as an original thinker. At the age of about fourteen years he accepted Jesus Christ as his Saviour and Lord, to whom he remained intensely loyal through all the vicissitudes of his long and eventful life. Many and severe were the trials through which he was called to pass, but neither prosperity nor adversity, ingratitude nor calumny dwarfed his noble instincts or turned him from his worthy ambitions. The Almighty, that "spake the world from naught, and guides the planets in their course," had, he knew, the power even to raise him up at the last day. He took his stand firmly and securely on God's promises, knowing that He could, believing that He would, fulfill every covenant made to those who trust and obey Him. He was ambitious; as a boy he had his castles in the air, many varied and fantastic, and when a man he looked forward through faith to what was more than a castle, a home whose maker and builder is God, the description of which transcends the language of man and the highest flights of human imagination, for "eye hath not seen, nor ear heard, neither have entered into the heart of man the things which God hath prepared for them that love him." He aspired to grow, develop and broaden, to work on and do good to the very end of his journey here, and at last to attain that state where somewhere in the boundless universe of God his mind could grow and grow forever, and forever bless.

The great desire of Thomas W. Phillips in his early life was to obtain a college education and become a preacher, but an injury to his lungs, compelling him to seek healthful outdoor employment, together with a number of other circumstances, prevented the realization of this ambition. He preached frequently when young, and on one occasion was forced to continue a meeting for

8

a few days after the evangelist had left. The subject of his closing address, delivered to a crowded house, was "Christian Union." At the close of the services Elder John D. Rany, who had heard Alexander Campbell and many other great preachers of the Restoration, congratulating him, said, "Campbell couldn't have done better." Mr. Rany did not know that although the speaker was only a boy, he had read all that Campbell had ever written on that subject, and much more in addition. Odd it is that a rather obscure passage in the Bible had much to do in determining the course of his career. To him, the unintelligible passage in Job, "And the rock poured me out rivers of oil," excited his imagination, and no doubt taxed his credulity. Soon after he learned that "rock-oil" had been found in this country, he drilled for it along the Mahoning River in Lawrence County, Pennsylvania. Either he did not have patience to drill to a sufficient depth with the crude spring-pole drilling outfit of that early day, or he was unfortunate in choosing the locations of his first ventures, for the rocks underlying the Mahoning Valley failed to pour him out even one little river of oil, and he lost all of his meager savings. Determined to find what he lost where he lost it, and fascinated by the uniqueness and possibilities of the petroleum industry, he went to Oil Creek in 1861, two years after Colonel Drake had made his historic discovery, and with his brothers engaged in the oil business. In this business, with varying degrees of success and failure, he remained until his death, completing the longest term of service that the oil industry had seen. He often remarked with reference to his experience in the oil fields, "Counting both good luck and bad luck, I have had plenty of it." The firm of Phillips Brothers at first met with great success, and within a few years their holdings were among the largest in the oil country. These brothers, generous by nature, used their profits largely to build churches, endow colleges, support missionaries, pay teachers, and help the poor, a very unusual course of procedure for men in the very beginning of their business careers. They were on the flood-tide of fortune when the Jay Cook panic occurred simultaneously with the discovery of great deposits of oil, the price of petroleum dropped from $4.55 to 65 cents a barrel, and the firm of Phillips Brothers found itself half a million dollars in debt. To the paying off of that debt, which, with interest, finally amounted to $800,000, Thomas W. Phillips devoted the next fourteen years of his life.

Practically none of this indebtedness could have been collected through process of law, and much of it he was under no moral obligation to pay, being made up of doubtful claims which were paid contrary to the advice of his attorneys and business confidants. He persisted in doing so, however, saying that he wanted his settlements to be such that there would be no man whom he could not look straight in the eye. Before the entire debt was paid his eldest brother Isaac died, and the firm of Phillips Brothers, originally composed of Isaac, John, Charles, and Thomas, had been dissolved, and for a number of years he continued in the oil business on a very large scale individually. Later the T. W. Phillips Gas and Oil Company was organized, with Mr. Phillips as president. The company, at the time of his death, owned some 850 gas and oil wells, about 900 miles of gas lines, and had besides a large amount of valuable oil and gas lands in Pennsylvania under lease. The oil industry in Pennsylvania probably benefited more from the presence of Thomas W. Phillips than from that of any other one man. He was a leader in every movement for its protection and improvement.

After the debts incurred by Phillips Brothers were all paid, Thomas devoted the major portion of his time and energy to work connected with religious, educational, and political questions, rather than to business. His activities and attainments might therefore be placed under the three heads of religion, politics, and business, and he considered his accomplishments in the political field secondary to those in the religious field, and his business attainments of less importance than his political attainments.

His political career was brilliant, and its influence far-reaching. He first came into prominent political notice in 1880. General James A. Garfield was probably his most intimate friend, and when Garfield was nominated for President, Mr. Phillips laid aside his business, and devoted his entire time to the canvass. He conceived, planned, and assisted in bringing out the Republican textbook used so extensively in that campaign, the first campaign textbook ever published, but which has since become a prominent feature in the campaigns of both parties. He was given credit for the organization of the party in Indiana, which carried the State for the Republican nominee for Governor, and for Garfield. His name was repeatedly mentioned and voted for in the Pennsylvania Legislature for the United States Senatorship. While he

10

was not elected he was instrumental in securing the election of a Senator favorable to the Garfield administration. In 1890 he was nominated for Congress, but was defeated owing to the presence of two Republican candidates in the field. However, in 1892 he was elected to Congress by a very substantial plurality, and in 1894 was reelected by a plurality of nearly twelve thousand, larger than that ever before received by any candidate in the Twenty-fifth Pennsylvania District.

As soon as Mr. Phillips was elected to Congress he planned to be appointed on the Committee on Labor, a committee at that time of comparatively little importance, but which he believed was the one on which he could render the greatest service. Through this Committee he was eventually able to secure the passage of a bill to establish a national Industrial Commission "to investigate questions pertaining to immigration, to labor, to agriculture, to manufacturing, and to business, and to report to Congress, and to suggest such legislation as it may deem best upon these subjects." Also it was to "furnish such information and suggest such laws as may be made a basis for uniform legislation by the various States of the Union, in order to harmonize conflicting interests, and to be equitable to the laborer, the employer, the producer, and the consumer."

President William McKinley appointed Mr. Phillips a member of the commission which his bill had created, and he was chosen vice-chairman, and presided at most of its meetings. His four years' work on this commission represents some of the hardest, most painstaking and most unselfish labor of his life. He was largely responsible for holding the commission to the purposes for which it was created, and he successfully opposed those who desired to make it a junketing commission. In order to more properly get his bearings for the great work he had undertaken, Mr. Phillips not only consulted an eminent authority on constitutional law, but at his own expense employed a competent attorney to aid him. The sinister and powerful influence exerted by the great monopolies, and by the *proteges* of special privilege, made his task most disagreeable, and would have driven a less courageous and determined man off the commission. He thoroughly believed, however, that the work he had undertaken, or a similar work by someone else, was absolutely necessary for the well-being and perpetuity of the nation, and that our republic could not continue to exist unless proper steps were taken to prevent the gulf between the classes and the masses from becoming wider and wider indefinitely. The final report of the commission was printed in nineteen volumes, and contains valuable and useful information which has been used extensively in formulating both State and national laws. In addition to the report of the commission in which he joined, Mr. Phillips filed and had printed in the nineteenth volume of the report a supplemental report which attracted more attention than the report of the commission itself. From his recommendations finally came the Bureau of Corporations and the United States Department of Commerce and Labor, both strong and essential arms of the Government.

Few men since the establishment of our Government have accomplished more along the lines of constructive legislation than Mr. Phillips accomplished, directly or indirectly, during the four years he served in Congress, and the four years he served on the Industrial Commission. Today there is no laborer, farmer, or independent businessman within the confines of the United States who is not in some measure indebted to Thomas W. Phillips.

A monumental service rendered to the cause of New Testament Christianity by Mr. Phillips was his prominent part in launching and financially backing the *Christian Standard*.

The Christian Publishing Association, formed in 1866 at Thomas W. Phillips' home in New Castle, Pennsylvania, consisted of the following fifteen men: Thomas W. Phillips, Isaac N. Phillips, John T. Phillips, Charles M. Phillips, A. J. Marion, J. P. Robison, G. W. N. Yost, James A. Garfield, J. H. Jones, S. C. Boynton, W. J. Ford, Richard Hawley, Harmon Austin, J. H. Rhodes, and Isaac Errett.

The aim and purpose of the Association was to publish a weekly Christian journal that would steadfastly advocate gospel extension by means of associated effort.

The name adopted for the publication was the *Christian Standard*, which, under the editorship of Isaac Errett, was first published in April, 1866, at Alliance, Ohio, later at Cleveland, Ohio, and finally at Cincinnati, Ohio. The *Christian Standard* soon came to the place of national and international leadership and influence which it has since maintained.

Through his entire subsequent life, Mr. Phillips was a close friend of and an honored contributor to the *Standard*, and no one more than he rejoiced at the growth and commanding influence that came to the paper as the years went by.

It would be difficult to enumerate all the benefactions of Thomas W. Phillips, for his life was one long act of charity and uplift. With tongue, pen, brain, energy, and purse, he worked continually for the relief of the needy, the comforting of the afflicted, the lifting up of the downtrodden, the guidance of the wandering, and the promotion of the best interests, both spiritual and temporal, of all those with whom he came in contact. With his brothers he built the noble edifice housing First Christian Church of New Castle, Pennsylvania. He aided many schools and colleges of the Restoration Movement, and without his generous support in making up deficits, in all probability Bethany College would have closed its doors or passed into other hands more than a generation ago. He established ministerial loan funds at Bethany, Hiram, Drake, Christian (Culver-Stockton), Phillips and Eugene (Northwest) which have enabled hundreds to preach the unsearchable riches of Christ, and to carry the gospel tidings to the uttermost parts of the earth, who otherwise could not have attained their worthy ambitions. The old Foreign, American, State, District, Church Extension, Ministerial Relief, and Benevolent Societies of the Christian Church were all special objects of his bounty. He contributed liberally of both money and service to the local, state, and national Y.M.C.A. and Y.W.C.A.

Thomas W. Phillips, despite all his great achievements in business, politics, and philanthropy, will probably be best known to posterity for his authorship of the book, *The Church of Christ*. While still a young man, and long before the innovation came in vogue, to use his own expression, "of teaching the Bible by the 'hop, step, skip and jump' method," he taught in the Bible school at New Castle the entire New Testament twice consecutively. During this teaching he made copious notes which were filed together with a few carefully prepared sermons which he preached when a boy or a very young man. After he had retired from politics and largely from business also, he collected all that he could find of his old notes and manuscripts and used them as a basis in the preparation of this epoch-making volume. On the twenty-third day of February, 1905, his seventieth birthday, he took his manuscript, just completed, to the Funk & Wagnalls

Company, and arranged for the publication of *The Church of Christ.*

The book was published in June, 1905, the author concealing his identity by attributing its authorship to "A Layman" in order that it might be read without prejudice, and judged solely upon its merits. Under the caption *The Church of Christ, by a Layman*, fourteen editions, comprising a total of more than 52,000 copies, were published. After the death of the author, his family purchased the copyright and plates from Funk & Wagnalls Company, and arranged to have a new edition, with much new material, published by The Standard Publishing Company. *The Church of Christ* is still widely read and used as a textbook in many colleges; it has been translated into the Chinese, the Japanese, the Hindi, and the Russian languages. Hundreds of commendations have been received from editors, professors, missionaries, and clergymen, who differed widely in their religious beliefs, which clearly indicates that the author handled his subject in a logical and convincing manner, having built upon the plain and unequivocal statements contained in God's holy and eternal Word. Probably no single volume has contributed more to the preservation and perpetuation of the Restoration Plea.

During his entire life Thomas W. Phillips occupied advanced positions on all the great questions of his day, and while in some respects he was so far in advance of the prevailing notions that he appeared almost visionary, yet business ethics, social justice, and religious dogma are steadily progressing toward the principles that always directed and dominated his life. His position on any important point of issue was usually well-nigh unassailable, because he had cultivated the faculty of considering questions thoroughly and from a disinterested viewpoint.

After Thomas W. Phillips' passing, with the unfolding developments of Divine providence, his sons Benjamin Dwight Phillips and his older brother, Thomas W. Phillips, Jr., became the chief stewards of this rich heritage. To them was given the high privilege of bringing to more complete realization many of the hopes and dreams of their remarkable father.

14

II

Gateways to Maturity

B. D. PHILLIPS was born in New Castle, Pennsylvania, November 20, 1885, at about the time his father had recovered
from the tragic consequences of the Jay Cook panic and the petroleum war. A new note of optimism and adventure pervaded the
home.

The business was booming and Ben's father was beginning to
devote a major portion of his time and energy to work in the fields
of religion, education, and politics. The youngest child of the
family received exceptional attention and he grew up in an atmosphere conducive to his maximal welfare.

The experiences of our infancy and early childhood make almost imperceptible impressions which have consequences important and of long duration in our lives. These first impressions at
New Castle helped to create in young Ben habits of virtue, industry,
activity, and spirit that fired him with an ambition to be useful
in the service of God and man. His mind was fixed on high and
noble objects and he came to have a supreme contempt for shame-
ful and unmanly vices.

The Phillips mansion was set on a hill, surrounded by acres of
wooded land, which were a temptation to out-of-door activity.
There were dogs and chickens, ducks and squirrels, horses and

15

sheep on the estate, to say nothing of the wild life that still lived in that area. Ben early developed an interest in pets. He often took his dogs on hunting forays. As he grew older he was allowed to have guns and became quite a marksman. So proficient was he that he joined with others in competitive events of all kinds, in which he was both honored and envied by his friends. This penchant for the out-of-doors and for competitive sports stayed with him all his life and gave balance to his career.

When he was six his father conceived the idea of taking the whole family on a trip to the Pacific Coast. In those days such a journey was a venture almost as thrilling as a modern trip around the world. Ben never forgot it. The journey was made by train and stage with stops at places of interest all along the way. T. W. had a brother in Pasadena who welcomed the family and introduced them to the mountains and the beaches of southern California. On week ends everybody went to church. The caravan ranged as far north as Tacoma, Washington, before their return home.

At Tacoma lived William F. Cowden, a former minister of the church at New Castle, who had succumbed to the "western fever." He saw a great future for the Northwest and was anxious that the "faith once for all delivered" should be widely disseminated in the area. With the financial and prayerful aid of his good friend T. W. Phillips, Cowden had planted a number of congregations and started a small academy for the training of church workers. His work and that of others who came later made it possible for the Restoration Movement to become for many years the leading religious influence in Oregon and Washington. Under the guidance of Cowden the Phillipses toured the frontier field. Ben was thrilled by the forests, the mountains, the game, and the streams filled with fish.

Little is a matter of record about Ben's early school days. He was a pupil in "Mrs. Stevenson's School" in New Castle. The good lady had a reputation as a highly cultured person who ran a small but greatly respected institution. The best people in New Castle sent their children there and had the confidence to believe that they would get the discipline and instruction which would make them respectable citizens when they grew to maturity. Here Ben got the rudiments of the three R's—"reading, 'riting, and 'rithmetic" and was introduced to elementary science, history, and

16

other cultural subjects. The daily sessions opened with Bible reading and prayer. The Ten Commandments were strictly taught and enforced, if necessary, with the paddle "which mends the gross mistakes of nature and . . . lays foundation for renown."

Ben's mother was dear to his heart. She led him first to God. Her words and her prayers implanted his faith in God's Word, gave him peace when troubled, and helped him in times of doubt. They were close companions, and when Ben mentioned her name in later years it was always with a note of awe.

Every Lord's Day (they called it that in the Phillips home, rather than the "sabbath" or "Sunday") the whole family went to church and sat together in the family pew. The father was the leading member of the First Christian Church in New Castle, often presiding at the Lord's Table, teaching in the Bible school, and even preaching the sermon if there was no one else to do it. It was a "New Testament Church," different from the other churches in New Castle, and the Phillips children knew why they went there. They learned "the Gospel plan of salvation" and they were taught to "give a reason for the faith that was within them." As a youth in his teens, Ben surprised the family one Lord's Day by stepping boldly down the aisle when the invitation hymn was sung, confessing his faith in Christ as Lord and Saviour and obeying Him in Christian baptism. No one in the family knew that he had even thought of taking this step. It was his own decision, his own act to which he was ever true.

It might be well to digress briefly at this point in our narrative to tell the story of this great church which had such an influence on the life of B. D. Phillips. It had its beginnings in March, 1856, when an evangelist by the name of P. O. Miller announced a series of meetings "in the Covenanter Church near the Neshannock Pool at the towing path bridge." On March 24 "a Disciples congregation" was organized and two years later was worshiping in a small meeting house, 18 x 28 feet, on North Street. The church had a checkered career until the Phillips family came into the picture. Late in 1864 the congregation was reorganized and took on new life. The Phillips brothers, led by T. W., bought lots in the center of the city and erected a structure which was almost cathedral-like in its proportions, with its clock-tower dominating the sky line of the city. It was dedicated by the distinguished editor of the *Christian Standard*, Isaac Errett. J. J. Pink-

17

erton, O. A. Burgess, and John T. Phillips were some of the great preachers who graced its pulpit. In 1871 a real sensation occurred in New Castle. William F. Cowden, pastor of the First Baptist Church, was converted to the "New Testament position" after weeks of discussion with T. W. Phillips. In the wonderful season of refreshing which followed, Mr. Cowden became the minister of First Christian Church and continued in that position until 1887. During his ministry over 500 were added to the congregation and it became the leading church in New Castle. Then followed a long list of outstanding pulpiteers—I. A. Thayer, Frank Talmage, Earle Wilfley, Crayton S. Brooks, W. L. Fisher, P. Y. Pendleton, W. W. Sniff, F. B. McAllister, and Gershom H. Bennett. For many years, because of the loyalty of First Church to the teachings of God's Word and its commitment to the principles of the Restoration Movement, and the outstanding leadership of the Phillips Family in the life of the brotherhood regionally and nationally, New Castle became renowned among the great churches of the nation.

To the T. W. Phillips home there came, through the years, outstanding leaders of the Church in missions, education, journalism, and every phase of church life. The latchstring was always out. Here took place many prayer meetings and discussions which helped shape the policies and programs of the brotherhood in the days of its greatest growth. The financial generosity of the Phillips Family often made possible the success of progressive undertakings, such as the launching of the *Christian Standard*, which brought marvelous blessings to the cause and greatly advanced the Kingdom of God.

And Ben was there. In later years he could recount having seen and heard many of the great leaders and having witnessed great decisions made in his father's house. His elders were probably unaware of the small boy who sat in the corner "all eyes and ears," but deep impressions were being made on his life.

Religion was not the only topic of conversation in the Phillips mansion at this time. Politics was becoming of greater and greater concern. Ben listened in awe as his father would recount the tales of his part in the nomination and election of James A. Garfield to the presidency of the United States. The young lad thrilled as his father told of happenings while friend, adviser, and supporter of Garfield as president of Hiram College, when he was elected to the Senate and during his brief but significant stay in the White House.

Judge Jeremiah Sullivan Black, elder in the church at Somerset, Pennsylvania, was another whose name was frequently mentioned in the Phillips home. Black had been judge of the Supreme Court of Pennsylvania, and Attorney General of the United States in the cabinet of President Buchanan. Then there were Senator George T. Oliver, Congressman W. H. Graham, and others of political renown in Pennsylvania who frequently visited the Phillipses. Russell Errett, editor of the leading newspaper in Pittsburgh (a brother of Isaac Errett, editor of the *Christian Standard*), was often in consultation with T. W. on matters pertaining to the welfare of the state and nation.

It was not strange that "in the course of human events" Thomas W. Phillips became, in 1892, a member of Congress from the Twenty-fifth Pennsylvania District. This meant quite a change in the affairs of the New Castle family. They still maintained their home there but they took up their abode in the new Shoreham Hotel in Washington, D. C. Ben became a student in the noted Sidwell School, a Quaker-oriented private institution in northwest Washington. Here he received "religiously guarded" elementary education, which meant that Sidwell put the Bible at the center of its curriculum and protected its pupils from "the evils of the world." The cultural ideals were the highest and the intellectual qualifications of the teachers were impeccable. Ben greatly prized his diploma from Sidwell.

Not long after the move to Washington, the family leased a house on Vermont Avenue near Thomas Circle. It was only a stone's throw from the new Garfield Memorial Christian Church where the brilliant pulpiteer, Frederick D. Power, was pastor. T. W. Phillips had been a leader in the move to erect a worthy edifice for the New Testament Church in the nation's capital. The idea of making it a living memorial to the brotherhood's most distinguished citizen caught on across the nation and soon the necessary funds were in hand to erect the impressive building. Here the Phillips Family, true to their tradition, sat together every Lord's Day and in many ways made their contribution to the growth and prosperity of the congregation.

The Phillipses moved in the best society in Washington. While they gravitated toward "the Republican side of the aisle" in their

19

close friendships, they were well received by all leaders in the life of the Government. Ben had a vivid recollection of standing in line at a Presidential Reception in the White House until he almost collapsed. The President was Democrat Grover Cleveland who gave the young man a crushing handshake and a pat on the back he never forgot. But in Ben's estimation the crowning event of his Washington experience was the gift of a new bicycle, a vehicle which was just then coming into its own on the American scene.

When the family returned home Ben continued his education at Hiram College in Ohio. The academy at Bethany was considered, but because of T. W. Phillips' admiration for President E. V. Zollars, Hiram had assumed special importance in the Phillips Family. Dr. Zollars had taken Hiram when it was little more than an academy and built it into an accredited college of liberal arts. Under his administration several new buildings had been erected, including the Association Building, Miller Hall, and the Teachout-Cooley Library. He had placed special emphasis on training for the ministry. In 1890 there were only twenty men studying for the ministry. Around one hundred were enrolled when Zollars resigned in 1901 to accept the presidency of Texas Christian University, and Hiram had become the leading school of the brotherhood in ministerial training. Before he left he raised a quarter of a million dollars for Hiram in a "Jubilee Year" campaign. Such success appealed to T. W. Phillips. He had accepted a place on Hiram's board and had given generously to its support. Dr. Zollars was gone, but Hiram it was, for Ben.

There was no question but that Hiram in those days was first and foremost a Christian college and thoroughly committed to the Restoration Plea. Every student went to the Hiram church on the Lord's Day. Bible reading and prayer were featured in daily chapel. There were periodic revivals in which many students confessed Christ and were baptized. Hiram's ministerial students preached in many of the small town and rural churches in northwestern Ohio. The college was also proud of the fact that it had prepared more missionaries for the foreign field than all the other colleges of the Christian church combined. In this atmosphere Ben Phillips was thoroughly at home, both in the academy and the college, and he grew in wisdom and stature.

James Alexander Beattie had succeeded E. V. Zollars as president but Ben never mentioned him in his letters home. His favorite professor was Edmund Burrett Wakefield. Wakefield was a Hiram graduate who loved the out-of-doors and was favorable to a strong athletic program. He had distinguished himself as a geologist. He was with the United States Geological Survey, a member of the original party that explored Yellowstone National Park. Finally, however, he entered the ministry, became the strongly evangelical pastor of the historic Warren, Ohio, church and then moved into a professorship (later the acting presidency) at Hiram. Wakefield had a great influence on the life of Ben Phillips both as a teacher and as a friend and guide.

Ben liked the idea of developing the athletic prowess of Hiram. With great enthusiasm and encouragement from Wakefield he went out for all forms of sport—baseball, basketball, tennis, and track. In a letter to his older brother, Tom, Jr., in 1901 he told about pitching for Hiram in a baseball game with Ravenna. He boasted that he had eight strike-outs and did not give a single base on balls. Ravenna won 7 to 5, a defeat he attributed to poor infielding and a muddy field.

It was in basketball that he shone. In those days it was a new sport and was played outdoors at Hiram. Hiram had always been considered "small time" in athletics among Ohio colleges, but in 1904 it won practically all its basketball games and went on to win the Intercollegiate Championship of the United States at the St. Louis Olympic Games. In B. D. Phillips' files to his dying day he kept a clipping about "the best team Hiram ever had." The lineup included: John J. Line, captain; Lester J. Hurd, Paul L. Wilson, B. D. Phillips, J. W. Smith, Earl W. Clark, Carl L. Clark, O. W. Harmon, and G. A. Vincent, manager.

The *Spider Web*, Hiram College student publication of that day, described the championship game. Basketball games today are high-scoring affairs, played by tall men on smooth wooden floors. The accent is on accurate shooting and finesse, not on defense or bodily contact. In 1904 it was different. Says the clipping:

The rains of the night before had left the clay field in a very slippery condition. Puddles all about the side-lines promised to make it unpleasant if the ball went out of bounds, but the sun blazing down from an almost cloudless sky foretold quick removal of this handicap.

Wheaton College had the heavier team but we on the sidelines saw the contrast between the brown, lean limbs of the Hiram team and the beefy ones from Illinois, and did not feel greatly depressed.

The pace Wheaton set at the start of the game could not be long maintained. Her lead was cut down point by point. Their cleated shoes were a hindrance, and they began making wild throws. To make matters worse, they noted each other's mistakes and did not hesitate to blame whoever was at fault.

Here it was that the real superiority of Hiram training asserted itself. Mistakes that cost points were accepted with cheerful resignation. When the timekeeper blew his whistle at the end of the second half, Hiram was a good five points to the good and the first game was won. The team and its supporters took it quietly for they knew that undue excitement tires one and is not conducive to good playing.

The second game was marked by the same consistent playing on the part of Hiram. While not so exciting as the first—owing to Hiram getting an early lead and maintaining it—it was marked by many brilliant plays and more effective team work than the first had shown. Through our enforced silence we were wild with inward excitement and only fear of banishment from the sidelines prevented our giving vent to our feelings. When the game was won and Hiram was declared the winner, our excitement ran a trifle high.

Even today Hiram athletes, in reminiscent mood, boast of the time when a Hiram basketball team won in the Olympics.

Then, suddenly for Ben, it was the Twentieth Century. There had been a good deal of argument as to whether it made any difference to write it 1800 or 1900 but there was a growing feeling that it did. Senator Chauncey M. DePew, speaking before a gathering of the nation's great in New York City said, "There is not a man here who does not feel 400 per cent bigger in 1900 than he did in the 1800s—bigger intellectually, bigger hopefully, bigger patriotically, bigger in the breast from the fact that he is a citizen of a country that has become a world power for peace, for civilization and for the expansion of its industries." The *New York Times* was saying, "We are stepping on the threshold of a new century, facing the brightest dawn in the history of civilization."

Ben was suddenly in a new world that was beginning to experience tremendous industrial development and immense financial prosperity. Recent inventions—steam engines, railroads, telegraph, ocean liners, telephones, electric lights, cash registers and others too numerous to mention—had paved the way for unprecedented progress. The years that were unfolding for Ben

22

might well be called the Confident Years, the Buoyant Years, the Spirited Years or perhaps the Golden Years for the nation. With a little imagination a man could make a fortune twice as easily as in the previous generation. There were stirrings for a revival in religion, for reform in the areas of economic and social concern. The nation's basic optimism was stronger than ever before as limitless opportunities presented themselves. Daily life had not yet become the complicated thing it is today and barriers to success were not impossible to scale.

Whether Ben fully understood this situation or not, a lad with his inquiring mind, alert to all that was going on about him, and eager for adventure must have caught something of the Twentieth Century fever. He must have heard his father and other forward-looking industrialists expounding their hopes and fears and plans for the future, and have imbibed the spirit of the times.

Despite the appeal of college days, Ben yearned for the time when he could go where the action was in the growing business which his father headed. The Pennsylvania oil fields were no longer productive as they once had been and the trend was toward gas. Oil men had ignored natural gas, often discovered as they drilled for oil. If oil was not found in a well, they lit the gas and allowed it to burn itself out. But some gas wells would not die. There were scores of "burning springs" left throughout the countryside that flared night and day and were declared a "public nuisance." Then the oil men made a discovery. Natural gas could be piped to industries and to cities for lighting and heating purposes at a reasonable price. It furnished a cheaper, cleaner, and more effective form of light and energy than coal, oil, or manufactured gas. When the Phillips oil operation converted to gas there were thrilling opportunities for expansion. Ben was excited about the prospects and was in the forefront of many expeditions organized to discover new fields and drill for natural gas. He loved roaming the mountains clad in dungarees and roughing it as tests and discoveries were made. His father was greatly pleased and encouraged Ben in every way possible. The young man soon learned the science of the new operation and became an expert in all the processes involved. Because Butler, Pennsylvania, was the center of the new industry, New Castle lost its appeal to him. He had visions of the day when he would go to Butler, live in Butler, and be deeply involved there in building the T. W. Phillips Gas and Oil Company into a great organization serving Western Pennsylvania in both the domestic and industrial markets. He applied himself in every phase of the operation until he knew it completely and then began to experiment in new ways to make it more efficient, effective, and productive.

Gateways to maturity had opened and B. D. Phillips was launched on what was to prove a great business career.

T. W. Phillips

FATHER

Pamphilia Hardman Phillips
MOTHER

Grace Phillips Johnson
SISTER

Thomas W. Phillips, Jr.
BROTHER

Artist's Sketch of the Home of Thomas W. Phillips, Sr., at New Castle, Pennsylvania

Later Mansion of T. W. Phillips, Sr. in New Castle

First Christian Church, New Castle, Penn.

Ben Phillips on Mountain Burro
(Photo taken near Tacoma, Washington)

A Hallowe'en Party in New Castle
(Ben Phillips Bottom Center)

Mature Businessman

Junior Worker
BENJAMIN DWIGHT PHILLIPS

Young Executive

1904 Hiram College Baseball Team

1904 Hiram Olympic Intercollegiate Champion Basketball Team

1904 Hiram College Tennis Team

Anna
Undine
Conant
Phillips

Stella Phillips (Ehrman)

B. D. Phillips, Jr.

Clarinda Phillips (Sprankle)

Victor K. Phillips

Undine Phillips (Weigand)

Donald Phillips

III

The University of Life

JEAN PAUL RICHTER once said, "Every man has two educations
—that which is given to him, and the other, that which he
gives to himself. Of the two kinds, the latter is by far the most
valuable. Indeed, all that is most worthy in a man, he must work
out and conquer for himself. It is that which constitutes our real
and best nourishment."

In the best sense of the phrase, B. D. Phillips was "a self-
educated man." What he learned in the "university of life" had
more to do with shaping his career than what he learned in the
academy or the college. He chose his own teachers, his own textbooks, his own curriculum and did his own research and laboratory
work on his own schedules. And the world gave him its *magna
cum laude*.

There is only one qualification to the above observation—B. D.'s
father. There is a sense in which the elder T. W. Phillips was
perhaps unconsciously the chief mentor and guide in all that his
son thought, learned, and did. Never was a father more loved
nor more highly regarded by a son.

B. D. saw in him an immensely successful businessman whose
methods were characterized by the most rigid honesty and in-

tegrity. He knew that no tainted dollars ever soiled his hands and that he was the implacable foe of those dishonest practices that enabled many great corporations to reap immense profits by legalized forms of robbery or by dishonest processes in evasion of law. His son saw in him the builder of a great fortune, created not at the expense of or upon the ruin of his competitors or by the sale of stocks of fictitious value, but by the honest production and sale of oil and gas and the initiation of new and progressive methods and strategies beneficial to the entire industry.

B. D. saw in him one of the grandest Christian men ever produced by the Restoration Movement. He saw his devotion to his Church locally and nationally and to the faith "once for all delivered to the saints." His whole life was built on the example of Jesus Christ and the saints of all time as recorded in the Holy Scriptures. He was the equal of the great preachers, teachers, writers, statesmen of the Church in his time, though he laid no claim to such attainments. He devoted all his talents and most of his wealth to the advancement of the Kingdom of God in every area of his influence.

Notwithstanding his father's immense business enterprises, B. D. noted his deep interest in building a better nation in which the welfare of capital and labor would be equally protected and advanced. He saw his father, on what proved to be his deathbed, actively concerned with the future welfare of his employees and the provision of public recreation facilities for the youth and children of his own city.

It is small wonder that B. D. Phillips preferred the encomiums of such a father to the academic honors he might have attained in the finest Eastern universities which he had opportunity to attend.

What were some of the courses and ideologies which were provided the young student in this unique "university of life"?

Next to the Bible, B. D. Phillips' most thumbed and worn "textbook" was the historic speech delivered by his father in the U. S. House of Representatives on May 21, 1896. The occasion was his presentation of the bill to establish the national Industrial Commission. It was as much a sermon as a legislative apologetic. It began:

Mr. Chairman, this bill calls attention to the fundamental principle of our Government—the equality of man—and seeks a more equitable distribution of the burdens and benefits of our free Government. While it is not the function of the State to guarantee individual happiness, it is its function to guarantee each individual the right to pursue happiness, and so enact laws that one class may not be compelled of necessity to work solely for another class, regardless of their personal comfort and improvement. Rights do not belong to one class and duties to another. Physical, intellectual, and moral ability can not be made equal, but each capacity may be met; each cup, be it large or small, may be filled. Circumstances can not be made equal, but law can be adapted to circumstances.

Mr. Chairman, the danger to this Government is not external, but internal. In the progress of human society the battles of the world are shifting from conflict with nations to a conflict within nations for better government and more equitable laws. We must recognize the fact that more are now peacefully organized and enlisted in the cause of industrial equity than in all the armies of the world. The people of civilized nations will not always continue to fight for national honor and supremacy while their individual rights are not protected within the nation. National glory must henceforth be based more and more upon the prosperity and happiness of the individual citizen. After more than six thousand years of experience the people are beginning to learn that government belongs to them; that they are not owned by the government, but that they own the government, and that it must respect their rights by meeting their just demands.

If laws are derived from the governed, they should meet the just demands of all the governed. This nation took the most advanced stand in civilization, and is the best prepared to meet the industrial issues of today by building on the foundation it laid more than one hundred years ago by conforming law to its declared principles of right, freedom, and equality, and thus organize our social and industrial system upon a more just and equitable basis than has yet obtained in the world.

Mr. Chairman, in entering upon the discussion of the subject-matter of this bill I wish to make three observations in regard to man, which are stated in the first chapters of Genesis.

First, the unity of the race and equality of man was shown in creation; God created man and gave him dominion as man. He was to "subdue the earth" and "have dominion over the fish of the sea, over the fowls of the air, and over every living thing that moveth upon the earth." But he was not given dominion over his fellow-man.

Second, before God created man it was said, "And there was not a man to till the ground."

In the third place, man was told by the Creator: "In the sweat of thy face shalt thou eat bread till thou return unto the ground." To all, therefore, who believe in the Bible account of creation, which I believe is also in strict accord with science, fact, and history, these three things are indisputable:

First. That when God created man, he gave him dominion as man, not over his fellow-man, but over beast and bird and fish; over all animate nature below him.

Second. That he was to till the soil as his chief occupation.

Third. That his life was to be sustained by labor.

All this agrees with reason; shows equality in creation; that sustenance comes from the ground; that labor is the normal condition of man; and it is a fact that no man enters into rest unless it is upon his own labor or the labor of others. The government, therefore, that does not strive to meet these three great cardinal principles of reason and revelation in the highest possible degree will perish from the earth.

The "preacher-congressman" went on to pay tribute to the four constituent elements of the body politic which he proposed to have equally represented in his proposed Industrial Commission—labor, agriculture, manufacturing, and business.

Of labor he said:

The importance of labor to our being and well-being can not be over-stated. Labor is one of the foundation principles upon which organized society rests. All kinds of labor are necessary, from digging in the ditch to measuring space and counting the stars, yet the lower forms of labor are more intimately connected with our existence and needs. The most despised is often the most useful. The man who digs the foundation is more important to the structure than he who frescoes its walls. Without the grading of the roadbed there would be no stockholders, no locomotives, or railroad president. If all manual labor were to stop, if all wage earners were to cease work, there would be no value in property and a large part of the race would perish. That our relations are most intimately bound up with the wage earner is shown by the many strikes and lockouts in recent years which have entailed great suffering and loss of property, as well as the sacrifice of life.

Of agriculture he said:

The agricultural industry is the most important of all industries. All civilized life depends upon the products of the soil. All food and clothing come from the soil; yet this most important industry is depressed. The constant settling in the value of farm products and farm lands in recent years in a large portion of the United States has made great discontent and unrest among farmers. Many of them cannot hope to have their children succeed them in husbandry, and they are exhausting their limited means to fit them for pursuits in the crowded city. No country can prosper when the agricultural interest is suffering.

Identifying himself with the representatives of manufacturing and business, he modestly paid but brief tribute to these important factors in the life of the nation. In fact, he became highly critical of his own kind in what he had to say.

28

Then he launched into a consideration of the dangers confronting the national welfare because of the selfishness of capital and labor. He showed a remarkable understanding of current conditions and a logical, intuitive, almost prophetic, foresight regarding the future. He said:

Mr. Chairman, the massing of capital and labor which has been caused by the scientific discoveries and the invention of machinery in our day has brought us face to face with new problems of the greatest magnitude. . . . This age is one of concentration, corporation and centralization. It is an age of organization. If organized capital deals with labor it must expect to deal with organized labor. Organization on the one hand implies organization on the other, so there may be two equal parties to the agreement, otherwise the first party would dictate and the other submit. Ours is a contract system, but men will not continue to contract as free men while believing they must submit as slaves. There must be two equal parties to an effective contract.

Industrial corporations largely control the production and exchange of this continent. Massed capital and massed labor are largely controlling production, manufacture and transportation, the very sources of supply and demand upon which all depend. These are now so frequently in conflict that all the relations of life are disturbed. Society has rights that must be respected by both these contending forces, and its good order and peace demand a settlement that must be equitable, just and durable.

The centralization of capital and labor has produced a war of competition in which labor suffers, fortunes are wrecked and homes are destroyed. Honorable competition is considered the life of trade, but the weapons which are more and more being used are cruel; they are reduction of wages, adulteration and counterfeiting. Low bids are made to secure large contracts, with no other hope to meet them than by reduction in wages, and labor has lost in all these battles. There are adulterations and counterfeiting in all we eat and wear, thus endangering health, comfort and life itself. While we have adequate laws to punish the counterfeiting of money, the more dangerous and damaging counterfeiting of the commodities of life goes unpunished. The first means only loss in value, the latter means loss in value and endangers health and life. Dishonest men engaged in the war for gain grow rich in selling counterfeit commodities while many honest competitors fail and their fortunes are wrecked.

Mr. Chairman, the war of competition as now waged, instead of being the life of trade, too frequently means the death of one of the contending parties or a combination in which the people lose. Property won by fair competition or honest toil will be respected; but won by special privileges, unjust competition or fraud in adulteration cannot be respected, and the time is fast approaching when such methods of acquisition will not be tolerated. The holder of such property cannot atone in acts of charity, returning in part to the few which he has taken wrongfully from the many. Philanthropy is one of the noblest traits of man; but it should be ex-

29

pended in teaching, in lifting up the race, in caring for the disabled, the suffering and the helpless. All that others require is an equal chance in the race of life with none to hinder and none to handicap. They require justice, not charity.

Mr. Chairman, it is most apparent that our laws have in no sense kept pace with the new discoveries, inventions, and developments of the age. The world has made more advancement in physical development and scientific discovery in the last one hundred years than it did in the preceding six thousand. While the founders of this Republic declare new principles, yet the laws they adopted were largely taken from a monarchy, and belonged to a darker age, when labor was oppressed, had no voice in the Government, and had not even the right of organization. We thus put our "new wine into old bottles," and they are bursting.

We say, "Government exists for the people," yet we adopted the laws of those who say that "the people exist for the government." New conditions confront us on every hand, in the concentration of capital and organized labor, in new improvements, in the instruments of husbandry, in the mode of manufacturing, transportation, travel, and communication. All these have been revolutionized within a generation. We have been offering premiums for inventions, discovery, and development, for labor-saving machines and devices of all kinds, until we have changed the whole order of industrial pursuits, of production and distribution. While we have had thousands inventing and discovering, we have offered no premiums for talent and energy; have had no men studying these new conditions and adjusting laws to our new environments; hence, there is friction, discontent, and violence, destroying peace, property, and life. . . .

Mr. Chairman, our big problem in this country is one of equality. The equality of man was shown in the creation, affirmed in redemption, and first declared as the foundation of human government in this new world in 1776. This is the greatest political question of the nation and the world. The barbarous ages are past, feudalism is gone, serfdom has been destroyed, and slavery has perished from the earth, but the question of equality has come to the front, and is pressing for solution with irresistible power. The history of the world teaches that God holds nations responsible to the standard they set up. Our standard was the highest erected since the dawn of time, yet it must now be apparent that this nation has been false to its declared principle of equality as it was to the declared principle of freedom. . . . We have exploited its resources and distributed its land and wealth most unequally. We have destroyed many of its forests, its animals, its birds, its fish, and instead of utilizing them for the benefit of man, are now trying to replace them. We have unequally divided the public domain; have been prodigal of land, giving it by millions of acres for development. With a continent vast in extent, incomparably rich in soil and mineral, teeming with animal and vegetable life; with its mechanically multiplied labor forces capable of sustaining hundreds of millions of inhabitants . . . we see large numbers out of work, seeking employment and finding none; many needy, hungry and poor; all this with

30

granaries and storehouses full of all the commodities of life; yet millions of laborers cannot earn and have no money to buy. . . . This can only be accounted for upon the ground of unequal opportunities, unequal privileges and unequal distribution. . .

Max Muller has stated that the word mankind is not found in human language before Christ. There was nothing in language to express the kinship of the race. It was Mede, Persian, Grecian, Roman, bond and free. But since the human race has learned its kinship and the word mankind has expressed its relation—this brotherhood—the laws of society must more and more recognize the obligations and rights growing out of this relation. Our Government is one government, our body politic being one body; when, therefore, any "one member suffers, all members suffer with it." When a number of the members of the human body suffers, and are not speedily healed, the body dies; so eventually will the body politic die if many members suffer. By not caring for others, we injure ourselves, as, for example, poverty and the want of sanitary conditions breed physical disease. This is true in a community, in a nation, and in the world. Even the world is bound together by ties of humanity which may not be disregarded without injury. . . .

In the last analysis of human government it will be found that it must be based upon principles which meet the highest wants and guarantees the best good of all in view of our common origin, common interests, and common destiny. No self-government can exist without a community of interests. Equality can not be denied nor favors granted. Every man according to his ability must contribute part, otherwise he becomes a privileged person. No man can obtain true success who lives and acts solely for self. A purely selfish existence is worse than no existence. The highest happiness is to be and do for others, and no government of the people and for the people can fulfill its mission unless it has constantly in view the highest good of all. We in this self-government have plighted faith to each other. Every loyal citizen must be protected in all his rights, because he is a citizen and a part of this Government. No discrimination in favor of any individual, company, or class can be tolerated in such a Government, yet the cry of discrimination comes to us from every State and district over the whole continent, and it demands prompt consideration and just action. . . .

Too much of our law is made up of compromise measures. All compromise laws, from the Missouri Compromise to the present time, if not in all time and in all nations, have been disappointing if not disastrous. If there be any great compromise law in nature scientists have not yet discovered it. If there be any great compromise law in the Bible theologians have not yet expounded it. We can not compromise truth or principle, facts or figures. If there be no great compromise principle in nature, reason, mathematics, or revelation, compromises should not enter so largely into our law.

I believe that in the last analysis of this industrial problem, in view of our common origin, interests, and destiny, the golden rule will be its solution, and that a large per cent of existing laws will be stricken from the records by inserting, "All things whatsoever ye would that men should do to you, do ye even so to them." This is in strict accord with our declared principles of freedom and equality, and we must return and build again upon this everlasting foundation of justice, mercy, and right.

The address was replete with government statistics, references to legal statutes and historical facts, to say nothing about the technical problems involved in the operation of the proposed Industrial Commission, but these quotations indicate something of its great moral and spiritual highlights and insights. If one were to ask, "What was the basic social, political, and business philosophy of B. D. Phillips?" the answer could be found in this pronouncement of his father in Washington on May 21, 1896. They lived that philosophy through their years together and it became an indispensable part of the Phillips tradition.

Another thumbed and worn textbook in B. D. Phillips' university of life was his father's book, *The Church of Christ* (page 13). He was greatly intrigued by this unusual theological adventure of a consecrated businessman and he eagerly read pages of the manuscript as it grew on his father's desk.

The Phillips Family was dedicated to Biblical Christianity as it had been presented by Thomas and Alexander Campbell, Barton W. Stone, and Walter Scott on the Allegheny frontier. They were in the forefront of the "movement to restore the New Testament Church in doctrine, ordinances, and life." This commitment was largely due to T. W. Phillips' clear and logical understanding of its basic principles, and his enthusiastic advocacy of it wherever he went.

The new book was to project that advocacy to the whole world. As the author put it in his Introduction—

The writer, believing that in Christ and His Church the mystery of life and death is solved and man's duty and destiny revealed, deems it most important that the teachings of Christ and His ambassadors be properly presented to the world. When we observe the divided condition of Christendom, we feel assured that there must be something fundamentally wrong in the presentation of Christian truth, because parties and sects of Christians, while differing can not all be right.

We are largely creatures of environment. The rule is that the child follows the faith of its parents. Demonstration of this is seen in both politics and religion. If a child's parents are Republicans, the child will be a Republican; if Democrats, the child will be a Democrat; and so with the

32

various political parties, no matter how divergent and contradictory in sentiment or principle such parties may be. The same is true in religion; a child born of Roman Catholic parents becomes a Catholic; of Episcopalian parents, becomes an Episcopalian. The same is true of the Baptists, Methodists, Presbyterians, and the multitude of different denominations; all have observed these influences of environment which appear on every hand; and yet many people believe that those who differ from them hold the most untenable and absurd views upon social, political, and religious subjects. We may well ask the question, Are we following blindly in opinions or faith because of our early training? Recognizing these facts the writer decided to reinvestigate his accepted religion, and, if possible, to make an original and impartial investigation of the subject pertaining to religious truth, considering it from the Heathen, the Jewish, and the Christian standpoints, the result of which is here given.

It is obvious that several hundred churches, denominations, sects, and parties in Christendom can not all be right. They may all be wrong, but no two of them can be right, if Christ's Church was a unit and divisions were forbidden by the statement, "That there be no divisions among you." Two men can not differ about any fact or truth and both be right; about any inspired command and obedience to it; about any divine ordinance and its observance, about officers under Christ and their duties, and both be right, any more than they can differ about the fact that the sun shines by day and the moon by night, and both be right. It is, therefore, the design of this volume to unfold the simple truth in regard to the Church of Christ, both in faith and practice. In doing this we place emphasis upon the completeness of the Christian religion as being adapted to all men everywhere and in all time.

Christianity is a new or an original religion. The proffer of absolute pardon to a world lying in sin was promised only through Christ. This great fact being of such importance, we have passed in review, in the order in which they occur, all the cases of forgiveness or pardon recorded in the New Testament, comparing one with the other in order to learn if the same terms were required of all, if there is one universal law of pardon, and if all persons come into Christ's Church upon the same terms. We know of no book covering this ground, which alone is deemed sufficient reason for presenting this volume to the public.

Again, reasons are given to show that all who come into the Church of Christ have the full assurance of pardon and acceptance with God.

Again, the Church of Christ is a complete organization, divinely constituted, without any authority given to man or set of men or ecclesiastical body to change any of its rites, its officers, or its ordinances.

Also, the church was a unit, Christians were one in Christ, being "complete in him." "There shall be one fold and one shepherd."

The book began by making its appeal to the authority of Jesus Christ, the Son of God and Saviour of the world, and His divinely-endowed Apostles, as recorded in the New Testament. The New

Testament and the New Testament alone was to be the criterion by which the nature, doctrine, and mission of the true Church of Christ were to be measured.

The author showed that the church had its beginnings on the Day of Pentecost, A.D. 30, as recorded in Acts 2. On that day the Apostle Peter, Christ's divinely-appointed spokesman, said:

> The last days have truly come. The starlight age has passed, the moonlight age is now closed. The law has waned to wax no more, "the sun of righteousness has arisen with healing in his wings," the everlasting gospel is being proclaimed for the first time on earth. "Ye men of Israel, hear these words: Jesus of Nazareth, a man approved of God among you by miracles and wonders and signs, which God did by him in the midst of you, as ye yourselves also know: Him, being delivered by the determinate counsel and foreknowledge of God, ye have taken, and by wicked hands have crucified and slain: Whom God hath raised up, having loosed the pains of death: because it was not possible that he should be holden of it." Peter then goes on to apply a prophecy of David to Christ, which says: "Thou wilt not leave my soul in Hades, neither wilt thou suffer thine Holy One to see corruption."

> He speaks of His ascension and concludes this wonderful discourse by saying in the most direct manner, "Therefore let all the house of Israel know assuredly, that God hath made that same Jesus, whom ye have crucified, both Lord and Christ. Now when they heard this, they were pricked in their heart, and said unto Peter and to the rest of the apostles, Men and brethren, what shall we do?" Never was there proclaimed to men greater facts, nor were they ever charged with greater crime. Nor from the depths of human conviction and anguish ever came a more direct, earnest and important inquiry, "What must we do?" This question demands and receives an answer about which there can be no mistake. Human language is incapable of making either the question or the answer plainer. "Then Peter said unto them, Repent, and be baptized every one of you in the name of Jesus Christ for the remission of sins, and ye shall receive the gift of the Holy Spirit. For the promise is unto you, and to your children, and to all that are afar off, even as many as the Lord our God shall call." "Then they that gladly received his word were baptized; and the same day there were added unto them about three thousand souls. And they continued steadfastly in the apostles' doctrine and fellowship, and in breaking of bread, and in prayers."

Here and now is opened before us the Christian age. Here we have the first gospel sermon preached by Peter under the ascended, ruling, reigning Christ. The gospel is now before us for the first time in its fulness. We have heard the first discourse based upon its great facts, listened to the first inquiry, "What must I do?" heard the first command given by the authority of Christ, and witnessed the conversion of three thousand persons, and their baptism into the name of the Father, Son, and Holy Spirit. It is evident from the preceding narrative, first, that these persons heard;

34

second, that they believed; third, that they repented; fourth, that they were baptized; fifth, that they received the remission of sins and the gift of the Holy Spirit. Upon these conditions they became subjects of Christ's kingdom. They entered His Church and are the first recorded who "continued steadfastly in the apostles' doctrine and fellowship, and in breaking of bread, and in prayers."

T. W. Phillips then speaks of the terms of pardon for sinful, guilty, and lost humanity as set forth in the New Testament:

Since the Lord reveals to man his sinful, guilty, and lost condition through the Scriptures we may rationally expect Him to give the knowledge or evidence of pardon through the same source. If the law declares the transgressor a sinner, why may not the same law declare the obedient righteous? If the Scriptures give evidence of man's guilt, do they not also give evidence of man's justification from that guilt through the obedience to the "Lord from heaven"? The Scriptures bear witness that the whole world (that is, those not converted), are guilty before God and included under sin, "for all have sinned and come short of the glory of God." It is Scriptural evidence alone that proves the disobedient guilty, and, therefore, it must prove the obedient justified.

Second, all who would become Christians must comply with the terms of pardon. It was shown that all persons, after the Church of Christ was established, were pardoned upon the same terms or conditions, there being no distinction made between Jew and Gentile, male and female, bond and free. All obeyed in the same manner and received the same blessings.

These terms may be briefly recapitulated here: First, all who come to the Saviour to obtain pardon are required to believe on Him. This, all who have knowledge of the truth can do. And "without faith it is impossible to please God." Second, those seeking pardon must repent. "Repent, ye, therefore, and turn again." They can and must turn to God with full purpose of heart. Third, all were required to be baptized. "Go ye into all the world and preach the gospel to every creature; he that believeth and is baptized shall be saved" (or pardoned), "baptizing them into the name of the Father, Son, and Holy Spirit." Faith, repentance, and baptism are the steps or appointed way by which persons come into the Church of Christ. Nor is there any other way appointed. Without complying with these terms there is no testimony that any one came into the Church, and all who thus came were promised the gift of the Holy Spirit, and by continuing faithful unto death were promised eternal life. To deny that persons who had thus come were pardoned and added to the believers would be to deny the sacred record.

How did they know that they were pardoned? The evidence was full and satisfactory. What is the evidence? "He that believeth and is baptized shall be saved." "Know ye not that so many of us as were baptized into Christ were baptized into his death?" "For as many of you as have been baptized into Christ have put on Christ." "For I know whom I have believed and am persuaded that he is able to keep that which I have

35

committed unto him against that day." "There is therefore now no condemnation to them which are in Christ Jesus. For the law of the spirit of life in Christ Jesus hath made me free from the law of sin and death."

In Chapters 23 and 24 the Church of Christ, as founded by Christ and the apostles, is described in New Testament terms:

We will now consider the Church of Christ as an organic institution. Paul says: "Now therefore ye are no more strangers and foreigners, but fellow citizens with the saints, and of the household of God; and are built upon the foundation of the apostles and prophets, Jesus Christ himself being the chief corner stone." "For other foundation can no man lay than that is laid, which is Jesus Christ." Peter said, "Thou art the Christ, the Son of the living God." Jesus' answer was, "Upon this rock I will build my church; and the gates of hell shall not prevail against it." These passages give the foundation of the church. It was organized by the apostles upon this foundation and governed by divine authority alone.

We now proceed to give a brief history of the Church of Christ. First, the name; second, the officers and their duties; third, the ordinances and their observance.

First, in regard to the name, we learn from the Christian Scriptures that they were called in their collective capacity: "The church"; "The church of God"; "The churches of God"; "The churches of Christ"; "The body, the church"; "The body (church) of Christ"; "Household of God."

In their individual capacity they were called "saints," "brethren," "disciples," "disciples of Christ," "Christians," "children of the kingdom," "saints of God," "heirs"; also such figurative terms as "sheep" and "branches" were used to designate the members of the Church of Christ, and are sufficient to describe them in their varied relations.

Second, we note the officers of this organization and their duties. This is very important in giving a description of any religious body, for churches frequently differ in this regard. We learn from the Scriptures that there were "bishops" or "elders," "deacons" and "ministers" or "evangelists"; and these were all the officers. This may be thought strange in view of the multiplicity of the officers in the organizations, sects, and parties that now exist, but these three classes were all the officers authorized in the organized New Testament church. . .

There are no higher titles than these given to any man in the churches. However, not satisfied with these the pope and priest have used the names belonging to Deity, "Holy Lord God the Pope," and "Holy Father." The priests call themselves Father in direct violation of the command of Christ: "Call no man your Father on earth, for one is your Father even he who in in heaven."

This is in a religious sense and strictly forbidden. Therefore no child of God should use any of these sacred names in speaking of a religious dignitary. We note further that "reverend" is never applied to man, not even to an apostle, bishop, elder, or minister, but to God only, and used but once in the Bible "Holy and reverend is his name." Therefore what right has any man to assume this title?

This, then, was a perfect organization. In every congregation there were bishops or elders to oversee the church and labor for its spiritual welfare —to settle its difficulties, strengthen the weak, encourage the timid, seeking to restore those who had wandered away from the fold, and to build up all in the most holy faith.

And they had deacons to superintend the temporal welfare of the congregation and to care for the needy; and ministers or evangelists bearing news of life and salvation to the world, planting new congregations and enlarging the borders of Zion. They were "to preach the word, be instant in season, out of season; reprove, rebuke, exhort with all long-suffering and doctrine." The officers of the New Testament church consisted of these three distinct classes and no more. It had no archbishops, cardinals, prelates, and no pope claiming political and ecclesiastical power. Thus it will be seen that no church that differs with the original one in officers and organization can be identical with the New Testament church. . . .

. . . In order to give a description of any religious body it is necessary to know its ordinances. The apostolic church observed one important ordinance which distinguished it from all other religious bodies. . . . It is called the "Lord's Supper," "the Breaking of Bread" and "The Communion of the Blood of Christ and of the Body of Christ." Christ told His disciples to do this in remembrance of Him. There is one fact connected with the founder of this church that partly, if not wholly, accounts for this singular, interesting, and important ordinance, and that is, He died the great anti-type, prefigured by every victim that had bled on patriarchal or Jewish altar. He came in the fulness of time and laid down His life as a sacrifice for the sin of the world; for "without the shedding of blood there is no remission." His death, then, was the noblest act of divine love. He died that man might have life; He died that man might not fear to die; He died that death might be disarmed and the gloom of the grave dispelled, that man might rise from the dust and ashes to endless life. It was therefore ordained that His death should be celebrated rather than His birth; for this great work of redemption was not accomplished until from the cross He said, "It is finished." And, therefore, to His death Christians will ever cling as the foundation of its brightest hopes. . . .

The Church of Christ celebrated the day upon which the Son of God triumphed over death. We are informed that "upon the first day of the week, when the disciples came together to break bread, Paul preached unto them" . . . . In accordance with the example of the early believers in Christ, Christians should now observe every first day of the week in memory of the resurrection of Christ.

The next ordinance to which we direct attention is that of Christian baptism. . . . In regard to the importance of baptism we observe that it is the final act by which persons come into Christ. "So many of us as were baptized into Christ were baptized into his death." It is sacred, uniting the names of Diety. It is the only act required to be performed in the Name of the Father, Son and Holy Spirit—the sacred names invoked upon persons who are baptized into Christ. Again, it is the only ordinance representing both the burial and the resurrection of Christ. The early Christians immersed, they were not sprinkled or poured. All scholars of note admit that immersion was the primitive practice, and many passages of Scripture will not make sense unless thus translated. All persons, therefore, who came into the primitive church were buried in baptism. Thus we read, "buried with him in baptism, wherein also ye are risen with him . . . from the dead." Again, "we are buried with him by baptism into death; that like as Christ was raised up from the dead by the glory of the Father, even so we also should walk in newness of life. For if we have been planted together in the likeness of his death, we shall be also in the likeness of his resurrection." There are some who have changed this ordinance and have utterly destroyed its meaning by instituting other things instead, which do not represent the burial and the resurrection of Christ. . . .

Divine wisdom has established all the ordinances, and they go on testifying to the great work of redemption, and the great facts of the gospel until time shall end.

Of church polity, Mr. Phillips observed:

The Church of Christ, as divinely established, was congregational. There was no higher organization, no synod, assembly, or ecclesiastical body placed over it or given legislative authority for it, for Christ is the "head of the church." Individual Christians are made "kings and priests unto God." They are called "a holy priesthood," "a royal priesthood." Being sovereign they have an absolute right, under Christ, to select their own servants or officers. Until Christians realize this vital fact, many will be in servile religious bondage.

There are, however, many reasons why there should be cooperation and union among the various congregations, not to legislate for the Church of Christ, which is prohibited, but to promote its welfare, and by united effort to spread the gospel abroad and build up the Kingdom of God on earth. By the classification mentioned in the Scriptures it is evident that the churches were divided into districts as "The churches of Galatia," "The churches of Asia," and "The churches of Judea." We are informed that "The churches of Macedonia" and "Achaia" joined together "in ministering to the saints," and there was a "brother whose praise in the gospel is spread through all the churches . . . and who was also appointed by the churches to travel" with Paul and Titus; and of them it was said, "They are messengers of the churches." This shows cooperation of the churches in the fellowship of giving and ministration.

The Church of Christ was so ordained and established, and its simple form of government was such that it could be planted in every nation and grow under any form of government. Hence the general form of cooperation among the various churches or congregations, for its spread seemed wisely to have been left to the good judgment of Christians under their various circumstances and surroundings in different nations and among divers peoples.

Christianity is a historical religion. The Church of Christ was complete, and so passed into history with the close of the New Testament. So far as revealed to us there has been no change made since, by any authority in heaven or upon the earth. Why can not the Church of Christ be reestablished everywhere now as it was then, in all its divine beauty and simplicity? Can not Christians build now on the same foundation, having the same Lord, the same name, the same officers, chosen in the same way, observing the same ordinances in the same way, telling the penitent believers to do the same things in order to become members, requiring the church members to live now as they lived then? If this be not the Church of Christ where can it be found? It is vain to search outside of inspired history to find the true church of the true Redeemer.

The concluding chapters of *The Church of Christ* called for the unity of all Christians and the exaltation of Jesus Christ not only as the Head of the Church but the King of Kings and Lord of Lords in the earth.

B. D. Phillips absorbed these teachings of his father and made them the expression of his own faith in Christ and the Church. During his lifetime he frequently quoted from the book. With its criteria he measured all the objects of his philanthropy, especially when it came to his generous gifts to institutions of higher education in the Christian Churches and Churches of Christ.

With enthusiasm he observed his father's efforts to advance the Restoration cause. He was with him when he made his decision to back E. V. Zollars in his plan to establish a university in Oklahoma and was thrilled as the vision of this new institution unfolded in the conversations of these two great leaders. It was in June, 1906, during the Commencement season at Hiram College, that B. D.'s father made his proposal to Zollars. He recognized the importance and the needs of the great and growing Southwest. Quick to discern crisis periods, he saw that the opportune moment had come for the planting of a Christian college in a region destined to be densely populated and an important economic factor in the life of the nation. The enabling act granting statehood to Oklahoma was passed the very day that the conversation took place at Hiram. T. W. Phillips said, "Brother Zollars, go out to the new State and talk to our brethren about establishing the school and I will stand behind you." This made the enterprise possible. It stimulated the people to attempt what otherwise they would not have had the vision or the courage to undertake.

Phillips' gifts called out matching gifts from the city of Enid, which Zollars chose as the best location, and from individuals in the area. Three splendid buildings were erected on a beautiful campus and Oklahoma Christian University came into being. At T. W. Phillips' death a grateful board of trustees voted to change the name of the institution to Phillips University.

In later years B. D. was also vitally concerned when his father made possible the establishment of Phillips Bible Institute. The elder Phillips was ahead of his time in seeing the value of normal school training for Sunday school teachers and leaders and the training of "lay preachers." He was an admirer of P. H. Welshimer, minister of the First Christian Church, Canton, Ohio, who had built up the largest congregation of the Brotherhood primarily through a great evangelically-oriented Sunday school, at that time the largest in the world. Phillips felt that rural and village churches had limitations that called for a special type of leadership which could be developed in the atmosphere of this great church. Welshimer gladly cooperated and Martin L. Pierce was called to direct the educational program. For five years Phillips Bible Institute functioned effectively. It produced hundreds of Christian leaders and workers and became the inspiration of a new type of ministerial education among the Christian Churches and Churches of Christ. When PBI was finally discontinued, a whole new system of "Bible institutes and Bible colleges" came into being. They are continuing to produce thousands of Christian leaders and workers for service at home and abroad. Many of these schools have been blessed by generous gifts from the son who saw himself as providentially helping to project the realization of his father's dream.

In both religion and business B. D. Phillips learned from association with his father that hard work, courage, sacrifice, and eternal vigilance were needed to preserve and defend the high ideals of truth and right to which he was irrevocably committed. There was no place for compromise or disloyalty in the Phillips Family tradition. One incident in the life of T. W. Phillips will illustrate this fact.

When Thomas W. Lawson was writing his famous treatise on "frenzied finance" a friend said, "You are making one mistake. You say that the Standard Oil Company always got whatever it wanted. That is not so. You have overlooked the confrontation

40

of T. W. Phillips and John D. Rockefeller." As the story goes, Lawson proceeded to do some research and changed the record in his book.

As B. D. Phillips liked to tell the story, John D. Rockefeller and a small coterie of men conceived the idea of monopolizing the petroleum industry. In collusion with certain leading railroad officials and political gangsters, they organized the South Improvement Company and got a special charter from the State of Pennsylvania which allowed them almost unlimited privileges. They secured a rebate arrangement with the railroads operating in the oil-producing country that gave them secret preferential rates, rebates, and kickbacks over all other shippers of oil. Between the railroad boycotts and cut-rate wars initiated by SIC the independent producers, refiners, and marketers were gravely threatened. At first, the protests of the "independents" and the public were so successful in countering the Rockefeller plot that the SIC went out of business and the Standard Oil Company came into being. There was no change, however, in the determination of Rockefeller to develop his monopoly. He adopted more subtle means. Scores of independent oil companies were forced into bankruptcy and hundreds of families lost their fortunes. (Ida M. Tarbell in her tremendous book, *History of the Standard Oil Company*, tells the whole story.)

At this point T. W. Phillips came into the picture. He was one of the biggest independent producers in the country. There were still about two thousand of them. Largely through his influence he organized the Producers Protective Association and was elected its first president. At this time Standard was not producing oil. Phillips proposed that the two thousand producers shut down a large portion of the production and drill no new wells. Then he called on Standard, with its 31 million barrels of oil in reserve, to join in an agreement that would be fair and reasonable to all parties concerned, and which would place the oil industry in a position above reproach in the business community and in the nation as a whole. For a time conditions improved for the independents, but Standard adopted new tactics to achieve its ends. It went into the production field, buying out many of the independents. Then, partly through personal jealousies and partly because of temporarily higher prices of oil, the PPA disintegrated. T. W. Phillips organized the remnant of the independents into the great Pure Oil Company, became its chief adviser, and until his death was a member of its board.

When he ran for Congress and wrote the bill creating a national Industrial Commission, he made possible the development of "Anti-Trust" legislation that led to the eventual conviction of Standard Oil for its evil deeds. Theodore Roosevelt once said, "Thomas W. Phillips gave me the 'big stick' I used to slay the dragons of special privilege."

This tremendous achievement made T. W. Phillips one of the most unusual men of his generation—a man of great wealth who built his fortune without claiming a dishonest dollar, and a Christian statesman without a stain upon his escutcheon.

This same incident had religious repercussions. John D. Rockefeller, seeking to make the public forget his violations of the civil and criminal laws of the nation, later entered upon a spree of philanthropies. Among them was a gift of $50,000 to the Foreign Christian Missionary Society, to which Mr. Phillips had long been a contributor. He branded this as "tainted money" and called upon the Society to return the gift. He claimed that the FCMS, by accepting the money, would become a partner with a man and a firm that were lawbreakers and would place the Society in a position of condoning their methods. The influential *Christian Standard*, of Cincinnati, joined him in his position. Then ensued a controversy that rocked the brotherhood of Christian Churches and Churches of Christ to their roots. Phillips carried the issue to the 1907 "National Convention" of the brethren at Norfolk, Virginia. He received a cool reception and the FCMS kept the Rockefeller money. This was the beginning of a ruthless reappraisal of the policies and programs of many of the agencies which the Phillips family had heavily supported. Where there was departure from the biblical, evangelical Christian faith and from the principles of the Restoration Movement, Phillips support was withdrawn.

T. W. Phillips told his son not long before his death that he should be vigilant to detect all departures from "the faith once delivered to the saints," because the day would come when the authenticity and the authority of the Bible would be questioned, when human opinion would be exalted above the Word of God, when the terms of pardon would be modified, when the churches would adopt the practice of "open membership," and when church unity would be sought by compromise and a return to Catholicism.

42

This was a prophecy which made a great impression on B. D. Phillips and caused him to crusade for the preservation and perpetuation of the true faith even at the expense of lost friendships, and honor and prestige among certain elements in the church.

B. D. Phillips often referred to many simple basic lessons he learned from his father. For instance, he learned that the only reward the philanthropist should expect for his gifts is the personal satisfaction afforded one's inner self. He realized that there is not over one chance in ten that his beneficence will be adequately appreciated. This unappreciative attitude on the part of persons and institutions, even though general, is no excuse for ingratitude. Because a majority of those whom our Lord cleansed from leprosy (nine out of ten) failed to return and express thanks was no reason for Jesus Christ to cease His healing ministries. B. D. learned from his father's example to show his appreciation for what others had done for him. He showed his appreciation of his father by supporting the altruistic work which he founded, supported, or in which he was vitally interested.

B. D. learned to be a gentleman from a real gentleman. His father was a man of natural polish and courtesy, but he was more than that; he embodied kindness, honor, and high principles without which qualifications no man can be a thoroughbred gentleman. He was so free from deception, duplicity, and treachery that it is unlikely he ever told a "white lie" even to fool somebody on April Fool's Day. When making an affidavit he usually "affirmed" rather than "swore" in harmony with the practice advised by our Lord in Matthew 5. His father's "yes" or "no" was as good and dependable as a thousand oaths, regardless of who might make them.

B. D. learned to be generous almost to a fault. His father told him that he could have been many times as wealthy as he was if he had been selfish and acquisitive, but he felt that all he had was the gift of God who had bestowed upon him health, the right use of his mind, business ingenuity and sagacity, and vast opportunities for development and service. These blessings created an obligation to share his wealth with enterprises that were seeking to do God's will and extend His cause and Kingdom. He gave, and true to Christ's promise in Luke 6 the Lord gave back to him "pressed down, shaken together, and running over."

B. D. learned to beware of bringing men into the business who were "lovers of money" and whose primary concern in life was "making money." His father told him that you never know the character of a person unless or until he has had the opportunity to take advantage of you in a large way in money matters without exposing himself to criminal prosecution. The thief or the embezzler calculates the risk and takes his chances; therefore, he is less despicable and less cowardly than one who takes advantage of your confidence and uses unforeseen and unexpected circumstances to benefit himself at your expense, when he knows his acts are beyond the reach of the law. "Avoid such men," for, said he, "the love of money is the root of all evil."

Benjamin Dwight Phillips was an apt scholar in the "university of life." The lessons he learned caused him to feel a deep-seated longing to make a worthwhile contribution to his day and generation in the highest and best tradition of his forebears. And God blessed him.

IV

The World of Business

"K EEP AN EYE on Ben.   He has what it takes to make a good businessman."   So said his father, T. W. Phillips, Sr., to a member of the family shortly before his death.   These were words of prophetic discernment which came true to a remarkable degree.

Business was life to B. D. Phillips.   Because of his deeply religious nature he equated business and religion.   Maltbie Babcock once said, "Business is religion, and religion is business.   The man who does not make business his religion has a religious life of no force, and a man who does not make a religion of his business has a business life of no character."   B. D. Phillips understood and appreciated that.

In dealing with people Mr. Phillips had a great knowledge of character with an unerring ability to know the right moment to act and the courage to take that action.   A discreet rapidity pervaded all the movements of his thought and action.   In a business deal, he was expert in getting all the facts, down to the last detail, evaluating them in the light of clearly-defined principles, making right decisions, and acting promptly and boldly.

He knew the Phillips gas and oil business from A to Z.   No one knew it like he did.   He liked to tell the story of it from the days of "blood, sweat, and tears" to the days of its immense success. T. W. Phillips, Sr., the founder of the business as we have seen (page 9), was primarily and originally interested in oil. However, as the oil in Western Pennsylvania began to be depleted in the late 1890's or early 1900's, and at least partly at the insistence of T. W. Phillips, Jr., the company began to move from an oil producing company to a gas producing company. At about this period, gas began to be used much more widely by individual consumers and by industry. The company continued to have some oil production until the late 1940's, at which time the last of its remaining oil wells and facilities were sold.

T. W. Phillips, Sr., began his activities in the oil industry about the time that the Phillips Petroleum Company was incorporated under the laws of the State of New York, in 1865. One old stock certificate of this company indicates that while the company was incorporated in the State of New York, its activities were largely conducted in Venango County, Pennsylvania. Mr. Phillips was recorded as being President of the company on March 1, 1865. On July 30, 1896, a Pennsylvania corporation was formed under the name of The Phillips Gas Company. According to its original charter, the activities of this company were confined to certain townships in the counties of Butler, Armstrong, and Allegheny, Pennsylvania. By amendment to the charter, dated July 31, 1900, Westmoreland County, Pennsylvania, was added to its operating territory.

Under date of May 31, 1900, "Articles of Association" were entered into by an association designated as T. W. Phillips Sons and Company. Members of this Partnership Association were T. W. Phillips, Sr., Mrs. Pamphila Phillips, Clarinda Grace Phillips (later Johnson), Benjamin D. Phillips, T. W. Phillips, Jr., Herbert C. Phillips, and Victor K. Phillips. The Articles of Association indicated that the operations of this partnership were to be carried out in Allegheny, Armstrong, Butler, and Westmoreland counties. On June 30, 1904, the Phillips Gas Company, by appropriate application to the Commonwealth of Pennsylvania, extended its operating territory to include the counties of Mercer, Crawford, and Erie, all in Pennsylvania. On September 30, 1930, the territory was further extended to include the counties of McKean, Potter, Tioga, Bradford, Clinton, and Lycoming, all in Pennsylvania.

On October 3, 1904, the T. W. Phillips Gas and Oil Company

entered into a merger agreement with Home Natural Gas Company and Enterprise Natural Gas Company of Freeport, Pennsylvania, the resulting corporation being T. W. Phillips Gas and Oil Company. The Home Natural Gas Company had certain producing properties in the east portion of Butler County and west portion of Armstrong County, which adjoin Butler County on the east. Enterprise Natural Gas Company of Freeport, Pennsylvania, had certain producing properties in the southeast portion of Butler County and southwest portion of Armstrong County, Pennsylvania. On July 11, 1906, T. W. Phillips Gas and Oil Company entered into a merger agreement with Mahoning Gas and Heat Company and Citizens Fuel Company of Punxsutawney, Pennsylvania. Both Mahoning Gas and Heat Company and Citizens Fuel Company had certain operating properties in Jefferson County, Pennsylvania. The Citizens Fuel Company served consumers in the Borough of Punxsutawney, Pennsylvania. The resulting corporation from this merger was the "T. W. Phillips Gas and Oil Company." On August 25, 1916, T. W. Phillips Gas and Oil Company entered into a merger agreement with Independent Natural Gas Company, the resulting corporation being T. W. Phillips Gas and Oil Company. Independent Natural Gas Company had certain producing properties in Butler County, Pennsylvania, which served a portion of the City of Butler. This last merger agreement indicates that in 1916, T. W. Phillips Gas and Oil Company had a total of 14,500 consumers.

Following the death of T. W. Phillips, Sr., which occurred July 21, 1912, his oldest son, T. W. Phillips, Jr., succeeded to the presidency of the T. W. Phillips Gas and Oil Company. T. W. Phillips, Jr., was quite active in the affairs of the company from the inception of The Phillips Gas Company in 1896 until he entered Congress in 1923 as a representative of his Congressional District, which at that time was composed of Butler and Lawrence counties. Upon the entry of T. W. Phillips, Jr., into politics in 1923, B. D. Phillips in his capacity of Vice-President of the company actually became the operating head of the company and continued in such capacity until the time of his death October 23, 1968. B. D. Phillips became President of the company in 1956, upon the death of T. W. Phillips, Jr. From 1923 until the time of his death in 1956, T. W. Phillips, Jr., retained a vital interest in the company and was consulted with respect to all major matters in the company's operations; however, from 1923 until the date of his death, B. D. Phillips assumed the responsibility for the day-by-day operations of the company. Under the management of T. W. Phillips, Jr., and B. D. Phillips, the company's operations had expanded from serving some 5,000 to 6,000 consumers in 1912, to some 14,500 in 1916. At the end of 1968, the company was serving approximately 42,000 consumers, including some sixty large industrial plants.

Mr. Phillips had the reputation of being "a detail man." His encyclopedic knowledge of the business extended to each gas well it owned. He knew the wells intimately. He had authorized their drilling, overseen that operation, gauged their output, arranged for their supervision, and kept a personal record of their productivity. He knew the supervisors (usually on a first name basis) and often talked with them directly about the problems of their individual wells. He knew the location of the wells, the terms of contract, the depth, the line pressure at testing periods. A huge chart in the Butler office showed all the wells and a comprehensive record of their status which gave him all he needed to know day by day and hour by hour about the individual and the total operation.

What was true of the wells was true of the pipelines, the delivery system, the major consumers, the administrative and service organization, governmental relations. When anyone asked a question about the business, B. D. Phillips had the answer. With remarkable precision this was true down to his last day at the office. He knew what he was supposed to know and he expected everyone in the organization to know what they were supposed to know and deliver. He produced and he expected everybody else to produce. When troubles and crises arose, he was cool, calm, and collected. Everybody in the organization had full confidence in his ability to find solutions and keep things moving in the right direction. Everyone stood ready to obey orders and do his bit.

While he operated a business machine, he was not unaware of the human element involved. He liked to think of the company personnel to a very large degree as a part of the Phillips Family. He knew his fellow-laborers and loved them. He dealt with them in a simple, frank manner, without any high pretensions of op-

48

pressive greatness, trying to understand their problems, obliging them when he could, and often being generous to a fault.

Mr. Phillips as the head of the business had a high sense of stewardship. He thought of himself as responsible to his consumers, his family, his stockholders, his church, and his community. He was proud of the fact that the T. W. Phillips Gas and Oil Company maintained the lowest gas rates of any company in Pennsylvania. It was operated impartially for each and every stockholder, expenses and overhead being kept to an irreducible minimum. As President of the company, he kept administrative salaries low, and tried to be even more careful with company funds than with his own. He felt that he was in a position of trust and confidence in relation to the stockholders of the corporation, and therefore had no right to engage either directly or indirectly in any activity likely to be detrimental to the interests of the corporation, its stockholders, and its consumers.

Mr. Phillips never had any ambition to become a business tycoon, to pyramid his business into a mighty monopoly of some sort, or to "tell the world" about Phillips Gas and Oil. Modern business expansionist ideas fell on a deaf ear. He had control of greater resources than many men who moved in that direction but he was content to do what he believed to be best for those who trusted him. At one time he was importuned to move his business headquarters to Pittsburgh and take his rightful place in the business community of this great financial and industrial center of the nation, but he refused.

In a letter written January 3, 1962, to one who questioned his policy, Mr. Phillips revealed something of his business philosophy:

The success of the T. W. Phillips Gas and Oil Company, from the very beginning, has been due to our ability to operate on an extremely moderate basis, securing the benefit of low costs, avoiding excess costs of all kinds, and making small wells profitable by having leases of graded royalty, permitting the retention of small gas wells, combined with seeking 24-hour industrial consumers of some size. I had wonderful training in this respect the first ten years I was in Butler, as we were hard-pressed for funds and had a large bond issue outstanding. Certainly nickels were watched, a trait I have not lost. However, by 1915 or 1916 we emerged from this condition with a splendid cash situation which was the envy of many other business concerns. . .

We are in a spendthrift age. Most companies are operated by employees who are particularly interested in heading a company of larger and larger

49

proportions, thereby receiving larger and larger salaries, or stock options or benefits; and pointing with pride to the volume of business the company is doing, reflecting to their glorification. The company is thereby burdened with a larger and larger overhead which must be reckoned with when conditions are unsatisfactory and the profit margin is reduced. In some cases under such a policy the stockholders receive no benefits at all. Our companies are operated for the benefit of their stockholders to the nth degree. I am just as careful about the expenses of these companies, as I am about my own expenses, perhaps more so. I feel that I have a trusteeship in acting for a large number of people connected with the family, and in some cases, at least, their dividends are of vital importance to their well being.

We have a small corporation with a small gross income, compared with many notable corporations of great size. A dollar spent or a dollar obligated should be given careful scrutiny, avoiding obligations that to a larger company with employee management would be insignificant and would be approved with stockholders' funds for the sake of generosity and personal good feeling. It is all too easy to be generous with other people's money under such circumstances. . . . This may be easy for some to do, but my conscience would never permit me to undertake such a policy and program.

In the above letter Mr. Phillips speaks of "companies" which he headed. In 1928 the Phillipses set up a corporation known as "The Pennsylvania Investment and Real Estate Corporation," chartered under the laws of the State of Delaware. Its charter privileges were very broad, permitting the company to engage in almost any type of business. The activities of the company from 1928 to date have, however, been largely confined to the purchase and sale of securities with somewhat nominal investments in real estate. The purpose for forming the company was twofold. The T. W. Phillips Gas and Oil Company as of 1928 had paid off its indebtedness incurred in its early years of existence and had accumulated several million dollars in value of outside securities. T. W. Phillips, Jr., and B. D. Phillips decided that it was unwise to expose these assets of the company to the hazards of the natural gas business. Furthermore, T. W. Phillips Gas and Oil Company, by reason of its being a public utility and subject to the jurisdiction of the then Public Service Commission (now Public Utility Commission), was formed by turning over to the investment company some five million dollars in securities owned by T. W. Phillips Gas and Oil Company. At that time, T. W. Phillips Gas and Oil Company had outstanding 60,000 shares of Common Stock. When the investment company was formed, it issued 60,000 shares of

Common Stock in payment for the securities obtained from the gas company. These shares were then distributed by the gas company to its shareholders on a share for share basis. T. W. Phillips, Jr., became President of the Pennsylvania Investment and Real Estate Corporation, but its investment portfolio was very largely handled by B. D. Phillips. Under his management, the assets of the company increased from its original capital of some five million dollars in 1928 to many times that amount by the end of 1968. In 1956, at the death of his brother, he became President of the Corporation.

Mr. Phillips was constantly alert to changing conditions in the operation of the gas business. He often startled his associates with new proposals for the good of the industry as a whole. One of the finest examples of this was in the development of the underground storage of gas. He was a pioneer in this development. The surface storage of gas had proved over a period of years to be impracticable for two reasons; first, surface facilities, such as tanks, provided a very limited capacity for storage purposes. Secondly, the storage of gas in surface containers was extremely hazardous. Some years ago the Equitable Gas Company of Pittsburgh had storage tanks located in the city and a very serious explosion occurred. Some years later, one of the Ohio gas companies had an explosion of certain storage tanks in the eastern part of the City of Cleveland, resulting in extensive damages and loss of some lives. The necessity for storage is likewise twofold; in the first place, during the summer months when no gas is used for heating purposes, the market for gas is very much smaller than it is during the winter months. In the second place, on the advent of the transportation of gas from the West to the considerably larger markets in the East, the necessity arose to provide facilities by which the gas could be taken in almost uniform daily amounts during both summer and winter. The transmission companies could not economically incur the tremendous expense of building pipelines from the southwest to the eastern coast without being assured of constant deliveries throughout the year. The result was that contracts for the purchase of Western gas provided that the purchaser must take his deliveries both summer and winter in almost equal amounts day by day, or in the alternative, pay for gas not taken. This meant that the purchasing company had to develop storage facilities in order to take its contractual allotment of gas during the summer months, as well as in the winter. The Phillips Company had several leases a mile or two east of the City of Butler upon which wells having a very large flow of gas had been drilled in the early 1900's. Other drilling in this same general area and on adjoining leases had indicated that the pool did not extend to these other leases and was, therefore, of very limited extent. Mr. Phillips concluded that this would be an ideal area in which to store gas underground, because of the existence of two requisites which were essential to the creation of a storage pool. In the first place, the very large flow of gas had indicated that the sand from which the gas was being produced was porous and permeable. In the second place, the wells drilled nearby on other leases indicated that the pool did not extend beyond rather certain, definite limits. Obviously, no one would store gas in an area from which gas might be withdrawn by other operators. Mr. Phillips had also observed from his intimate knowledge of the wells owned by the company that there were indications at times when wells were producing from several sands that gas was moving from the sand having the higher pressure to the sand having a lower pressure. He, accordingly, concluded that gas could be ejected into a particular sand where there were indications that the sand was porous and permeable and of limited extent. In 1942, he arranged for the installation of a compressor in the area above mentioned just east of the City of Butler, and began the pumping of gas brought from other sources into the sand present in the area mentioned. This permitted the company to withdraw gas from wells some fifty to sixty miles away from Butler, and have the same near at hand and readily available for the winter market in Butler. The experiment proved quite successful and the small compressor which was originally installed was soon replaced by a compressor having a much larger capacity. In later years other storage pools were developed in the company's operating areas and by the end of 1968 the company had eight underground storage pools in operation. The underground storage of gas, of course, became a vital factor in the natural gas industry and has involved the expenditure of many millions of dollars. According to the *American Gas Journal*, at the end of 1968, there were 308 underground storage pools in operation, spread throughout twenty-five states.

Mr. Phillips knew how to meet competition. Probably the biggest challenge he met during his long business career was that of the Anderson Natural Gas Company. This is the thrilling story:

The early operations of the T. W. Phillips Gas and Oil Company were confined largely to Butler County and several adjoining counties. As these areas gradually became less productive, it was necessary for the company to expand its operations to additional counties, mainly to the east and north of its original operating territory. The result was that the company had to transport its gas from increasingly greater distances to supply its market in Butler, which was at the extreme western end of its system, as the company had no production west of the City of Butler. During this same period two of the company's largest industrial consumers, namely, Pullman Standard Car Manufacturing Company and Armco Steel Corporation, were expanding their operations and increasing their use of gas to the point at which Phillips was unable to supply their total fuel requirements, and it was necessary for these companies to use either electricity or oil as supplemental fuel. During the late 1940's, Western gas was not available because of the limited capacity of lines coming from the West, and furthermore, at that time Phillips could not purchase out-of-state gas without subjecting itself to the jurisdiction of the Federal Power Commission.

Taking advantage of this situation, a group of men took an option on the entire outstanding stock of the Anderson Natural Gas Company, a local corporation which had a limited number of customers in the Butler area but practically no production. The prospective buyers thought they could get a supply of Western gas through out-of-state pipeline companies, transfer the same through certain facilities of the T. W. Phillips Gas and Oil Company to the Anderson Natural Gas Company which would supply all the considerable needs of the Pullman and the Armco plants in Butler. To force Phillips into this arrangement all sorts of threats were made but to no avail. Finally, the cabal brought pressure upon Phillips to buy into Anderson for $500,000. Mr. Phillips knew that the outfit had paid only $10,000 for their option on Anderson; that the $500,000 would represent less than fifty per cent of the stock ownership; and that his competitors would not only control Anderson but the lion's share of the Pullman and Armco business. It looked for a time that Mr. Phillips was caught in a dilemma. Then he sent his very capable attorney son-in-law,

Rolland L. Ehrman, to Harrisburg, the State capital, to examine the files of the Pennsylvania Public Utilities Commission in an effort to discover whether there was some other natural gas company chartered to operate in the Butler area, aside from the T. W. Phillips Gas and Oil Company and the Anderson Natural Gas Company. Mr. Ehrman, after long and painstaking explorations, discovered the existence of the Acme Natural Gas Company which had the charter rights they were looking for. He visited their principal stockholders who resided in the Kittaning community. At that time it was a very small concern, having five or six wells and some twenty or twenty-five consumers in Gilpin township, Armstrong County. A deal was made with Acme by which the entire stock of the company was purchased in the name of the Pennsylvania Investment and Real Estate Corporation. Exercising the charter rights of Acme, a supply of Western gas was obtained, and a contract made with Manufacturers Light and Heat Company of Pittsburgh (one of the companies of the Columbia Gas System) to deliver it to Acme at Ellwood City.

Acme, after obtaining approval of the Federal Power Commission, extended a line to Butler, completed contracts with the big industrial users and was in business before Anderson's schemers knew what happened to them. Anderson had no real contracts for Western gas, no real permissions from the Federal Power Commission, no real means of bringing gas into Butler, and no real contracts with the big industrial users in the Butler area. Completely outwitted, they withdrew from the scene. Mr. Phillips, who was quite active in the whole competitive situation and in the acquisition of Acme, took a tremendous satisfaction in his Company's victory. Likewise he came to see "little Acme" become quite successful in its own right. During the year 1968 Acme's revenues amounted to around three million dollars. Since the days of this battle, and as a result of subsequent legislation, Phillips Gas and Oil remains free of the jurisdiction of the Federal Power Commission and is fully prepared for any new contingencies that may arise in fair business competition.

During his lifetime B. D. Phillips was the chief adviser to members of the Phillips Family respecting their investments involved in the Phillips corporations. As an example of this, he was largely responsible for the affairs of the T. W. Phillips, Jr., Charitable Trust. This fund was comprised of 42.5 per cent of the

54

assets of his brother's estate and represented some five to six million dollars, according to the will dated July 21, 1955. Trustees were named as follows: Mrs. Greta Phillips, B. D. Phillips, Sr., B. D. Phillips, Jr., R. L. Ehrman, and F. L. Weigand, Jr. The will specified that "It shall be the duty of my Charitable Trustees at their discretion to distribute the income (of the fund) among churches, educational institutions, and other institutions of the Disciples of Christ, the Church of Christ, and the Christian Church. My suggestion is that all of the (fund) be exhausted by application through the aforesaid institutions within twenty (20) years after my death." The grants made from this Trust involved a great deal of painstaking work on the part of B. D. Phillips. He took a personal interest in the distributions and in the objects for which they were allocated. Very often he would match these gifts with liberal payments out of his own personal funds. In later chapters of this volume there will be repeated reference to these Phillips philanthropies.

Mr. Phillips, acting for himself and for the Phillips interests, manifested a great concern for the Butler YMCA, the Butler County Memorial Hospital, and other community enterprises. He deliberately refrained from accepting positions of public leadership in any of them, but they knew they could count on him for advice and counsel and generous financial support. He was for many years the largest contributor to various building campaigns for both the Y and the Hospital. Annually his name led all the rest in contributions for the Community Chest. He served on the Y Board and was extremely active on the Building Committee at the time of the erection of the McKean Street building in downtown Butler. He could be counted in favor of every movement for the enlargement and betterment of the Butler community.

While Mr. Phillips was deeply immersed in the world of business, he saw it as only one phase of the supreme business of serving in his Father's world. Here he was a living demonstration of the fact that a man can be a business success and a good Christian at the same time. Many times the Word of the Lord to Joshua must have come to him: "This book . . . shall not depart out of thy mouth; but thou shalt meditate thereon day and night, that thou mayest do according to all that is written therein: for then thou shalt make thy way prosperous, and then shalt thou have good success." He made the Holy Scriptures a vital part of his life. Many times he must have remembered the admonitions of his saintly father and mother and considered the fact that if it had not been for their Christian examples and their early training, there might not have been any T. W. Phillips Gas and Oil Company and he might not ever have known the peace and joy which come from certain knowledge of the everyday and everlasting love and power and the guidance and strength of Jesus Christ his Lord. He saw himself as only a steward of all he possessed, and in that stewardship he was always found faithful. Like John Wanamaker, Robert A. Long, J. Howard Pew, J. C. Penney, R. G. LeTourneau, and many others in the galaxy of successful Christian businessmen of his generation, B. D. Phillips always thanked God and gave Him the glory for his business attainments.

V

A Man Among Men

THE REMARKABLE versatility of B. D. Phillips extended to every important phase of life—the spiritual, mental, physical, and social. He was a full-orbed man who measured up to the highest standards man sets for man.

This may surprise some who thought they knew him. In certain circles he was known as the businessman and industrialist par excellence with few interests beyond the daily grind. To others, he was the churchman and philanthropist deeply concerned with Christian higher education and the extension of the Kingdom of God.

Mr. Phillips had no penchant for seeing his name in headlines or his picture emblazoned in magazines or on television screens. He avoided reporters and authors bent on getting exclusive interviews. His comparative anonymity so far as the public was concerned was the natural result. Only his intimate companions and friends really knew the magnitude of his interests and his attainments in the many fields of his concern.

This characteristic reveals to a very large degree the quality of the man. Bulwer-Lytton once said, "The distinguishing trait of people accustomed to good society is a calm, imperturbable quiet which pervades all their habits and actions, from the greatest to the least. They eat in quiet, move in quiet, live in quiet, and lose their wife, or even their money in quiet. It is only low persons who cannot take up either a spoon or an affront without making an amazing noise about it."

He was the businessman and industrialist. He was the churchman and philanthropist. But he was much more. He was also a sportsman of parts and was nationally-known among other sportsmen of repute. He was a hunter who ranged the United States and Canada in pursuit of rare game. He was a naturalist of distinction. He was a noted collector of stamps, of rare books, of jade and china. He was a builder who left his mark upon some of the finest structures in the nation. He was a man of broad community and social interests. He was a member of the most exclusive social clubs in Pittsburgh and other American cities. He was a patriot who knew the principles which made America great, kept abreast of every political and social development, knew the major conservative leaders of the nation and backed them in their efforts to make and keep America great.

Let us explore this little-publicized side of the life of Benjamin Dwight Phillips.

To start with, something that might appear to be rather inconsequential: Mr. Phillips was a nature lover. He especially loved flowers. Rolland Ehrman tells about an incident that happened in Switzerland. The train had stopped at a way station in the Alps. Mr. Phillips got out and wandered up a glen. When the time came for the train to leave, they called him and whistled for him, but he was nowhere to be found. The train had to pull out without him. Later, when he joined his party in Paris, he rather sheepishly admitted that he had discovered so many new varieties of flowers that he had been enticed from one to another until he was temporarily lost in the forest. This side of his nature is further revealed (page 87) in the magnificent collection of flowers, shrubs, trees, and vines that he brought to Elm Court. Practically every known ornamental plant that will grow in Western Pennsylvania is there. His knowledge of their names, both common and scientific, often amazed those who strolled with him in the park-like surroundings of Elm Court. He literally loved every sprig of them.

We said Mr. Phillips' love of nature might be considered "inconsequential," but maybe not. It was London's great Baptist

58

preacher, Spurgeon, who said: "To understand and appreciate nature you must begin with nature's God. Once you believe Him and love Him, it is surprising how easy it is to hear music in the waves, and songs in the wild whisperings of the winds; to see God everywhere in the stones, in the rocks, in the rippling brooks, in the trees, in the beautiful flowers, and hear Him everywhere, in the lowing of cattle, in the rolling of thunder, and in the fury of the tempests. Get Christ first, put Him in the right place, and you will find Him to be the wisdom of God in every experience of life." Possibly herein lies the secret of Mr. Phillips' interest in his Father's world.

Mr. Phillips' Hiram College days revealed his innate interest in competitive sports of all kinds (page 21). He starred in baseball and basketball. His baseball team chalked up a record season when he was its "southpaw" pitcher. His basketball team won the one and only Olympics championship in Hiram's history.

At Hiram, or soon after, he became a devotee of tennis and earned quite a name as an amateur. As a young man he played every day the weather permitted on a court behind the Ritts home on McKean Street in Butler. He would arrive with his good friend and business associate, Ross McCafferty, after a long day of work in and out of the office in the gas fields, for a real tennis workout. Then, as throughout his tennis career, he was always more interested in singles than in doubles. He was always in a hurry and there was an arrangement with the owner of the court that he could play promptly upon arrival. He always used new balls. At the conclusion of the play he would give them to the children of the neighborhood who stood around watching the proceedings in bright-eyed wonder.

In 1929 he built his own red *en tout cas* tennis court of the very finest construction and he spent many hours on it during the 1930's and 40's. One of the expert players he welcomed on the court was his future son-in-law, Frank Weigand, Jr. He was always generous in permitting serious tennis players to use the court, placing limits only to preserve it for high quality play.

During the 1920's and 1930's, B. D. had the reputation of being one of the best, if not the best, player in the Butler area. According to observers his game was not always orthodox but he had finesse, substantial power and he used the element of surprise to win many points. His whole game was undergirded with a will

59

to win that was far beyond the ordinary. Ross McCafferty was also noted as an excellent player. In 1930, one of the top New England preparatory school champions from Phillips Exeter Academy visited Butler. He played a match with B. D. which became a tradition among Butler tennis fans. B. D. had just returned from New Orleans the day of the match after driving all night and the day before, but he went into the game with all the zest of a professional and won in a dazzling finish.

During the baseball season Mr. Phillips would occasionally try his hand at pitching with scrub teams around Butler, but active participation soon became too much of a chore, took too much time from his work, and did not offer the sporting excellence he desired. He transferred his affections to the Pittsburgh Pirates and became a frequent visitor in the Forbes Field stands, only forty miles away. He knew all about the Pirates—past, present, and future, and rooted for them with an enthusiasm seldom matched by anyone who actually lived in the old "Smoky City."

It is not surprising, therefore, that he eventually became a part owner of this famous National League baseball team. It came about on this wise, according to Mr. Phillips' son-in-law, Joseph Sprankle, Jr.:

In the fall of 1946, Frank E. McKinney, an Indianapolis banker and a principal in the Indianapolis Baseball Club, one of the Pirate "farm" teams, learned that William E. Benswanger, owner of the Pirates, was disposed to sell the club. He contacted his friend Thomas Phillips Johnson, B. D.'s nephew, to find out if he might be interested in joining with him to purchase the Pittsburgh Baseball Company, owners of the national franchise and the Pittsburgh Athletic Company, owners of Forbes Field. Tom became interested and presented the opportunity to his uncle for consideration. B. D. decided to join with them in the purchase. He mentioned a number of times that his decision was based on the business merits of the proposition with Mr. McKinney, a businessman with knowledge of baseball, being President and running the show. "Bing" Crosby also joined them as a minor shareholder.

Now that the Pirates had new owners, changes were expected by the fans. A new manager was hired for the team, players were traded and one of the new young ones, Ralph Kiner, soon developed into a "home-run" hitter of national repute. But after several years the efforts were apparently not succeeding and even-

60

tually Branch Rickey was hired as general manager to rebuild the Pirates. Perhaps it was about this time, or soon after, that Mr. McKinney sold his interest and John W. Galbreath became one of the owners and President. Later, Forbes Field was sold to the University of Pittsburgh under a redevelopment program of the University and leased back to the Pirates for a period of years. This real estate transaction undoubtedly was profitable and returned a fair amount of the original capital to the owners.

Finally in 1955, B. D. sold his interest in the Pirates. His concern for the development of the team continued and his attendance at games didn't change. It is possible that he bought into the Pirates purely as a business proposition and not primarily because of baseball as a sport. The team's record during his tenure was only fair with more "off" years probably than good ones, and he hadn't the patience to wait for a winner. A more likely reason might have been that the heavy costs involved in rebuilding the team, along with the management of the expenses, conflicted with his business interests and principles. It is interesting to note, however, that the rebuilding program succeeded. The Pirates became World Champions in 1960, when they defeated the Yankees in seven exciting games. Although others wondered, B. D. never seemed to regret that he was no longer one of the owners when victory came. He was in there cheering and "went wild" with all his Pittsburgh friends at the record-breaking celebration. Until his dying day he enjoyed nothing more than driving down to Pittsburgh for a Pirate game, having dinner at the Athletic Club, and driving home to Butler.

Hunting occupied an important place in Mr. Phillips' sports calendar. It demanded such complete concentration on its objectives that he found in it an immense relaxation from business cares. The spirit of the chase was still there and there was the added freedom of the woodland or the wide open spaces. Once or twice each year he went out on hunting expeditions, which ranged from the Appalachians to the Rockies.

He always enjoyed taking his sons on their first hunting trip (page 79). This practice became a habit. The boys relished the sport and soon became as expert as their father in handling their guns and bringing down the game. This competitive spirit added zest to the expeditions.

From trips to farms near Butler and Hiram, the hunting forays extended east to Maryland and Virginia. Mr. Phillips joined the exclusive Woodmont Rod and Gun Club, of Hancock, Maryland, and was a member until its natural hunting policy was changed to artificial deer drives, turkey and pheasant shoots. Wild turkey and wild deer abounded here and the Phillipses, on their own, trekked uncounted miles in pursuit of their game, carrying in the shoot themselves. This seemed like hard work for the boys, but B. D. relished it and thought it merely invigorating exercise.

As in his business, Mr. Phillips hunted with precision and efficiency. He had a plan for every day and pursued it to the last detail. He was very proud of the number of shells he used to get his game. He did not want to waste ammunition and never shot promiscuously. He had a reputation of being a good shot, despite the fact that he sometimes neglected his practice in marksmanship. He maneuvered purposely, always took deliberate aim and usually hit his mark. When going to Woodmont, he would often leave Butler right after lunch, arriving at the Club at dark. In the morning he would be up before dawn and hunt all day. If he happened to get his game early, he would not stay over night, but would start for home, driving all night. Arriving in Butler, he would head for the office first. Sometimes he would get there at 3:00 a.m., having been on the road since 8:00 p.m., but he wanted to "check those wells" before doing anything else.

Then the western fever got him. He had heard so many hunting tales about the West that Woodmont began to look pretty tame. His first venture was to British Columbia and the Canadian Rockies. Let Ben, Junior, tell the story:

"We left from Mahoningtown B. & O. Railroad Station, New Castle, transferring in Chicago to a Canadian Pacific train for Ashcroft, British Columbia. We arrived at Ashcroft on a Friday evening, met Mr. Bryson, our guide, and slept at a western tavern that night. As I remember it, it was a very barren hotel—wood floors and sparsely furnished. Saturday morning, we left in Mr. Bryson's open topped Studebaker for Horse Fly Lake. It took all day driving 175 miles on the Caribou Trail. We stayed at Bryson's house Saturday evening. I can remember the very delicious creamed blueberries Mrs. Bryson served us that evening.

"Sunday morning, we packed two boats, one equipped with an outboard motor which towed the second boat with our gear, and spent the day traveling to the end of the lake. Here we met Bryson's outfitter and the pack horses and stayed in an old log hut over night. There must have been six or seven hands and a like number of horses. We all slept on the floor in sleeping bags, except Bryson and Dad. They placed their sleeping bags on two old cots and slept above the floor. During the night or early morning, I heard a pistol shot over my head and down fell a pack rat. Bryson had shot it.

"Monday morning, we started out from the camp after we had breakfasted on bannock and strawberry jam, heading for the base camp. Victor and Dad rode and I walked, carrying my 22 rifle. En route I shot half a dozen "fool hens" (a species of partridge) which we ate that evening. We traveled all day and made camp about 4:00 p.m. on pine boughs, sleeping in our sleeping bags under the stars that night. The next morning, we got up at the crack of dawn and made our way farther into the interior. Victor was so stiff he could hardly walk, although Dad was doing very well. I remember hearing the thundering hooves of a moose nearby, but didn't see it. We arrived at the base camp at about 2:00 p.m., where they had a wooden picnic table set up and we prepared for luncheon. Above the timber-line of the Rockies, we could see mountain goats and grizzly bears. I was eager to get started and asked Bryson if we could go after one of the grizzly bears; but he said it would take until sundown to get above the timber-line, although with the field glasses, I could see a couple of large bears rooting.

"The next morning after breakfast, we started out for the climb above the timber-line. Bryson and I went up one draw with Bruno, his Airedale dog. Dad and other guides went up another draw. We were prepared to stay above the timber-line over night. As I was quite young and active, Bryson moved off fast and we were above the timber-line by 11 o'clock that morning, and had also spotted a grizzly bear quite a distance away from us in another draw. We worked our way around to the bear; the Airedale scenting kept us above the bear. Bryson, crouching and easing his way out between a few pine trees, spotted the bear about fifty yards below. He motioned me to come forward, warning me not to reveal myself to the bear or he would move out fast and we would never get a shot. The way I was crouching was hard and I decided to raise up more and look out. The bear at this moment raised its entire head (a bear's eyes do not roll upward or downward as a human's; they must lift the head to look up) and I immediately shot and hit the bear in the throat with a 30-06, killing him. He went over backwards—Bruno, the dog, was at the bear's side immediately. I remember the bear taking quite a swat at the dog with his paw. Bryson said it was about a three-year-old bear, weighing approximately 300 pounds—a nice specimen. In fact, the bear still had a patch of cub hair on its back which was lighter and looked like a saddle. We skinned the bear and then proceeded to return to camp with the hide and head. We arrived in the camp in the middle of the afternoon, and made a rack on which to stretch the bear hide. It was about this time we heard a terrific amount of shooting way off in the upper draw. I counted at least 48 to 49 shots; then I gave up as there were more. The next day, we learned that Victor and Dad were shooting at goats and had shot two. Victor did most of the shooting we heard. Victor returned to the base camp that day, but Dad remained on top of the timber-line to hunt grizzly bear. He was getting a tremendous kick out of the trip!

"The weather was turning bad and Victor decided to stay in camp with the guides while Bryson and I packed up and made our way to the top again to hunt mountain goat. By this time, fog was moving in and out and there was a fine mist making it very miserable and the visibility poor. It took most of the day to get above the timber-line to the place where we pitched camp. It was about 3:00 p.m. and the weather was very depressing and miserable. We pitched our pup tent and laid our sleeping bags out. Bryson cooked some chow and we crawled into our bags at 5:30 p.m. for the night. Now, if you don't think this was 'some night': the wind howling—the fog boiling in and out—raining—cold—and pitch dark! I will never forget the length of that night. We arose at daybreak; the weather hadn't changed a whole lot, although it wasn't raining. After having some breakfast, we started out in search of goats. The terrain was mostly rock and we had to climb from one rock to another. About 8:30 a.m., Bryson spotted a billy goat about eight hundred yards away lying on a rock ledge below us. Between the breaks in the fog, we could see the goat and with stormy weather conditions such as they were, Bryson said the goat would not move. He told me if I was willing, he could get me within fifty yards of the goat for a shot. However, it would take quite a hike over the top of the mountain to do so. I, of course, agreed to it and we started out. Had I known what I was getting into, I never would have done it. I had a pair of boots on and Bryson had spikes on his boots. He would go along and make footholds for me on the ledges which were covered with tufts of grass here and there and snow—at times, very slippery. One slip or miscue would possibly slide you over a cliff or wall over 800 feet below. As we progressed, I became more frightened and found myself crawling on my hands and knees, my gun slung over my shoulder, grasping onto the grass with my hands. By 11:30 a.m., Bryson and I had maneuvered below the goat and the goat was lying on the ledge. He got up and just as he turned to go behind the rocks, I shot. The first shot missed; however, with the second one, I hit the goat in the rear quarters and noticed his leg slipping. He came out farther on the ledge above us and just as I was ready to aim again, Bryson said not to shoot as the goat was weaving. In a few minutes, he toppled forward and was caught in a little pine tree between the two of us on a ledge with a drop of some 250 feet. Had the goat hit one of us, we would have probably been killed (although at the time, I never gave this a thought). We skinned the goat out. Bryson carried the skin and head. I carried a ham and rolled the remaining carcass down over the precipice some 250 feet below us. The weather by this time had cleared somewhat and we stayed at the shelter camp again that evening in our sleeping bags.

"The next morning we ran into Dad and his party on top of the mountain. They decided to stay up another day and see if they could get a grizzly bear. Bryson and I left for the base camp. We found Victor at the camp and spent the rest of the day with the guides. Dad came down the next morning and as the weather was not getting any better, we decided to break up the camp the next day and start for home. We thought it best to get out of the area. We returned by horse and boat getting to Horse Fly Lake on Sunday. I recall Dad, as usual, was in a very big hurry to get home and of course we had a 175-mile motor trip to make to catch the train. Bryson was not about to attempt this hazardous drive in the evening, and Dad was insisting that we make the two o'clock morning train out of Ashcroft. Bryson said there might be one fellow that would drive this trail at night. Dad was all for finding him. Fortunately we weren't able to find the wild-eyed driver and Dad had to stay at Bryson's over night. As it turned out, this was the wise thing to do. We then had a nice trip home, finding no particular trouble occurred while we were gone and the weather had been beautiful in Butler. Dad and the rest of us were fully converted to hunting in the West."

After the British Columbia experience Mr. Phillips became especially interested in antelope hunting and made numerous trips to the "antelope country" around Casper, Wyoming. He became acquainted with a noted outfitter and guide by the name of Otto Heath. He was a very fine Christian gentleman and both he and his wife, Helen, became warm friends of the Phillipses through many years. Bob Grieves, owner of the Diamond Ring Ranch (a 250,000 acre spread); Jim Greaves, owner of the Dumbell Ranch; Tom Sun, owner of Independence Rock Ranch, and Ben Rourke, a noted hunter, were all well-known to Mr. Phillips. Hunting ranged over these ranches and beyond. Poison Spider, the Yellowstone, the Platte, the Pedro Mountains, Rattlesnake Mountains, Alcova and Pathfinder Reservoirs, the Sweetwater and other areas became household words. In later years, the Heath's Hotel Murietta at Merced became a noted hostelry. Here came many of the nation's great. One time, President Kennedy and forty White House aides were guests. On that occasion there were several direct telephone lines set up to Washington. Later-to-be-President Nixon was once a guest along with his sizable retinue.

Very often Mr. Phillips, upon his return home, would write out detailed summaries of his hunting trips and put them on file. One of these tells the story of a Wyoming expedition in 1932.

SUMMARY OF WYOMING TRIP

Saturday, September 17
    Left New Castle at 1:00 p.m.

Sunday, September 18
    Left Chicago 1:50 a.m. (2:50 a.m. Butler time) after a layover in Chicago of about five hours, one hour's layover at Omaha at 4:00 p.m. Very warm and dusty.

Monday, September 19
    Arrived Rock Springs, Wyoming, at 12:37 p.m., two hours difference in time. Elevation 6200 feet. Lester Leek at station. Arrived at Jackson about 6:00 p.m. Elevation 6200 feet. An automobile trip of a little less than 200 miles; for the most part a wide improved gravel road, passing through about 100 miles of so-called desert, flat and rather uninteresting. Saw several sage hens; resemble very much in color and form a half-grown

turkey. Also passed along the road probably about 50 dead jack rabbits, which are killed by automobiles at night. These had been killed in the last day or two, as they are taken away quite rapidly by coyotes, hawks, etc. Leek claimed that one time when driving to Rock Springs he counted over 100 dead jack rabbits along the road. Also saw a lot of prairie dogs along the road. It was a rather bleak, cool evening—an overcoat felt comfortable. Had supper at Jackson, made a few purchases, and before leaving met Jim Simpson. Left about 8:00 p.m. and arrived about 10:00 p.m. at Turpin Meadows Lodge about 40 miles from Jackson, along improved gravel road. Elevation about 7500 feet. The sky was clear and the air seemed very cool. This was the end of the automobile trip.

Tuesday, September 20

Left the Lodge by pack train about 11:00 a.m. Arrived Buffalo Creek camp site (elevation about 8000 feet), about 14 miles, at 3:00 p.m. Took a four or five mile ride with Simpson between 4:00 and 6:30 p.m. Saw cow and calf moose in willow flats.

Wednesday, September 21

Left with Simpson about 9:00 a.m. Had lunch near Swede Lake about four miles from camp. Failed to locate elk. Went into woods up mountain, with fine fir and pine timber, about 3:00 p.m. Heard elk bugle. Saw two or three cow elk. Finally, the fellow that bugled appeared and I shot him about 3:30 p.m., two shots. Estimated weight about 700 pounds. Took picture, dressed elk, returned to camp about 6:30. Saw three moose on way in. A fine, clear, reasonably cool day.

Thursday, September 22

Before breakfast went to willow flats, saw nine moose. On way to or from willow flats, which lie about a mile below the camp and extend for two or three miles along the creek, we evidently scared some moose out and a bull moose, cow and calf were within 200 yards of camp for quite a while when we were gone. Returned to camp, had breakfast, then riding our own horses and taking two pack horses we returned to where the elk had been shot. Skinned and quartered it and returned to camp about 3:00 p.m. On this trip I lost the small orifice sight belonging to my gun, which I could not replace, and which caused me to lose confidence in my shooting. Saw two moose on way back. Left for willow flats about 4:30. Saw two moose, cow and calf, and returned to camp about dark.

Friday, September 23

Rained until about noon. Took all morning to pack train. Left for Yellowstone Flats camp site about twelve miles distant at 2:00 p.m. Accompanied by Young and Lester, left pack train on Yellowstone Flats about two miles from camp site. Saw about twenty moose, including four bulls. Located large bull moose across flats near camp site about dusk. Pack train arrived at camp site about 7:30 p.m. (dark). Had supper about 9:30, including broiled elk steak. Foggy night on flats. Yellowstone Park and about eight miles from the southeast corner of the Park.

Saturday, September 24.

Located bull moose seen the previous evening. Killed same about 7:30 a.m. Horns had a 44-inch spread; very large moose; estimated weight, 1200 pounds. Young, Lester and I left for sheep camp at 11:00 a.m. Summers and Simpson remained to skin, quarter and pack moose. Arrived at sheep camp at dark. Summers arrived about half an hour later, Simpson having taken the moose back to Buffalo Creek camp site. Elevation of sheep camp more than 10,000 feet, very close to timber line, and quite a good deal cooler than the other camps.

Sunday, September 25

Left about 8:30 a.m. alone for deer hunt. Clear, cool morning. Saw a very large eagle, dead, caught in trap and fastened to limb of tree. Evidently the trap had been set for some animal, the eagle was caught in it and had gotten the trap loose and flown perhaps several miles, then had gotten the chain entangled in tree. Returned about 11:30. Young and Lester had left about 9:00 a.m. on sheep hunt. It snowed a little and looked rather stormy. Took a nap and went deer hunting about 3:00 p.m. Returned about 5:30. Simpson had arrived. Young and Lester returned about 6:00 p.m. Saw some sheep, got into quite a snow storm, found it very cold and windy on the higher elevations and Lester froze one of his ears.

Monday, September 26

Young and Lester left for same location as previous day. Simpson and I went to top of mountain overlooking head of Thoroughfare Creek. Had lunch. Was quite cool if you were exposed to the wind, but reasonably comfortable if protected from the wind. Failed to locate any sheep. Saw two herds of elk. Returned about dusk. Young and Lester returned shortly afterwards. Located sheep after a long trip. Tried to get to them, but after taking a long, circuitous and very rough route found them gone.

Tuesday, September 27

All left together, going up the creek from camp past Young's peak. Located sheep in high, rocky cliffs. Also saw two sheep cross a long, rolling piece of ground for half-mile, about a mile away from us. Also saw another sheep standing out against the sky line on rocky cliff. Retraced our steps so as to approach the cliff on the leeward side from the sheep. Tied the horses, had lunch, started up the cliff. Got up to place where Simpson had spotted sheep and were looking around for a moment or two, about 2:30 p.m., when ram appeared apparently from nowhere, standing looking at us, probably about 60 or 70 yards away. Shot too quickly and missed. Shot five or six times more, but ram bounded up cliff, appearing in sight from time to time as he came out from behind rocks, but missed. Trying to get final shot at crest of cliff 250 or 300 yards away, when another ram appeared apparently from nowhere, about 75 yards away. Shot it through back and it tumbled down—9 years old and weighed more than 200 pounds. This was away above the timber line at an elevation of considerably over 11,000 feet. Dressed and skinned ram, cut it in two, loaded it on horses and started for camp about 4:00 p.m., walking and leading horses. Saw large bear about sunset along crest of mountain 500 or 600 yards away, but on account of long walk ahead and delay, did not think it worth while to get the gun out. Had 1½ hours' walk in dark over very rough ground to camp; arrived about 8:30 p.m. Young had also killed a sheep, bringing back only the head, and arrived about dark.

Wednesday, September 28

Went with Young and Lester to get Young's sheep; beautiful day; fine trip. Met "Jonesy" and another man with Valley Ranch party. Had lunch in Valley, shielded from wind along stream; little flakes of snow falling occasionally, but we were quite warm. Returned to camp about 3:30 p.m. Hunted deer with Simpson, but saw none.

Thursday, September 29

Left for Yellowstone camp site about 10:30 a.m. Shot grouse on way to camp. Arrived shortly before dark.

Friday, September 30

Left Yellowstone camp about 10:30; arrived at Buffalo Creek camp site about 3:00; left there about 4:00 and arrived at Turpin Lodge about 8:00. Saw probably 40 elk on way from Buffalo Creek camp site to Lodge. These were all on reserve, but heard several bulls bugle, and very fine sight. Had not seen daily paper since Sunday, September 18. At the Lodge (on Friday evening) they had a Salt Lake City Monday's paper.

Saturday, October 1

Left Lodge by automobile for Rock Springs about 9:30. Stopped to see the taxidermist at Jackson and arranged to have head of elk and sheep mounted and hide of sheep tanned with hair on. Arrived at Rock Springs about 5:30 and left there at 6:35 p.m.

Sunday, October 2

Very warm, dusty, dirty trip.

Monday, October 3

Arrived Chicago 7:00 a.m. Left Chicago 8:30 a.m. Arrived New Castle 8:20 p.m.

With the advent of the great continental highways the Phillips party would drive to Wyoming from Butler by automobile. It was usually pretty much of a "push" going out and coming back. There was little or no time for sight-seeing or formal meals. According to B. D.'s schedule it should take two and a half days of hard driving each way, and always *that was what it took!* There were picnic lunches along the way, consisting of sweet pickles, fig newtons, and grapes—plenty of grapes. The grapes would always have to be washed at the store where they were purchased, so they would be ready to eat when the time came. For years this was the pattern.

On his last hunting trip, in Wyoming (1964), B. D. manifested all his accustomed enthusiasm and agility. One day on the last trip, the party had about given up getting any game, when a nice buck antelope passed in front of their jeep and stopped some distance away. Ben, Junior, and B. D. both aimed and shot simultaneously. Ben thought his shot had killed the buck, but B. D. said, "When you examine him you will find out that he was shot through the neck. That is where I aimed." Surely enough, he had made a remarkable shot and Ben had missed. This fine demonstration of his hunting ability was the last in Wyoming and this was the last antelope he ever killed.

In his home at Elm Court is a mounted antelope head and in a large unfinished garret room are still several stuffed trophies of his hunting days. He liked wild meat, often kept a stock in a deep freeze, and had it served when his guests expressed a desire to sample it. He was proud of the fact that he had provided the meat with his own gun.

Mr. Phillips was one of the foremost philatelists in America. In common parlance—he was a great stamp collector. Beyond doubt, in his day he was in the class of the late Colonel E. H. R. Green and President Franklin D. Roosevelt, outstanding specialists in the acquisition of United States stamps. At one stage in his philatelic career Mr. Phillips was said to have the finest USA collection in the world.

He began collecting stamps as a hobby when a mere lad. As in everything else he undertook, he became a perfectionist in this field. He knew the history and principles of philately. He spoke its language. Mention a perforation, grill, a double transfer, a double impression, a coil, a block, plate numbers, inverted centers, surcharges, bisects, mints, se-tenants, tete-beches, miniature sheets, souvenir sheets, or any other descriptive term about stamps and he knew all about them. Under his fine lens he could detect errors, woven screens, watermarks, various fibers of stamp papers, prelures, batonnes, granites, silk-threads or "what have you?"

Just to give an example of the fine points of stamp collecting, take the varieties of the 1-cent green stamp of the United States issued first in 1912. It was watermarked "single-line USPS" and perforated 12. Also, there were vertical and horizontal coils, perf.

70

8½. In 1914, still watermarked, it was issued perf. 10, but there were some that were issued perf. 10 vertically and perf. 12 horizontally, and some perf. 12 vertically and perf. 10 horizontally. There were also vertical and horizontal coils, perf. 10. In 1915, the same two coils were issued from plates curved to fit a rotary press; each stamp thus became approximately one millimetre larger in the direction of the curvature. In 1916 they were again issued, this time, on unwatermarked wove paper, still perf. 10 and also two coils. There were some also issued imperforate, for use in patented mailing machines. Finally, in 1917, they were issued on unwatermarked paper, perf. 11. The same stamp to all outward appearances, but 15 varieties to the philatelist! Mr. Phillips, the "detail man" in business, was in the "Promised Land" when he sat down to work with his collection after a busy day at the office, or as respite from wrestling with a deep problem in his business. If he could discover an "error" or acquire a stamp of great rarity, he would "walk on clouds" for days.

He handled each specimen with loving care. It was prophylactically cleaned and enclosed in a separate cellophane envelope, mounted in its proper place together with an accurate scientific classification and description. He did all this detail work himself. Raymond and Roger Weill, internationally-famed stamp specialists and close friends of Mr. Phillips, marvelled at the perfection with which he maintained each and every philatelic detail. His catalogue listings were maintained with the same meticulous care.

His collection of Provisional Issues of postmasters, which antedated the general United States issues, was superb. It included not only complete Alexandrias, Annapolises, Baltimores, Philadelphias, Saint Louises, New Havens, New Yorks, but many maverick issues by postmasters along the routes of the mail-carrying stagecoaches and pony expresses that spanned the nation in those early days. Somewhat in this class were many rare issues of Confederate post offices during the Civil War days.

His collection of Fig. 4 and Fig. 4A, the first-issue stamp of the United States, was as nearly complete as ever known. So was his collection of the Trans-Mississippi commemorative issue, especially the rare $1 stamp "Western Cattle in a Storm." He loved that stamp so much that he acquired the original painting from which the picture was reproduced. This same thoroughness featured hundreds of single-issue collections. The United States "24-cent

71

Inverted Center Airmail" was one of the rarest in modern U.S. When the United States Post Office discovered the error (engraving of an airmail plane printed upside down within a correct border) everything was done to retrieve the total issue. But a clerk who had bought a whole sheet of the stamps for his firm in a routine postage purchase by chance discovered the error before he was to deliver his stamps to the mailing room. He retained the sheet, reimbursing his firm with a sheet of regular air mails. Years later, when the existence of the sheet was made known, many stamp dealers offered to purchase sections of it at fabulous prices. The clerk insisted on selling the whole sheet or nothing, so it embarked upon a long and interesting philatelic history. Mr. Phillips wanted that sheet and got it. For many years it was his prize exhibit to a select number of fellow stamp collectors.

Occasionally he would venture beyond his specialized field in securing foreign rarities. At several times in his philatelic career his acquisitions were featured in color reproductions in such magazines as *Life, Time,* and *Fortune.*

Probably, if the B. D. Phillips collection of thousands upon thousands of United States stamps had been kept intact, it would have gone down in philatelic history with the Green, Roosevelt, Newbury, Lichtenstein, Steinway, Casparri, Tapling, Smithsonian, and Brown University collections. But, as was always typical of the man, he desired no such place in any hall of fame.

Mr. Phillips was a confirmed bibliophile and possessed one of the finest private libraries in Western Pennsylvania. When he was comfortably ensconced in Elm Court he began to build his unique collection. With the advice of experts he acquired a foundation of the best American literature including the writings of Emerson, Hawthorne, Holmes, Longfellow, and Whittier—all these in rare editions beautifully bound. Then he added works of American history—John Fiske's histories that treated the development of the country from the discovery of America to the adoption of the Constitution. Then came the American Statesman series (40 volumes) dealing in biographical form with developments from the time of Benjamin Franklin through the nineteenth century. Included in this section of his library were Beveridge's *Life of Marshall* and *Life of Lincoln,* and the 22-volume Montezuma edition of Prescott. Three great American naturalists—Thoreau, Burroughs, and Muir—occupied a prominent place in his collection. Of British authors, Mr. Phillips acquired rare editions of Shakespeare, Carlyle, Dickens, George Eliot and Sir Walter Scott, Lord Macaulay, William Wordsworth, Alfred Lord Tennyson, Rudyard Kipling and others. In the field of the great Classics he included Homer's *Iliad* and *Odyssey*, Virgil's *Aeneid*, Dante's *Divine Comedy* and Goethe's *Faust*. From this basic collection his acquisitions ranged far afield in many areas to which he was especially attracted by whims of the moment. Here, at random, appear such great names as the Brownings, Disraeli, Gibbon, Hugo, Hardy, Adams, Irving, Theodore Roosevelt, Surtees, Riley, Conrad, Ruskin, Motley, Verne, Tolstoi, Turgenieff, Tarkington—all of which reveal the wide-ranging literary taste of Mr. Phillips and something of the "other world" to which he could retire after trying days in the office and find complete refreshment of mind and heart.

His concern for the Movement to restore the New Testament Church is reflected in a large collection of volumes—practically everything of the Campbells—involving theology, history, and polemics—greater than that to be found in many ministers' libraries.

Also in his library he had a collection of original signatures of every signer of the Declaration of Independence and other rarities which added to the richness of this Elm Court treasure trove.

Mr. Phillips was intrigued by jade. He did not go deeply into a study of it or the development of a collection, but it was very appealing to him. It is interesting to note that the greatest rulers of the East treated this stone with a reverence attributed to no other material. The poems of the emperors have been recorded on tablets of jade and the great fish bowl in the noted Bishop collection, weighing 120 pounds, has the poem of an emperor on its inner base. The respect and reverence placed in this stone by the the Chinese was well-deserved. Jade in different colors was used in China for the six precious tablets employed in the worship of heaven and earth and "the four cardinal points." Jade is to be found in axes, adzes, knives, and other utilitarian instruments, but chiefly in ornamental features such as rings, earrings, beads, vases, cups, plates, bowls, candle-holders, or lamps. In Mr. Phillips' library are several books on jade and he could carry on a very interesting and informative conversation with anyone who admired his holdings. Most of his specimens, both large and small, were

73

of a rich emerald green color and of Chinese or Mexican origin. He was alert to the imitations—saussurite, fibrolite, stillimite, jadeite, bowenite, prase, plasma, chrysoprase, jasper, and prehnite—and was proud of the fact that in his collection he had nothing but pure jade. Possibly the intricacy of detail involved in acquiring only authentic pieces had a special appeal to "the detail man" of Phillips Gas and Oil.

Mr. Phillips seldom mentioned his exclusive club relationships but he delighted in surprising his family, friends, and visiting dignitaries with invitations to dinner at Pittsburgh's Duquesne and Athletic Clubs. It is likely that his memberships in these clubs were motivated primarily by business reasons. Many deals were made over gourmet meals for which such dining rooms are famous.

A little background on the Duquesne Club will serve to show the significance of such connections. The Duquesne is "ultra-ultra" among social-business clubs, not only in Pittsburgh but in the nation. Its members like to think of it as primarily a business club. Its progenitors were prominent in public utility and railroad circles and its early members held high government positions. Their families were the social arbiters of the city, so that Duquesne memberships became highly desirable socially. A survey of its memberships today, however, shows that perhaps forty-five per cent are business oriented, forty-five per cent political, and only ten per cent social. Osborn Elliott once wrote, "It is where you go upstairs at the Duquesne that you begin to enter the substratosphere of executive power." On the second floor there are no fewer than five dining rooms, including the main one; and in each of these, day after day, the same people sit at the same tables. As you enter the main dining room, the Gulf Oil table is across the way; Gulf's chairman sits facing the door, surrounded by his senior vice-presidents. In the corner over to the right is the Koppers table—and next to it is the U. S. Steel table where sales vice-presidents gather. In other small rooms nearby, Pittsburgh Coke and Chemical's president, chairman, and vice-presidents break bread together; in another central spot is Pittsburgh Plate Glass; while Alcoans hold forth in the corner, next to the Heinz' worthies . . . The field marshals are to be found on the fourth and fifth floors, where thirty-five suites are rented out by the year to such companies as U. S. Steel, Gulf Oil, Jones and Laughlin, Blow-Knox and Alcoa —to name just a few. These attractively decorated apartments usually have at least one bedroom and a dining room. They are used by the companies' topmost brass for meetings and lunch almost every day and for dinners perhaps two or three times a week when a "visiting fireman" or perhaps the "fire chief" comes to town. In these company suites new products and mergers are planned, bargaining strategy for labor relations are hammered out, multi-million-dollar financing arrangements are made. Here and in the public dining rooms below, the professionals of production get together and exchange ideas every day. It is often said that Pittsburgh would not be the production name it is—indeed, Pittsburgh would not be Pittsburgh—without the Duquesne Club. And Mr. Phillips was always treated with the utmost respect when he visited this "sanctum sanctorum" of American business.

In Butler Mr. Phillips was often chided for not being a Mason. Masons make much of their tradition never to ask a man to join a lodge. He must humbly and contritely make application, he must be minutely screened and investigated, well-sponsored and finally, with a show of reluctance, admitted to the lowest order of distinction. His brother, T. W., Jr., who was a high Mason, often urged him to join the Butler Masonic Lodge, telling him if he put off such a move too long, he might later be black-balled. He considered this carefully, but told him that he simply did not have the time to give to such matters. Mr. Phillips had nothing against the Masons; in fact, he admired them and the principles they stood for. He had a multitude of friends, both socially and commercially, who were Masons. Finally, a group of these intimate friends conspired to obtain for B. D. an honor seldom bestowed upon any man — to make him a "Mason at sight."

There was in Mr. Phillips' personal files a copy of the program for a "state dinner" celebrating the Hundredth Anniversary of the Butler Masonic Lodge No. 272. This program, dated September 18, 1953, contains a brief history of the Lodge which was constituted on August 3, 1853. The program included the following notation: "An unusual event occurred on April 6, 1933, when Brother Benjamin Page, the Right Worshipful Grand Master, visited the Lodge and raised Brother Benjamin D. Phillips to the sublime degree of Master Mason, having made Brother Phillips a Mason 'at sight'." He treasured this honor very highly. Few people in the history of Masonry in Pennsylvania were ever accorded it.

It is next to impossible to give an adequate view of the many facets of B. D. Phillips' wide interests beyond his business and his church, but that which is recorded here will give some intimation of this tremendously energetic and versatile person.

Frank L. Weigand, Jr., his trusted friend and son-in-law, senior attorney for the United States Steel Corporation, pays him this high tribute:

> B. D. Phillips directed his almost super-human energy to a wide variety of activities. His business life was itself an intricate mosaic in which he involved himself with minute details. The same must be said of his philanthropic activities, his interest in various forms of art, literature, stamp collecting and other avocations. In the creation of Elm Court he poured himself into planning and often into construction details. The breadth of his application of himself to these intricacies is, in my opinion, the uniqueness of the man, and probably the basic explanation for his unique type of impact on the world.
>
> Back of all this were his faith motivations. He was, in my opinion, motivated and guided by a vital Christian faith which was initially generated by parental influence. He seemed to go far beyond the "honoring of father and mother" commandment. He seemed at times to almost worship his parents. It was certainly from them that he derived his dedication to the Restoration Plea. He was a very practical man and the practical application of his faith enabled him to weather the types of storms of life that would spell disaster for the strong as well as the weak. It also seemed to provide him with a continuing ignition and discrimination with respect to his varied activities. To put it in another way, his life of faith bore witness to the promise of the abundant life, even in the face of adversity. So far as his life of activity was concerned, he was the epitome of faith-inspired effort. His knowledge of the Holy Scriptures helped him in directing his energy and making his choices. They guided him in the use of the property which he accumulated with a constantly-growing awareness of the responsibilities of the faithful Christian steward. As I think of his career I can see the Bible, and the Book of Proverbs, especially, coming to the surface in every phase of his varied concerns.

B. D. Phillips was "a man among men," but he was distinctly and uniquely a man of God.

VI

Home and Family

THERE WAS SOMETHING of the patriarchal in the Phillips concept of home and family. The father was the "chief of the tribe" and he took all the responsibilities of that stance with an intense seriousness. He sought to make the home base magnetic enough to hold the interest of every member of the family and to provide for their welfare in religion, education, health, recreation, and work.

In our day this concept of the companionship family is rapidly disappearing. In an urban civilization most of the decisions for living are made without regard to a personal God, His moral law, or parental authority; and the home, like society, tends to become thoroughly secular. Indeed, the American family is today disintegrating as a social unit and spiritual matrix wherein persons discover that individual freedom is derived only at the price of subordination of self to the common good.

It is refreshing, therefore, to recount the home-and-family story of Benjamin Dwight Phillips, a tremendously successful businessman and "man-among-men," who nevertheless found time for companionship with and guidance of those he loved.

His first marriage, in 1909, was the culmination of a Hiram

College romance. The young lady was the daughter of a prominent family in the Western Reserve — Anna Undine Conant. Professor E. B. Wakefield, his favorite faculty member, performed the marriage ceremony. The event came at about the same time that Ben decided to move from New Castle to Butler to be nearer his work. Their first house in Butler was modest but adequate and comfortable. What it lacked in sumptuousness it possessed in peace and happiness. As James Hamilton once put it, "If God be there, a cottage will hold as much happiness as might stock a palace."

Six children came to bless the home, three daughters and three sons: Stella, Clarinda, and Undine; Benjamin Dwight, Jr., Victor, and Donald. Most of the names were traditional to the Phillips family. A daughter carried his wife's name. A son bore his own name. His father's first wife was named Clarinda, the name chosen for his second daughter. He had an older brother named Victor who died while a young man; he perpetuated the name in his own Victor. It is interesting to know that this naming custom has been carried on in the families of his children and grandchildren.

Health and recreation occupied a large place in family affairs. In the spring, Mr. Phillips would take his family on wild flower hunting expeditions, usually on the Nugent farm east of Butler in Clearfield Township. First came the trailing arbutus. They grew in pink beauty close to the ground and were hard to find. On one of these trips Undine (now Mrs. Frank L. Weigand, Jr.) stepped on a yellow jacket's nest and was stung so badly that she required medical attention. Such incidents might temporarily cool interest in flower searching, but by next season everybody was all out for adventure. In late April or May the pack would return to the Nugent farm to look for wild honeysuckle. Usually they only viewed the beautiful blossoms. Dad did not want the children to gather them and take them home since this would require snapping limbs off the bushes and mutilating the growth. South of Butler, along the "Three-degree Road" on the McCalmont Tract, a property owned by the Phillips family, grew many mayflowers. Here the youngsters were allowed to collect the flowers and the mayapples. Indeed, there would usually be a contest to see who could collect the most. In June Mr. Phillips would take the gang to East Brady, a village north of Butler, in Armstrong

County. In the surrounding area grew what he contended to be the finest specimens of the Pennsylvania state flower, mountain laurel. This trip was the crowning event of the season. Several hundred of these flowers were later transplanted in the grounds surrounding the Elm Court estate in Butler.

In the fall the boys enjoyed chestnut hunting on the Nugent farm. They were armed with a half dozen broom handles which they would throw into the trees to bring the chestnuts down. This event usually took place after a heavy frost when the burrs would open. Everybody would get splinters in their hands which B. D. would take the time to tenderly remove with his pen knife. In the evening the family would gather around the old iron-plated gas stove for the feast. Dad would "x" each chestnut with his knife to insure that when they were properly roasted they would burst open with a delicious flavor

The trips above-mentioned took place under quite primitive conditions. The "Three-degree Road" mentioned above was one of two routes from Butler to Pittsburgh (now known as Route 8 South). It was in those days a dirt road running through the 900-acre McCalmont Tract acquired by T. W. Phillips, Sr., and still in the family. The other road was known as the "Butler Plank Road" which was a dirt road that had been improved with planks buried in its base. It was the only reinforced road in the area until 1916 or later. This plank highway was the main road to Pittsburgh and was a toll road. It was always interesting to the children to drive to the swinging toll gates, numbering at least four and attended by toll collectors and helpers, "pass the time of day" and move on to the next leg of the journey. Most of the traffic was made up of horses or horse-drawn vehicles with only an occasional motor car.

The boys were at an early day taught how to use guns. This was preliminary to squirrel hunting expeditions. Let Ben, Junior, tell the story:

"When my brother Victor and I were quite young, Dad used to take us with him to hunt squirrel. In the early '20's hickory and chestnut trees were in abundance around Butler. We were coached to walk behind Dad quietly, as he was particular about absolute quiet as we waited for the squirrels to appear. Usually we would get the limit allowed by the game laws. Always, after he shot a squirrel or two he would let Victor and me run and pick up the game, which was a real thrill. He would usually give us the squirrel tails after he had removed the tail bone with a pair of pliers.

"I particularly remember a squirrel hunt near Hiram College. We were staying at his brother-in-law's home, the Udall farm. They had a large sugar maple grove on the farm. In fact, we spent more than one spring at the Udall Sugar Camp, collecting the sap and helping (?) to make maple syrup. We got a big kick out of riding a sled through the snow behind a team of work horses as we collected the sap and brought it to the furnace. Well, it was a beautiful fall day—the sun falling very bright on the colorful maple leaves. As we approached the Sugar Camp, Dad spotted a large fox squirrel. The tree was full of leaves and the squirrel was hard to see, but Dad saw just a bit of his tail hanging over a limb high up in the tree. He had Victor and me walk around the tree on the side opposite him. This, of course, made the squirrel move around on Dad's side of the tree and just as he did there was a loud blast and down came Mr. Fox Squirrel, one of the finest specimens I ever saw. We continued our hunt through the woods and, as I recall, we bagged seven or eight squirrels that day. On that day Victor and I spotted a kingfisher. As boys will do, we begged Dad to shoot the bird for us, and he obliged.

"One of the things I recall that was peculiar to Dad was that he always wore kid gloves when he skinned a squirrel. I paid little attention to this habit as a boy, but later, as I became older and did some hunting of my own and dressed my own game, I realized the value of this protection. He taught us how to skin a squirrel. He began with a sharp knife, splitting the animal down the back, and pulling the hide off starting at the neck and removing the head. It was an art as he did it. We learned from an expert."

The grounds of the Phillips abode on Second Street were spacious and the children were encouraged to have pets of their own — dogs, cats, ground hogs, rabbits, pheasants, pigeons, etc. They were held strictly accountable for the health and discipline of the animals. Besides the immense enjoyment they had in their wards, they learned many lessons in personal ownership responsibility and understanding. Mr. Phillips always had a dog of his own, usually a German shepherd which was his favorite. (The last one missed him so much after he died that she refused

80

to eat, developed acute heart trouble, and had to be anesthetized.)

While there was an abundance of recreation and fun in the Phillips household, work was given an important place. Mr. Phillips believed that patience, persistence, and power to do are only acquired by hard work. He often said, "Hard work, steadily and regularly carried on, never hurt anybody." He abhorred laziness or idleness. One of his grandsons recalls his saying, "If I had no work to do, no matter how much money I had, I would run a peanut stand on a street corner just to keep busy." To which the lad added, "I'm sure that's true, Granddad, and I'll bet you'd have made money at it."

Every child had a job to do around the house and grounds. When they were old enough to earn money, they got a chance to do so. Even the single girls were included in this work philosophy. Mr. Phillips wanted to make sure that his progeny would not be labeled "playboys" or "playgirls" by an often critical public.

The boys were trained to take an interest in the Phillips business enterprises. There were family talks about the services rendered to the public and the problems encountered in carrying on an efficient and profitable operation. B. D. often took the boys on scouting expeditions in the oil and gas fields. They witnessed well-drilling and were thrilled when new wells were brought in. They saw how the offices operated and the hundreds of people that came and went in the course of a day's work. They came to realize how important their father was in the life of the community and how their conduct was involved in the respect in which he was held. When opportunity came for association in the business they considered it an high honor to take their place at his side.

In the summer there would always be a family vacation trip to some interesting part of the nation. The more they saw of America the more they came to love and respect their native land. Mr. Phillips never failed to inculcate a lively patriotism in his flock whenever opportunity offered. Some time after his oldest daughter, Stella (Mrs. Rolland L. Ehrman), was married, he took the Ehrmans and his sons, Ben and Vic, for a comprehensive tour of Europe. When the party returned, Mr. Phillips said he would not care to go abroad again. For him, America had everything worthwhile that foreign lands possessed — and more! Like Thoreau he felt that "only that traveling is good which reveals to me the value of home and enables me to enjoy it better." Nevertheless, he wanted his family to have every advantage that travel could bring and encouraged them to see the world if they so desired.

There was wise solicitude for the education of each child in the Phillips Family. Both public and private schools were utilized. No expense was spared to give each one the type of preparation for life which he desired. Stella received her training at Holton Arms School in the nation's capital. She also studied at Wellesley. Clarinda also attended Holton Arms and the Emma Willard School in Troy, New York. Undine studied in the Emma Willard School, Garland Junior College in Boston, and Miss Connley's Secretarial School in Pittsburgh. Ben Junior and Victor were graduates of Culver. Ben took further work at the Robert Morris Business School in Boston. Donald, whose health was frail, received his education in private schools in Phoenix, Arizona, and Asheville, North Carolina.

The Phillips house majored in religion. The Bible was not only "center-piece" on the parlor table. It was frequently read. Every child knew that it was the source book and guidebook for the head of the house and that it should be his. Christ was lifted up as Lord and Saviour. When each child reached the age of accountability it was only natural for him to give his heart and life to Him and obey Him in all that He had commanded.

There was a Phillips family pew, although the North Street Christian Church was not a pew-rental church. Each member of the family knew where it was, naturally gravitated to it, and when worship began each one was in his place. It is said that one Lord's Day morning little Ben, Junior, "played hooky." Discovering his absence, Ben, Senior, got up, left the sanctuary, found the "sheep that went astray" and marched him down the center aisle to his accustomed seat amid the knowing glances of the parishioners. There were no more absences unless duly accounted for.

Each child was instructed in his duties as a Christian. They learned and sang the great hymns of the church. They knew why they went to the North Street Church rather than the Lutheran or Presbyterian churches around the corner. As they became old enough to participate meaningfully in the Bible classes and other church organizations, they took their places in the

82

affairs of these groups and often accepted positions of leadership. It is interesting that this loyalty to Christ and the Church has persisted through the years and that all the children are still members of the Christian Church.

One thing that contributed to this family loyalty was the fact that the household was frequently visited by noted leaders of the Restoration Movement who came from all parts of the nation to visit Mr. Phillips, to benefit from his advice and from his always generous largess to institutions which merited his concern. The children became acquainted with these capable and inspiring personalities. They would often sit in awe as affairs of the Kingdom of God were discussed and the Holy Scriptures were expounded. B. D.'s home, like that of his distinguished father, was a gathering place for the great and near-great, with benefits accruing to the whole family.

It was during the youthful years of his children that Mr. Phillips, along with his brother, T. W., Jr., decided to give the North Street Church a new building adequate to the cause it represented and the services it was supposed to render to its members and the Butler community. L. D. Riddell, Mr. Phillips' favorite pastor, noted for his loyalty to the Word of God and to the Restoration Plea, was then leading the congregation. The old church building was razed and a new Gothic edifice—a veritable architectural gem and one of the most beautiful buildings in Butler—was erected in its place. The art-glass windows, the gold-leaf decorations and rich furnishings provide ideal surroundings for worship services. It houses one of the finest pipe organs in Butler County. Many other rooms provide facilities for educational and social activities. It may be noted that 1,110 persons united with the congregation during "Brother" Riddell's twenty-year ministry.

In due course all the children were married and launched on careers of their own. Close relationships were kept alive by frequent family gatherings at the parental home. The special annual gathering was of such significance that it will be treated in some detail later in the chapter. The remarkable sense of family companionship which marked childhood experiences was not allowed to wane as the years fled by.

As B. D. Phillips came into new responsibilities and status in the business world, he began to realize the importance of maintaining a residential establishment worthy of the Phillips family.

He wanted the Phillips name reflected in the dignity, distinction, prestige, and nobility of which it was worthy. It was then he began to plan for the erection of Elm Court.

Possibly there was something in his blood of his noted ancestor, Thomas Phylyps, the "Chief Builder and Supervisor of Buildings in the Town and Marches of Calais" which found expression in Elm Court. He was determined that no expense would be spared to erect a manor house of real distinction.

Eleven acres of beautiful woodland overlooking the city of Butler were acquired for the site. Eventually every known shrub and tree that would grow in this area of Pennsylvania was planted in this garden spot; likewise, every woodland flower from trailing arbutus to mountain rhododendron. Trails wound through the tract—mere traces and stone-stepped—enticing the viewer to ever-new vistas of nature's loveliness. Roads and driveways centering in the mansion were so placed as to provide an impressive approach.

In consultation with the noted architectural firm of Janssen, Cocken and Hoffman of Pittsburgh, English Tudor was chosen as the medium of expression. Mr. Phillips had been much impressed with views of the older areas of Hampton Court palace; Moreton Old Hall, Cheshire; and with Corpus Christi College and the hall at Magdalen in Oxford. He was much taken with the King's gateway and the Great Court at Trinity. In the area of England from which his ancestors came, many of the old manor houses reflected the Tudor style.

In ecclesiastical architecture, of the Tudor period, there was much use of the Gothic. In secular exterior manifestations, Tudor was characterized with large groups of rectangular windows; rich oriel or bay windows; interesting and sometimes fantastic chimney treatments; complex roofs with many gables; much brickwork, frequently in patterns and lavish half-timber. In interior work this period saw an extraordinary development of wood paneling which was frequently used to cover all four sides of a room, and often enriched by linen-fold decoration and lavish use of molded plaster-work for ceilings, cornices, and walls. Elm Court abounds in splendid examples of many of these Tudor distinctives.

Construction—under direction of Harry Wimer, construction engineer—began early in 1929 and the structure was not completed until mid-1930. Everything that went into the building

84

was of the finest quality. Brick was especially molded. Stone work was all hand-carved. Workmanship was often imported to Butler to insure structural perfection. Each door in the house was elaborately carved and patterned after a different famous door in England. All windows were made in England, to assure architectural authenticity. Most of them were of steel casement type with leaded glass bearing art-glass symbols appropriate to the rooms in which they were installed. Every room had a fireplace, ranging from a huge greystone one imported from an English castle to miniature ones in small guest rooms. With the exception of the great fireplaces which were equipped to burn both wood and coal, all were fitted with *gas-burning* coals or logs!

Elm Court is a three-story forty-room structure built around a court and nestled in a hillside. Its approaches fail to do justice to the massive proportions of the building. The setting was deliberate, as Mr. Phillips wanted Elm Court to appear as a home and not as a palace. Only from the air is it possible to get an adequate realization of the capaciousness of the edifice.

We invite the reader to take a tour of Elm Court: After entering the massive gates and the foyer, one goes down steps to a first landing dominated by a magnificent cathedral-like Gothic window. From this point stairways lead up to guest rooms, suites, and apartments; and down to the Living Hall and the Drawing Room. To the right are the Library, the Study, and powder rooms. Forward through the long Living Hall one comes to the Sun Room where intimate friends are received and conferences with church leaders occur. Here the casement windows bear the signs of the zodiac. To the right, again, are the dining areas—the private dining room or "breakfast room" fronting on the court with its vines and flowers; and the formal Family Dining Room where, on special occasions, as many as forty-four guests can be comfortably accommodated.

The appointments of the Living Hall and the Drawing Room best reflect the sumptuousness of Elm Court. In the former is the huge greystone fireplace extending from floor to ceiling and bearing on its apron the sculptured Phillips coat of arms with its motto *"Ducet Amor Patriac"* (The Love of Our Father Leads Us). The oak furniture is of the Tudor period and was made from wood imported from England especially for Elm Court. The rugs are of authentic oriental weave. On the walls are beautiful and appropriate tapestries and paintings. A choice Skinner pipe organ graces the beautiful room.

The Drawing Room has a richness in every feature exceeding the Living Hall. Here is the fireplace imported from an English castle and said to be two hundred years old. Above the fireplace are two niches holding jade lamps. Mr. Phillips was especially interested in the collection of fine jade and many classic examples appear throughout Elm Court. Chinese vases and bowls of ancient origin—collectors' items—are set in appropriate spots everywhere. Paintings from the Arab Scout by Schreyer to Tennier miniatures grace the walls alongside rich tapestries from Belgium and France. Crystal chandeliers add formal dignity to the room. Hunting scenes appear in the stained-glass medallions of the casement windows.

On the second floor are seven guest suites. Also on this floor are a music room, the large master bedroom with two adjoining dressing rooms, a sewing room, and a study. The medallions on the windows depict scenes from English literature. There are music symbols in the music room and King-and-Queen windows in the master bedroom. All bathrooms are marble-lined and the plumbing fixtures are of silver and gold plate. Eleven telephones provide communication to all parts of the house.

Behind the scenes are a multiplicity of rooms providing for the needs of the household staff and the services essential to the establishment. On the ground floor, there is a recreation room and the immense heating system. Two identical hot-water gas-fired furnaces assure unbroken functions in case one might be disabled. On the first floor adjoining the dining rooms is a kitchen large enough to serve a good-sized restaurant, with every gadget for the production of gourmet meals. Here also are a large serving room, a small pantry, and a small dining room for employees. Off the serving room is a large walk-in cubicle where are kept many sets of dishes appropriate for all sorts of servings. They are "a joy to behold." Also in this area of the house is a sitting room for employees which has been nicknamed "the courtin' room" because several of the women employees used it for that purpose before marrying. Also on this level and connected with the main house are the garages and shops for minor repair work. Beyond is a spacious paved and walled area for deliveries and recreation. On the third floor are adequate living quarters for employees who

86

are required to or who prefer to live on the premises.

At this point it might be appropriate to say a word about the sizable company of those who labor to keep the establishment going. One young woman, Annabelle Gruver, who came to work when the house was built, remained with the family for thirty-seven years. She loved the place. Although she married young she said, "I want to work at Elm Court until they carry me out." She worked until two days before her last illness when the best hospital care was provided. Oscar Bartley worked on the house when it was under construction and remained to become the overseer of the grounds. He stayed for thirty-eight years when ill health forced him to quit. A laundress worked for twenty-two years, and her daughter for fifteen years. A seamstress has stayed for thirty-three years. A maid for twenty-three years. Every effort was made to provide ideal working conditions, brotherly kindness, and sympathetic understanding, and to give medical, nursing, and hospital care when needed.

No description of Elm Court would be complete without reference to the beautiful gardens. Like the great English gardens, this Pennsylvania place has been developed in an architectural direction. The landscape has been sculptured into a series of interlocking terraces which are an extension of the house itself. Plant material has been selected almost like furniture for a room—that is, for its permanent shape, structure, and color. The courtyard garden is frankly derivative in design, with a central and geometric pattern echoing European cloisters. Basic planting is boxwood, ivy, and yew, with potted plants for summer color. The great sunken garden with pool occupies a broad area between the sweep of the main driveway and what is known as "Linden Avenue" with its rows of beautiful linden trees. This garden is entered from a terrace down broad stone steps. Around the green garden in spring, summer, and fall there is a riot of color where Mr. Phillips' favorite flowers—roses, iris, and day lilies—reign in all their glory.

Elm Court's gardens in their heyday were recognized to be among the finest in America. James F. Fitch and F. F. Rockwell in their *Treasury of American Gardens* gave several pages to a map and pictures. This lavish book surveyed every major region and climate of the country with sections on public gardens, but majoring on private gardens, hitherto seen only by their owners or a privileged few. The pictures were taken by noted garden photographers and the subjects ranged from suburban acres to great estates. It was indeed an honor for the gardens of Elm Court to be included.

The *Treasury of American Gardens* said of Elm Court:

With the rising acceptance of contemporary design, the tendency to duplicate or recreate the forms of old gardens from other lands has all but disappeared. So-called "period design" in landscaping, as in architecture, is a thing of the past. But twenty-five years ago when the B. D. Phillips estate was laid out, modern architecture was still a thing of the future. Given the reference frame of Tudor England, the designers here have created an impressive complex.

Like all Renaissance and Renaissance-inspired designs, these are "pleasure gardens" in the truest sense of the term. And designed, above all, to give pleasure to the eye. They are also, as plan and pictures reveal, essentially architectural in their character. Walls, garden houses, terraces, and pools are dominant elements in the design. Plant material, while handsome— especially after years of care — is of secondary interest. Architectural elements are, of course, expensive and this is perhaps one of the main reasons for their disappearance from the American scene. But they date from a period in which expense was a secondary consideration. And they have created a kind of monumental splendor which, within its own terms, is admirable. A touch of Elizabethan England has been brought to America in Elm Court.

While not so apparent to the casual visitor, there is another dimension to the Phillips estate—the development of the natural woodland surrounding Elm Court proper. Existing trees have been preserved and against the fine skeletal background have been planted dogwood, both pink and white. Blended with these are rhododendrons and pale pink evergreen azaleas. There are plantings of ferns and evergreen shrubs and ground covers to create the feeling that one is on a path treading natural woodland. Lovely in May when the shrubs and flowering trees are in bloom and shades of young green on deciduous trees contrast with evergreen foliage ranging from chartreuse to deep forest green, such a scene is even more exquisite in autumn. Then the reds and golds of maple, elm, sweet gum, and oak are supported by the richly-colored foliage of berried shrubs and accented by the shadowy greens of the rhododendrons and other broad-leaved evergreens. In winter the bare forms of the tall trees, set among the evergreen shrubs, lend a rugged beauty to the scene. As has already been indicated in this chapter, Mr. Phillips was a real lover of nature. He took

Bird's-eye View of B. D. Phillips Elm Court Mansion, Butler, Pennsylvania

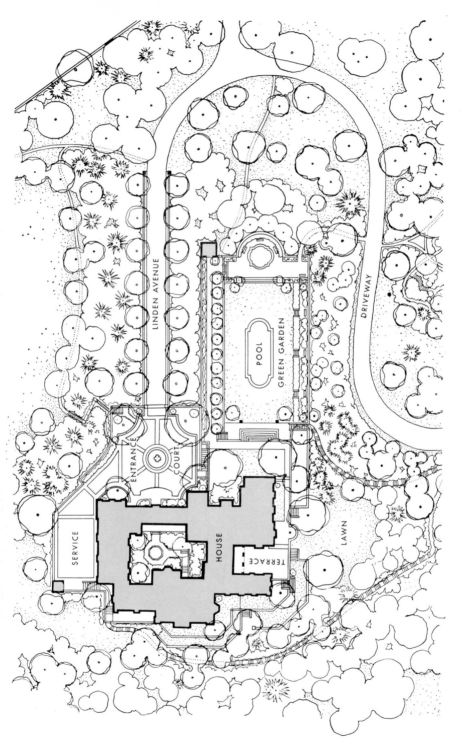

Map of Buildings and Grounds, Elm Court

The following labels appear within the map:

LINDEN AVENUE

DRIVEWAY

POOL

GREEN GARDEN

ENTRANCE COURT

SERVICE

HOUSE

TERRACE

LAWN

View of the House from Sunken Garden

Where the Mansion and the Terrace Meet

The Pool and the Green Garden

The Inner Patio

Gate to the Entrance Court

A View of the Terrace

The Grand Staircase and Entrance

The Family Dining Room, Elm Court

Glimpse of Mr.
Phillips' Study

Pipe Organ in
Living Hall

Greystone Fireplace
with Phillips
Coat-of-Arms

Domestic Scenes of
B. D. and Mildred Phillips
Taken at Butler

Sheep Camp 500 Feet Below Timberline

B. D. Phillips with Buck Antelope He Killed

Phillips Pack Train Ready to Leave on Hunting Trip

Ram's Heads — Trophies of Wyoming Hunt

great pleasure in walking through his gardens and wooded estate alone, or with his wife or a close friend, observing the changes that had taken place in a day's time and meditating on the wonders and blessings of God's creation.

When Elm Court was completed it became the center of typical Phillips hospitality. Mr. Phillips especially enjoyed weekend or overnight visitors. There was a steady flow of church leaders, businessmen and other men and women of affairs. Conversations were not ordinary "chit-chat" but dealt with current issues in depth. A large number of guests were presidents of colleges or others interested in the cause of Christian higher education.

There were many social affairs of community importance. Topping the calendar were two family affairs—one on Mr. Phillips' birthday for his children and their mates, the other a New Year's dinner for their children and grandchildren. There was another annual dinner, for the directors of the T. W. Phillips Gas and Oil Company on the evening of their board meeting, following the annual stockholders' meeting.

The minister of the North Street Church and his family were always welcome. Louis Riddell, who baptized and married most of the Phillips children, often visited at Elm Court with his delightful family. N. Quentin Grey, who was Mr. Phillips' minister for fifteen years, often brought his family to enjoy the Phillips hospitality. His oldest daughter, Nancy, often says that one of her most pleasant childhood memories was that of being at Elm Court for an Easter dinner when the ice cream served was in the shape of a rabbit with ice cream Easter eggs around it.

The Phillipses had been in Elm Court scarcely four years when Anna Undine Conant Phillips died. The loss of his wife cast a shadow for a time, but Mr. Phillips' eldest daughter, Stella (Mrs. Rolland L. Ehrman), stepped into the vacuum and became for almost thirty years the gracious hostess at Elm Court. The Ehrmans with their delightful family of girls added a lively youthful touch to the home.

Mr. Phillips now plunged more deeply than ever into business affairs and the development and expansion of the family fortune. This was forced to an even greater degree by the death (January, 1956) of his brother, T. W. Phillips, Jr., who had been president of the gas company, and B. D.'s succession to that position. In all of this, however, he never lost to the slightest degree his commitment to Christ and the Church and his concern for Christian higher education.

It was in connection with a plan to erect a splendid new library at Milligan College as a memorial to his good friend, P. H. Welshimer, nationally-known minister of the great First Christian Church, Canton, Ohio, that he became intimately acquainted with Mr. Welshimer's daughter, Mildred, then Dean of Women at Milligan (page 189). After a brief courtship they were married at the Lemoyne Christian Church, Harrisburg, Pennsylvania, in July, 1963. Thus began a relationship which brought new happiness to Elm Court and eventuated in a new and enlarged vision for educational philanthropy in the Christian Churches and Churches of Christ.

Mildred Phillips, a graduate of Hiram College, began her teaching career in the high school of her home town, Canton, Ohio. After a period of time, during which she was on the staff of The Standard Publishing Company of Cincinnati, Ohio, she joined the faculty of Milligan College in Tennessee, where for sixteen years she served as Dean of Women.

While with The Standard Publishing Company, Mrs. Phillips lectured widely among church and educational groups across the nation. She also made valuable contributions to literature, especially in her books and articles for young people. Her published works include *The Young People's Bible Teacher and Leader* and *Special Addresses*. The latter volume, released in 1967, carried these introductory remarks: "Few, if any, have spoken in so many churches, taught more Sunday School classes, addressed more students."

Mrs. Phillips' father, P. H. Welshimer, was minister of the Canton Church for more than half a century. With its seven thousand members, this was the largest local congregation in the history of the American Restoration Movement. Mrs. Phillips sister, Helen Welshimer, was a nationally respected poet, journalist, and essayist whose works appeared in such journals as *Good Housekeeping* and *Parent's Magazine*. She contributed for many years to the columns of the *Chicago Tribune*. Her books of poetry include the popular *Singing Drums*.

In the brief five years of their marriage, before Mr. Phillips passed to his reward, the guest book at Elm Court showed the names of 533 out-of-town visitors who enjoyed its hospitality.

Among them were two of Mr. Phillips' closest business friends, Carl Brelos and Milton Hulme of Pittsburgh. Another business associate who came to Elm Court was Joseph Hirschorn of New York City, who recently gave his fifty-million-dollar art collection to the United States government. He had lunch in the Phillips home just a few days after he had been a guest in the White House and completed arrangements with President Johnson for the gift and its housing in a large Art Museum in Washington to bear the Hirschorn name. Raymond and Roger Weill of New Orleans, the most noted philatelic dealers in the world, were frequent and most welcome guests. One of the guest rooms was known as "Raymond's room." Since he liked a "hot-dog on a bun" before retiring, B. D. always made sure there was a supply on hand. Usually Mrs. Phillips herself "did the honors." Clinton Davidson, a New York investment banker and active member of the Church of Christ, always mixed religion with business when he came to Elm Court. When Mr. Phillips' business friends came he would often recall his close association with the late Elias Ritts, who had been president of the Mellon Bank in Butler, and Ross McCafferty who had been his "right hand man" in the gas company for many years.

Of church leaders there was, according to the Phillips tradition, always a long list in the guest register. Lawrence Kirkpatrick, of New York City, secretary of the World Convention of Churches of Christ, was always a welcome guest. James DeForest Murch and his wife, Olive, of Washington and Cincinnati, friends of long standing, were often invited. They, too, had their special room whenever they came. Mr. and Mrs. Burton Coffman, of the Madison Avenue (Manhattan) Church of Christ, New York City, other visitors, had much in common with the Phillipses. Mr. Phillips enthusiastically participated in the erection of their new church edifice, the first new Protestant structure built in that area in fifty years. When B. D. and Mildred were in New York on "prayer-meeting night" they always went to Madison Avenue for the service.

Among college administrators who frequented Elm Court in this era were Dean Walker and Jess Johnson of Milligan; Perry Gresham of Bethany; W. F. Lown of Manhattan; Woodrow Perry of Cincinnati; Earl Hargrove of Lincoln; Don Earl Boatman of Ozark; Hallie Gantz of Phillips; Kenneth Stewart of Pacific;

Joseph H. Dampier of Emmanuel; Norvel Young and William Banowsky of Pepperdine, and Robert M. Bell and Floyd Clark of Johnson.   Among others in a similar category were Paul Carpenter of Culver-Stockton and Henry Webb of Milligan.

One of Mr. Phillips' favorite guests was the late Frank Albert, a member of the faculty of Christian Theological Seminary and the former School of Religion at Butler University.   Dr. Albert was converted by Mrs. Phillips when both lived in Canton, Ohio. Mr. Phillips would always insist that Frank bring his wife and four boys with him when he came to Elm Court.   Their visits were more like "family reunions."

Elm Court might well be said to be "the lengthened shadow of a man."   Everywhere one goes in the great mansion the handiwork and the spirit of B. D. Phillips are reflected.   After a visit there, Gail (Mrs. Don Earl) Boatman wrote "The Man of the Mansion" which expresses this thought:

"He's a creator of good revealed by 'Elm Court' which he designed.
Observed from visiting within, 'twas the dream of someone refined.

The house has a sturdy foundation like its creator staunch and true.
Its stone walls offer protection when the storms of life come
     through.

Because of his masterful planning, beauty glows within this
     magnificent place
Where one's spirits are filled with courage the unknown future to
     face.

I know he's a wonderful person, a lover of all that's fine
With an appreciation for beauty around him, and an inspiration
     divine.

Within his court each flower and tree is tended with loving care
Where the creatures of God's creation together with man might
     share.

'Tis not a mansion alone, but a man's revealed forethought
To be a good and profitable steward toward God as man ought.

Choosing a wise and gracious wife with whom to share his golden
     years
Projects his goals to heights sublime as he reflects the future
     without fears.

92

Permeating their home of beauty is the warmth of joyous
    hospitality
Where the soul feels a kinship of spirit concerning God's reality.

Their forefathers continue a spiritual crop to yield
As together they assist workers in Christ's harvest field.

For beyond this physical creation of the mansion graced with
    flowers that bloom
Their faith is the conviction of things hoped for, the assurance of
    dispelled gloom.

When I think of the blessing they make possible, to them I feel
    akin
Because Christians striving together enable Christ's Church to win.

Though the marble and stone invested in his monumental build-
    ings of the past
Will crumble and fade away, his evidences of faith will forever
    last.

Fortune did not change this man, but only revealed his soul
Where his thoughts and desires accumulated to gain this precious
    goal."

But, speaking of family reunions, nothing could equal the annual birthday and New Year parties in the great Family Dining
Room at Elm Court. When all were assembled Mr. Phillips
would lead in a prayer. He would pray for their health, for wisdom and guidance, and that they would never forget their Christian heritage. At one of the New Year parties, where the grandchildren were special guests of honor, a grandson was heard to
remark, "It was worth coming all the way from New England to
Butler just to hear Grandfather's prayer."

Usually, on these occasions, after a delightful meal with plenty
of "seconds," Mr. Phillips would make a full-length "patriarchal"
address dealing with matters of special concern to the Phillips
Family. He kept in his file memoranda of what he had said.
Many of his remarks were of a personal and confidential nature,
but it is a pleasure to record some sage words of advice which
reveal the character of the man and his deep and sincere desire
that the high ideals of his father and mother be perpetuated by
future generations, both in their homes and in their business relationships:

I well know some of my family, and undoubtedly others, feel that I have devoted too much time to business, neglecting to some extent social gatherings and outside acquaintances. However, I believe this cannot be truthfully said regarding my six children in the early years of their lives.

Perhaps I have devoted too much time to business, but I feel well-compensated in this effort, because we have what very few of you appreciate or realize—a wonderfully stable business, as well as an extremely wide base of investments, not out of proportion in any one interest or corporation. All of this has required a time-consuming effort on my part. As a result, I am very sensitive where far-reaching policies are considered and consequently apprehensive when the future is contemplated, especially when little thought is exercised, particularly by those who should be more concerned with the future than I can possibly be.

I have read that after the Constitutional Convention Benjamin Franklin was asked, "What do we have now?" He replied, "A Republic, but the question is: Can it be kept?"

I might ask the same question in regard to the two companies we have: Can they be kept? Certainly by "kept" it is implied that they be operated efficiently and satisfactorily. This is a question about which I have been much concerned for many years, in fact several years before T. W.'s death. If those in my family, who are involved in the operation of these companies, will engender a spirit of humility in their attitude toward each other and lose sight of the fact there are others not engaged in the business who perhaps are benefiting to the same or to a greater extent, many petty considerations and jealousies can be avoided.

Those occupying these positions should derive a real sense of pride in the company in which they have a part—a company which they have every reason to feel is a credit to the name it bears and which is of great monetary benefit to the communities and the industries it supplies—keeping in mind at all times the name the company bears is an honorable one and for two generations has exemplified honesty, integrity, and truthfulness.

Has it ever occurred to you what kind of community you would live in if there were no churches and no church influences, directly or indirectly? I am certain you would not consider living under such conditions in that community and positively it would not be a community in which you would consider rearing a family; yet I have known a number of people who to all intent and appearances have no interest whatever in any church, contribute nothing to any church, and rarely, if ever, attend a church service. However, they are enjoying untold and indirect benefits from the influence of the church and therefore are "spongers" to the nth degree.

Through diligent effort and intense application, combined with family integrity which was an inherent quality of my father and mother, I have been able to accumulate property having value of some consequence. My father and mother and also T. W. were greatly concerned about what use would be made of their property when their heirs took possession. I am

94

greatly concerned with a similar situation. Will my property be frittered away and presumably a reasonable amount of pleasure of a very transitory nature obtained by those to whom it is left? Or, will my heirs make some use of it in line with what was done by my father and mother, by my brother and sister, and by me, and continue benevolent and Christian work, confined almost entirely to the church with which we have been identified for two generations?

I am not interested in leaving property to my children, to their children, and to their grandchildren, unless my grandchildren and great-grandchildren will be nurtured in religious beliefs similar to and in most cases identical with the policies that had such a tremendous influence on my parents, on their children, and on my children. I owe too much to my family and have treasured too highly its influence on me to permit funds to pass into the possession of my children and in turn their children, if their children show a tendency to have little or no consideration for the principles that were instilled in me from the time I was quite young and have had a tremendous influence on my life.

I have had instilled in me certain Christian fundamentals:
(1)   The inspiration of the Scriptures.
(2)   The divinity of Christ.
(3)   Christ's bodily resurrection.
(4)   A life after death.

When these beliefs are questioned, one gets into serious difficulties, and if followed through to the ultimate can readily lose interest in the fundamentals of the Christian religion. I realize that unfortunately some of my grandchildren presently are living in large cities and undoubtedly have very little, if any, Christian religious association, either for themselves or for their children, of a nature that is compatible with what I have had almost my entire life.

The following question was asked of a person who was active in church work and had church background for a generation, based on the church founded on Pentecost and described in the book of The Acts: "What would you do, if you lived in a community where there was no church embracing the Restoration Plea?" The answer instantly was: "I would organize in my own home a church as described in the New Testament, perhaps with only members of my family and endeavor to interest others" —a pattern that has been followed in the formation of many churches.

How many of you would make a real effort every Sunday to drive ten or fifteen miles, either in the country or in a large city, to attend a church of the New Testament pattern? This is being done by many who perhaps have had less religious training than you have had, but are dedicated and believe wholeheartedly in the Restoration Plea; in other words, the church that was founded on Pentecost, which is free of all man-made creeds and human ordinances.

Contributions to church and benevolent work, particularly church work, should not be considered with the idea of easing one's conscience. Contributions of this kind should be analyzed and scrutinized just as carefully as you would an investment you intended to make with funds on which you hoped to obtain a return or enhancement in value.

Mr. Phillips had a simple but deep spiritual nature. He abhorred seeing anyone making a show of his piety. He never prayed merely to be heard or seen of men. Often when he and Mrs. Phillips would return from a trip he would pray out loud, after they had retired for the night, thanking God for His protection and their safe return. Almost always he would also pray, asking wisdom and guidance not only for himself but for each member of the family. One of his last acts for the family was to send each of his six children a copy of *The Analytical Bible*, expressing his personal hope that they would read and study it and make it their guidebook for life.

Goldsmith has well expressed the spirit of Elm Court:

> Blest be that spot, where cheerful guests retire
>   To pause from toil, and trim their evening fire;
> Blest that abode, where want and pain repair,
>   And every stranger finds a ready chair:
> Blest be those feasts with simple plenty crowned,
>   Where all the ruddy family round
> Laugh at the jest or pranks, that never fail!
>   Or sigh with pity at some mournful tale,
> Or press the bashful stranger to his food
>   And learn the luxury of doing good.

VII

Education With Dimension

C HRISTIAN HIGHER education was of major concern to B. D. Phillips in his philanthropic program. In this concern he shared the Phillips family tradition.

His father, Thomas W. Phillips, believed that the Restoration Movement would challenge the religious world only to the extent that it could produce an educated leadership worthy of its distinctive plea. He was thoroughly committed to Alexander Campbell's idea of what a Christian Church college should be.

In his early fifties Mr. Campbell announced his plans to establish Bethany College, and promised to devote a major portion of his time to the project. Dr. Robert Richardson, in his *Memoirs of Alexander Campbell,* said:

In the College (Mr. Campbell) proposed a liberal course of studies, giving somewhat more prominence than usual to the physical sciences, and contemplating the most liberal provisions for thorough instruction, so as to prepare young men to enter upon the study of the learned professions. In this department, however . . . moral and religious training was to form a principal feature and the Bible was to be made one of the regular textbooks, so that no one could receive the honors of the institution without being thoroughly acquainted with the Sacred Oracles, which were to be

97

taught regularly every day—not with the design of evolving from them any system of doctrines, but for the purpose of familiarizing the mind with Bible facts and institutions.

Campbell conceived of the Bible as the basis of all moral culture. He felt "the relations of the great principles taught in the Bible to human rights and political and social freedom" were being ignored by the educators of his time. "No one had assigned to it its proper position in respect to moral science, which had, as yet, found no better foundation than philosophy, and the study of (that) had been postponed to the latest period" in the curriculum. The Bible, in Campbell's thinking, was the center around which any true Christian college must be constructed, and with its sacred truths accepted as the normative and modifying standard for the entire educational operation.

Alexander Campbell himself became professor of "mental philosophy, evidences of Christianity, moral and political economy." His morning classes on the Bible soon became famous. He began each school year with lectures on Genesis and closed with lectures on the New Testament. They were not particularly critical or exegetical, but rather discursive, highlighting the great moral and religious principles which he considered essential to the building of Christian character.

In Campbell's time it was an entirely new idea to build a liberal arts college with the Bible as its chief textbook and to emphasize its teaching as more important than the teaching of all the other books in the world. This was higher education in a new dimension, giving new meaning and purpose to the life of every student enrolled. Thus at Bethany was born the idea that created a whole family of Bible schools, colleges, and "Bible chairs" distinctively characteristic of the early work of higher education among the Christian Churches.

Thomas W. Phillips "bought" this idea and gave much of his time and money to perpetuate Bethany College and other schools of the Brotherhood committed to its educational philosophy.

Times changed in the interim between Thomas W. Phillips' day and that of his son, Benjamin Dwight. The scholastic improvement of the colleges reflected a rise in the general cultural level of the nation and better public educational facilities. The state poured millions into great secular educational institutions which offered unusual inducements to young people preparing for a life work. A society which originally owed much to Christianity was inundated by a veritable deluge of secularism and scientism. Being rich and greatly increased in goods, America came to trust in Mammon and find its hope in its industrial potential, its scientific abilities, its democratic processes and institutions and paid a sort of lip service to a tribal God. In this atmosphere many church colleges "gave up the ghost," or went along with the tide, to become themselves "church-related" secular educational institutions.

B. D. Phillips saw the changes, was fully aware of the need for improvement in scholastic quality, academic respectability, broadened curricula, and adequate buildings and equipment in Christian Church institutions. He was for betterment and progress provided there would be no compromise of the distinctive nature and mission of the schools as indicated in their charters and in the minds of their founding fathers.

Mr. Phillips had no sympathy with the modern educational theories which insist that it is the function of the school to turn out good citizens for a world democratic society with well-adjusted personalities, who will accept revolutionary change with calmness, even if it means the abandonment of all the traditions of the past. Equally foreign to his views was the insistence of "liberals" and "progressives" that it is the duty of higher education to create a scholastic and economic millennium. Such humanistic conceptions of the purpose of education could have no place in his educational philosophy. Education to him was a basic means by which man prepares himself to glorify God in his life in that vocation for which his divinely bestowed talents best suit him. All other purposes muse be subordinated to this all-consuming and one-prevailing goal. Mr. Phillips looked with abhorrence upon the Greek ideal that knowledge is virtue and that educated people are morally better simply because of their intellectual achievements. In his estimation, Christian colleges could not accept these modern theories and remain Christian in the true sense of the term.

A study of Mr. Phillips' voluminous correspondence with Christian Church educators and his many conversations with ministers and educational leaders concerning the basic issues of Christian higher education makes possible an outline of his educational philosophy.

Mr. Phillips believed that a Christian institution of higher education worthy of the support of Christian Churches should (1) be built upon a thorough-going Christian philosophy of education, (2) have a faculty thoroughly committed to its distinctive philosophy, (3) have a curriculum that is Bible and Christ centered, (4) have a student body that can actively support its moral and spiritual philosophy and aims, and (5) produce an intelligent, indoctrinated leadership for the Christian Churches and Churches of Christ. It was this larger dimension which made a college Christian.

Mr. Phillips placed the same premium upon the Bible in relationship to higher education that Alexander Campbell did. He believed that no valid philosophy of education can be formulated and that no Christian college can be operated successfully without taking into account the teachings of the Word of God. Why? Because the Bible answers the questions of life with answers which cannot be discovered by scientific investigation but only by divine revelation. The Bible teaches students how to live in their total environment which is, after all, the Kingdom of God. The Bible provides a unifying center for all knowledge. The Bible is a perennial source of vision, dynamic, idealism, moral purpose, faith, and hope. The college that uniformly fails to inculcate respect and understanding of the Scriptures and to win commitment to the Christian way of life has failed of its mission.

Mr. Phillips also believed that no student should graduate from a Christian Church school or college without having been exposed to a clear understanding of the relationship of the Restoration Movement to the Church at large. He insisted that there should be at least one required class in the history and principles of the Restoration Movement in every course leading to a baccalaureate degree. He felt that there was no reason why Christian Churches and Churches of Christ should be called upon to support and maintain a system of schools and colleges of their own if their distinctive position was not taught in their classrooms and boldly advocated by their administrators and faculties.

There were always two questions Mr. Phillips asked college officials when solicited for financial support—"How many of your students have committed their lives to preparation for full-time Christian service?" and "How many of your alumni are ministers, Christian educators, missionaries, and evangelists?" There were always many other questions dealing with the fiscal status of their

100

institutions, their methods of administration, their scholastic standing, their buildings and equipment, their doctrinal commitment, etc., but these two pragmatic questions seemed to have priority in his thinking. If the schools were not producing, and their product was not contributing to the ongoing of the Movement to restore New Testament Christianity, he was not interested in giving for their support.

During most of his life, Mr. Phillips was disposed to trust those who had been given positions of authority in the church colleges which had a long history of loyalty to the faith. He assumed that boards of directors or trustees of these institutions were thoroughly committed to the Word of God and to the Restoration Plea, and that they would make sure of such commitment on the part of those to whom they entrusted administrative and instructional authority. When approached for financial aid he was always assured that this was so. When rumors of unfaithfulness came to his attention he was disposed to discount them if they had no official backing. He dealt with the men at the top, the "responsible authorities," and had no time for "reactionary scandalmongers." Unfortunately his faith and trust were sometime misplaced.

Mr. Phillips was often offered positions on college boards where he might have had great influence in keeping such institutions loyal to the faith, but after his Hiram College experience (page 118) he turned down all such invitations. He felt that anyone accepting such a responsibility should make it his business to keep closely in touch with all phases of the operation, attend all meetings of the board and committees to which he might be assigned, and in other ways take an active interest in the affairs of the institution. His increasing responsibilities in a rapidly expanding business made this impossible and so he declined "with regrets."

He also declined the kudos of the many colleges and universities, religious and secular, who vied with each other for his largess. On many occasions he frankly wrote that he did not think himself worthy of the honors and that he did not want to be placed in a position of special obligation because of them. It is estimated that some twenty-five or thirty institutions offered him honorary doctorates and distinguished service awards.

The interest of Mr. Phillips in higher education with the larger dimension of the Christian faith and the Restoration commitment was purely unselfish. He carried this attitude to the extreme of

101

insisting that his name not be used in named funds nor upon the magnificent buildings which his giving made possible. He was willing for the Phillips name to be used, but when this was permitted he had in mind primarily his father and after that the family as a whole. Not until after his death was the name "B. D. Phillips" inscribed over the entrance of any college hall.

One must survey some of the larger Phillips gifts to the schools and colleges of the Christian Churches and Churches of Christ during his lifetime to realize how deep was this interest. A recounting of his munificence is appropriate at this point in our narrative.

Hiram College was his first love. There he had received his college training. There he had been guided by such spirits as E. B. Wakefield in making life's choices. There his father had been a member of the Board and had fellowship in every financial drive. Hiram's presidents from Garfield to Zollars had been guests at New Castle and were warm friends of the family. So from the beginning of B. D.'s business career he had his part in the generous gifts of the Phillips Family for new buildings, endowments, and every forward movement for the good of the institution.

Bethany was, however, the chief educational concern of the Phillips Family, largely because of Alexander Campbell's mark on the College and because of his concept of what higher education should be in the Restoration frame of reference. Both Thomas W. Phillips, Senior and Junior, had been on its Board. Other members of the Phillips Family had also served in this capacity. Phillips money had virtually "flowed" into coffers of Bethany for more than a generation before B. D. came into control of the family fortune. On one occasion, when B. C. Hagerman was president, Phillips money kept Bethany from closing its doors and merging with Hiram. It was natural for Mr. Phillips to respond generously to appeals for Bethany development. The first of these was in 1929 for the remodeling of Phillips Hall which had been given by the family in 1891 for use as a dormitory.

Then came the Thomas W. Phillips Memorial Library worth today more than $2,000,000. It contains Bethany's splendid collection of books in a setting designed for its protection and use according to the latest library science. Mr. Phillips made many trips to Bethany during its construction to be sure that every detail of the structure met the high standards of quality assured by the

102

architects and construction engineers. When the contemporary structure was completed he was so enthusiastic about it that he consented to break his long-established custom and made a few remarks at the dedicatory exercises, June 4, 1960. He said:

It is with a feeling of veneration I came to Bethany today, as a representative of the Phillips Family, to present to Bethany College this library building. There is no other community and no other college in these United States that to the Phillips family would be more fitting for this gift, than Bethany and Bethany College.

The college was founded by Alexander Campbell, who was and remains almost a century after his death the greatest writer, debater, and religious leader that lived all his adult life in this country—and here in Bethany. It was largely through the influence and leadership of Alexander Campbell and his father, Thomas Campbell, that we have the largest membership of any church indigenous to the United States.

Commencing the year Alexander Campbell died, 1866, my father became a trustee of Bethany College and continued as a trustee until his death in 1912, at which time my brother, T. W. Phillips, Jr., succeeded him and continued as a trustee until his death in 1956—a period of ninety years.

We consider it a privilege to place this building at the disposal of Bethany College. Our sincere desire is that it be availed of to the fullest extent practicable for those who seek knowledge generally, and to implant and inculcate in a great many the principles proclaimed by the Campbells and others of our pioneers, who proposed the restoration of the primitive church established on Pentecost.

Not long afterward a great new Science hall was to be erected. The campaign for financing the project started with a large gift from the Benedum Foundation, but it soon became evident that unless Mr. Phillips would come forward with a very generous contribution the drive would fail. The unusual oval structure was to occupy a prominent place on the campus and be the image of Bethany's concern for scientific education. It was to have been named for a noted West Virginian who was not a member of the Christian Church. Mr. Phillips held back his decision on a gift but finally he proposed that the hall be named after Dr. Robert Richardson. Richardson was a distinguished physician and a scientist of parts, teaching courses in science offered by the College in its early years. He was also the author of theological works and the definitive life of Alexander Campbell. The appropriateness of his suggestion was so patent to all concerned that the change was made and Mr. Phillips gave the funds necessary to complete the great building. Today the Robert Richardson Hall of Science stands on the Bethany campus largely because of Mr. Phillips' generosity.

Conscious of the historic values to the Restoration Movement inhering in Bethany and its environs, Mr. Phillips had made contributions from time to time to the maintenance of the Campbell Mansion, the Campbell Cemetery, and the old Bethany Church where the Campbells and other Restoration pioneers had preached for many years. He was conscious of the fact that Bethany was only a few miles from the site of the old Brush Run Church, the first independent congregation organized in the American effort to restore the New Testament Church in doctrine, ordinances, and life. The original structure had long ago disappeared, but foundation stones still remained in a grove some distance from the highway. Mr. Phillips proposed to Bethany College that property be purchased, making possible easy access to the site. He gave the funds for the purchase, the building of a road connecting with the main highway, fencing and other improvements, and perpetual care. Nearby was the site on Buffalo Creek where the church conducted its baptismal services. Mr. Phillips bought an acreage there, fenced it, improved it, and arranged for perpetual care. Thanks to his interest Bethany pilgrimages now include the Brush Run trip, and classes in church history in the college are inspired by their journeys to "the birthplace of the Restoration Movement."

One of Mr. Phillips' plans for the future was to have fellowship in the project to restore and reconstruct the original Bethany Church building. Whenever he entered the old structure he said he felt as if he were walking on holy ground. He envisioned there a veritable "cloud of witnesses," "heroes of the faith" long gone, that inspired him to new efforts in the furtherance of the common cause they espoused. He hoped that visitors for years to come would be similarly inspired.

Phillips University at Enid, Oklahoma, was, from its beginnings as Oklahoma Christian University in 1907, always in the annual Phillips' benevolence budget. The story of its origin, recounted in Chapter III, had a proud place in the Phillips tradition.

Thomas W. Phillips, Sr., and Thomas W. Phillips, Jr., to say nothing of the rest of the family, could be counted on to undergird every forward move made under the leadership of Phillips' presidents from E. V. Zollars to I. N. McCash. The salary of E. V. Zollars in the founding years was paid by the Phillipses. When the first three permanent buildings were erected on the Enid Campus, Phillips money made them possible, especially the Library which was the outright gift of Mrs. Thomas W. Phillips, Sr., Thomas W. Phillips, Jr., and B. D. Phillips.

B. D. kept up the family tradition. There were investments in Athenian Hall, the Intramural Center, the Student Center, and (after the disastrous fire that leveled "Old Main") the Marshall Building, The Science Building, the Isaac Newton McCash Building, the Administration Building, and other structures necessary to a well-equipped college.

In his later years checks from his own personal funds, the Thomas W. Phillips Charitable Trust, and the T. W. Phillips Gas & Oil Company came from his office in Butler with considerable regularity, totaling in given years around $100,000 for current expenditures.

Mr. Phillips was particularly proud of the development of the "Bible College" which under Frank H. Marshall, C. C. Roberts, and other "stalwarts of the faith" came to enroll the largest number of young men studying for the ministry in any college of the Disciples. At one time some five hundred ministerial students were enrolled. Its graduates were known to be "well grounded" in Bible doctrine and were among the most zealous advocates of the Restoration Plea to be found anywhere. Phillips men were in great demand and they measured up to the standards of the largest and most influential churches in the Brotherhood.

For fifty years there was wonderful progress in the three basic areas of students, faculty, and facilities. The administrations recognized the broad responsibility to students, offering the very best in accredited instruction. An atmosphere was created in which young people became academically equipped to pursue high purposes in life. A growing number of qualified applicants for a Phillips education come from the Christian Churches and Churches of Christ in the geographical area served and, so favorable was the reputation of the school in other states that the institution's enrollment took on a national complexion. By and large, Phillips graduates had learned the importance of a distinctly Christian faith and life and were aware of the need for the dissemination of the Gospel. Many dedicated themselves to full-time Christian service because of the impressions made in the classrooms by well-equipped and thoroughly committed Christian teachers.

105

The last sizable investment of Mr. Phillips in the Enid institution was in a million-dollar library dedicated to the memory of his father's friend, Ely Vaughn Zollars. It provided space for 125,000 volumes, contained an assembly hall seating 325, and afforded accommodations for a number of classrooms until other academic buildings were constructed. He was glad to perpetuate on the Phillips campus the name, and, hopefully, the faith and the spirit of one who gave his life and his all for the perpetuity of the Restoration Plea.

Culver-Stockton College of Canton, Missouri, was virtually unknown to Mr. Phillips, it never having been in the orbit of the higher education concerns of the Phillips Family. It had a long and interesting history under the pretentious name of "Christian University." It was the first coeducational college west of the Mississippi River, organized in 1852, chartered in 1853, and opened to students in 1855. For many years it had a hand-to-mouth existence and was nearly bankrupt when the Culver and Stockton families endowed it in 1910 and made possible a reorganization and building program. Although always a small school, it was to make a considerable contribution to the Brotherhood at large by its cradling of the Disciples of Christ Historical Society and as the birthplace of Restructure in a meeting of "The Panel of Scholars" (page 167). In 1960 the institution planned to erect a million-dollar building bearing the name of Alexander Campbell and providing a spacious auditorium and administrative quarters. Mr. Phillips was approached through relatives and friends for a large gift. The name of the building had strong psychological appeal. Promises were made of a new historical and doctrinal emphasis on the Restoration Movement. Without too much investigation Mr. Phillips gave $200,000 to the project and might have given more had he not learned of certain liberal policies and programs of the college which seemed to nullify all his hopes for its future. Nevertheless, his giving made the new structure possible and it stands prominently on the campus today as a testimony to Campbell and his plea for a united church.

In 1941 the Disciples of Christ Historical Society was organized largely through the vision and notable abilities of Dr. Claude E. Spencer, then librarian of Culver-Stockton College. He found in Dr. Henry Barton Robinson of the faculty an enthusiastic supporter of the plan to develop a comprehensive collection of the

106

literature of the Restoration Movement and make it available for educational research. Dr. Robinson donated his own extensive library to the project. The holdings of the Society grew to such proportions that adequate housing became essential. Through the generosity of interested brethren in Nashville, Tennessee, a modest, poorly-located property was acquired and DCHS headquarters were transferred to that southern city. The Society would probably have remained a rather insignificant factor in the life of the Brotherhood had not Mr. Phillips' interest been elicited. So many conflicting stories have been circulated about the importance of his contribution to the development of the Society that his own account of his concern is of more than passing interest. In his files under date of March 30, 1968, was the following:

Mr. James E. McKinney, then Executive Director of the Disciples of Christ Historical Society, called on me in Butler, Pennsylvania, in December 1954, regarding the proposed building for the Society. As I recollect, certain papers and documents pertaining to our Movement had been forwarded to Nashville from Culver-Stockton College, Canton, Missouri, and were stored in the cellar of one of the Vanderbilt University buildings, Dr. Claude E. Spencer having charge of them. An option had been obtained, or a down payment made, on a property on which there was a very ordinary yellow brick house, within a block or two of the Vanderbilt campus. It was tentatively proposed to place on this lot a building of the same type of brick, merely four walls and a roof, in which was to be housed the Disciples of Christ Historical Society material and the curator presumably was to live in the house.

At that time Mr. McKinney was told that with some of my family I expected to go south early in 1955, via Nashville. As a result, we stopped at Nashville and spent an afternoon and most of the following day canvassing the situation, after which Mr. McKinney was told we would not be a party to establishing library facilities at Nashville in a building located on a side street. I explained to him that we possess an entirely too important heritage, as heirs of the Restoration Plea, and for which we should have much greater respect and reverence, than might be evidenced by the proposed location and building. I further stated we would have nothing to do with the project, unless an adequate site were secured in a prominent location, preferably on the Vanderbilt campus. On that day we selected the site and authorized purchase of it, which site was later acquired.

We now have on this site what in many respects is perhaps the finest building, with possibly one exception, owned by those who trace their origin to the Restoration Plea. One of the outstanding features of this building is the cenotaph at the entrance, depicting our four pioneers—the Campbells, Scott, and Stone—with quotations from each, all done in granite. This monument should have an enormous influence and remain intact for hundreds of years. . . .

When Mr. McKinney first mentioned Nashville to me, I was of the opinion it was hardly the city that should be chosen. However, after a visit there we had more appreciation of the culture of the city and of the influential position and the numbers of those located there and in the surrounding territory, who traced their beginning to the Restoration Movement, and came to the conclusion that Nashville had been well chosen. Location was especially important if the Society was to be recognized as a unifying influence throughout our entire brotherhood, regardless of whether the various individuals had closer attachments to the so-called "organized work" or "independent work," or of the so-called "Church of Christ" (non-instrumental).

We recognized the great growth and advancement in the number of church buildings and colleges that had been made by what used to be known as the "Antis." They had not lost their evangelistic zeal or their adherence to the New Testament Church, and I was hopeful they would be given appropriate recognition on the Board of the Disciples of Christ Historical Society. This, as a matter of fact, influenced us greatly in deciding to accept the Nashville site. . . .

Plans for a "Thomas W. Phillips Memorial" building were announced in 1955. Ground was broken in November of that year and the cornerstone was laid in April of 1956. The building was ready for occupancy in April of 1958. Its total cost was around $1,500,000 and the entire expense was underwritten by B. D. Phillips and other members of the Phillips Family, the late Thomas W. Phillips, Jr., and Mrs. Grace Phillips Johnson. By far the greatest contribution was made by Mr. Phillips himself.

The Nashville structure, more than any other edifice Mr. Phillips had given the Restoration Movement, became "the apple of his eye." He spared no expense to produce a building that would not only adequately serve the Society but be a notable architectural contribution to the college and university community in which it was located and to the City of Nashville. He consulted with the architects and builders; he frequently visited the site during construction; he proposed unique decorative ideas; he checked and double-checked for high quality of materials, and made provision for every modern gadget of modern library science that would assure superior service to scholars and researchers. So important was the "Thomas W. Phillips Memorial" to B. D. Phillips that any story of his life would be inadequate that did not include a comprehensive story of its conception and completion.

The architects of the building were Hoffman and Crompton of Pittsburgh. The Memorial was designed by Kenneth R. Crompton, who did not live to see the building completed, but his ideas and his designs were faithfully carried out and executed by members of his firm. In an article which was written in 1955, Mr. Crompton said this of the architecture of the Memorial: "The conception and design style of the Memorial to Thomas W. Phillips is fundamentally Tudor Gothic. The Gothic style of architecture is primarily a live and virile style in that it is inspirational and creative, as well as emotional. There are many well developed motifs for use in this style. Their combination and arrangement in harmonious composition is almost unlimited."

The Gothic style flourished in Europe and England during the twelfth through the sixteenth centuries. The Continental influence was brought to England about 1140. There it developed and thrived, becoming distinctly English in concept during the fifteenth and sixteenth centuries.

Selection of this particular style for the Memorial Building answered many questions of relationship between the Society and its home. It presented an ecclesiastical atmosphere and combined harmoniously with the neighboring college and university buildings of Scarritt and Vanderbilt. Throughout the design of the building and its parts, one will see the reflection of features borrowed from the Old World, from important buildings of the period, ecclesiastical and domestic.

It is impossible in the space at our command to give anything like an adequate description of the Memorial Building. The material is of the very finest, and the workmanship is excellent beyond description. The sheer beauty of the building, both the exterior and the interior, defies description without going into infinite detail concerning art, sculpture, stained glass, etc. Nothing has been left out and nothing has been left undone to make this building outstanding in its field. The Nashville, Tennessee, newspapers referred to the building as "a perfect jewel." The building is air-conditioned throughout and is equipped for various meetings, for study groups, visual educational programs, etc. One is deeply impressed by the strength and sheer beauty of the building inside and out. It certainly is a fitting tribute to a man who gave of his strength and the beauty of his own life to his community, his nation and his Church.

In the entrance porch of the Memorial occurs the following inscription:

THOMAS W. PHILLIPS
1835 - 1912

BUSINESS PIONEER OF
WESTERN PENNSYLVANIA,
CONGRESSMAN AND CHRISTIAN
STATESMAN, AND CONSECRATED
LAYMAN OF THE DISCIPLES OF
CHRIST, HE COUNTED FIRST
HIS LABORS FOR THE
KINGDOM OF GOD

BY HIS ACTIVITIES IN INDUS-
TRY AND GOVERNMENT, HE
ELEVATED THE STANDARDS
OF BUSINESS ETHICS AND
POLITICAL MORALITY AND
ENNOBLED THE CONCEPTS OF
INDIVIDUALISM, FREE ENTER-
PRISE, AND SOCIAL JUSTICE

HIS EARTHLY SUBSTANCE HE
LARGELY EXPENDED IN WORKS
OF CHARITY AND EDUCATION—
TO BUILD CHURCHES, FOUND
AND ENDOW CHRISTIAN COL-
LEGES AND PUBLICATIONS, AND
MISSIONARIES AND TEACHERS,
AND SUCCOR THE UNFORTUNATE

AUTHOR OF WIDELY READ BOOK,
"THE CHURCH OF CHRIST
BY A LAYMAN,"
HE WAS A FERVENT ADVO-
CATE OF NEW TESTAMENT
CHRISTIANITY AND A STUDENT
OF CHURCH HISTORY FOR
WHOM KNOWLEDGE OF THE
PAST ILLUMINED THE PRESENT
AND INSPIRED THE FUTURE

TO HIS MEMORY
THIS BUILDING STANDS

110

Also in the entrance porch of the Memorial occurs the following inscription:

DISCIPLES OF CHRIST

EARLY IN THE NINETEENTH
CENTURY, IN THE LAND OF
THE WESTERN WATERS, A
NEW CHRISTIAN MOVEMENT
WAS BORN

IMPELLED BY CONVICTION THAT
GOD COULD REQUIRE OF THIS
HIGHLY FAVORED NEW WORLD
NOTHING LESS THAN A
THOROUGH REFORMATION
IN ALL THINGS CIVIL
AND RELIGIOUS,

ITS PIONEERS, MEN OF THE
ADVENTUROUS SPIRIT OF THE
NEW AGE OF FREEDOM AND
ENLIGHTENMENT, HELD THESE
TRUTHS TO BE SELF-EVIDENT:

THAT MEN ARE ENDOWED BY
GOD WITH EQUAL RIGHTS TO
THINK AND ACT FOR THEM-
SELVES IN ALL MATTERS
OF RELIGIOUS BELIEF
AND PRACTICE:

THAT A DIVIDED CHURCH
IS SIN AND THE SPIRIT OF
LOVE AND UNITY, LIBERTY AND
CONCORD, IS TO BE RESTORED
BY CASTING OFF THE SHACKLES
OF HUMAN TRADITIONS AND
RETURNING TO THE ORIGINAL
FAITH AND ORDER OF THE
CHURCH OF CHRIST

THAT BELIEF IN JESUS THE
CHRIST AND OBEDIENCE TO HIM
AS LORD IS THE ONLY TEST OF
CHRISTIAN CHARACTER AND
THE ONLY BOND OF
CHRISTIAN UNION

111

The Cenotaph is a strikingly-sculptured stone monument dominating the Forecourt at the entrance to the grounds of the building.

The Cenotaph, which was Mr. Phillips' idea, is a permanent tribute to four of the fathers of the Restoration Movement in America.

On each side of a square shaft that rises from an octagonal base is carved the bas-relief bust of one of the "Big Four"—Thomas Campbell, Alexander Campbell, Barton Warren Stone, and Walter Scott. Beneath each bust the pioneer leader is identified by his name, dates, and pertinent short quotations usually taken from his writings that serve to underscore his particular contribution and interest.

The carved sections of The Cenotaph are of Westerly granite from Vermont, warm gray in color with underlying tints of pink to harmonize with the buff-to-gray tones of the building. The octagonal base, which serves as a seating area in the center of the Forecourt, is of Indiana limestone, the same stone as that used on the exterior of the Memorial.

Crab-orchard stone walkways, in shades of pink and beige, surround The Cenotaph and lead to other sections of the grounds around the building where visitors may view carved stone shields, symbolizing brotherhood events, places, and concepts, built into the walls of the structure.

The Cenotaph is the result of the efforts of many persons. Its basic size and shape was determined by the building designer, the late Kenneth R. Compton, partner in the Pittsburgh architectural firm of Hoffman and Crompton. His associates, R. L. Hoffman and C. A. Gaus, completed the design.

A prominent Nashville sculptor, Puryear Mims, Professor of Fine Arts at Vanderbilt University, was commissioned to prepare models of the bas-relief busts of the "Big Four." Working from all available portraits, daguerreotypes, sketches, and descriptions, Mr. Mims prepared plaster models, larger than life size, which were reviewed and approved by Society officials, including the members of the Fine Arts and Inscriptions Committee, established to supervise this and other artistic elements in the building project. The plaster models were shipped to New York where the firm of Rochette and Parzini had secured a large section of flawless Westerly granite, determined to be the best medium for the carving.

112

Thomas W. Phillips Memorial, Disciples of Christ Historical Society

Main Entrance to Building

The Cenotaph

Thomas W. Phillips Memorial, DCHS, Nashville, Tennessee

Entrance to Grounds

The Four Sides of the DCHS Cenotaph: Commemorating Four Early
Leaders of the Restoration Movement in America

Left: Entrance
Above: Sanctuary
North Street Christian Church
Butler, Pennsylvania

Main Offices, T. W. Phillips Gas & Oil Company, Butler, Pennsylvania

Phillips Hall, Bethany College

Thomas W. Phillips Library, Bethany College

Robert Richardson Hall of Science, Bethany College

Rear View Phillips Library with Campbell Tower in Background

Original Buildings Oklahoma Christian University (later Phillips University)

Marshall Memorial Graduate School

Zollars Memorial Library

Phillips University

The artisans of this prominent firm faithfully followed the models in exact detail, hand-carving the monumental figures and the accompanying inscriptions. Rochette and Parzini sculptors also carved the granite urn that completes the top section of the eleven-feet high monument.

Miss Eva Jean Wrather, Chairman of the Fine Arts and Inscriptions Committee, and her associates, Dr. Howard E. Short and Dr. Ronald E. Osborn, gave painstaking attention to the selection of quotations that would adequately summarize the contribution and thought of each of the "Big Four." Suggestions came from many sources. Quotations were widely distributed to Brotherhood leaders and Church history scholars for comment and suggestion.

In some instances, it was relatively easy to select quotations. Some statements came to mind automatically. For example, Thomas Campbell's.

THE CHURCH OF CHRIST
UPON EARTH IS ESSENTIALLY,
INTENTIONALLY, AND
CONSTITUTIONALLY ONE

WHERE THE SCRIPTURES
SPEAK, WE SPEAK;
WHERE THE SCRIPTURES
ARE SILENT, WE ARE SILENT

A selection from the writing of Barton W. Stone, representing the man and his contribution, was agreed upon quickly.

LET THE UNITY OF
CHRISTIANS BE OUR
POLAR STAR

LET EVERY CHRISTIAN
BEGIN THE WORK OF
UNION IN HIMSELF

Expressing concisely the central theme of Walter Scott's message was relatively simple.

THE GOLDEN ORACLE:
THE GRAND SAVING TRUTH
IS, "THAT JESUS IS THE CHRIST"

THE TERMS OF THE ANCIENT
GOSPEL: FAITH, REPENTANCE,
BAPTISM, REMISSION OF SINS,
GIFT OF THE HOLY SPIRIT

It was not so simple to select from the voluminous writings of Alexander Campbell some short statement adequate to include all the many interests of this guiding spirit of the Restoration Movement. Finally, the committee selected two quotations that indicate interests not caught up in the inscriptions for the other pioneers and which, at the same time, illustrate two of Alexander Campbell's principal concerns.

COLLEGES AND CHURCHES
GO HAND IN HAND IN THE
PROGRESS OF CHRISTIAN
CIVILIZATION

THE SPIRIT AND SOUL OF
ALL REFORMATION IS FREE
DISCUSSION

It is appropriate that these four men of faith, whose efforts largely determined the direction of a great American religious reform movement, should be honored together with this imposing monument to their lives and work.

It is especially fitting that such a monument occupy the central position at the entrance to the Thomas W. Phillips Memorial.

The building was dedicated during appropriate services September 12-14, 1958. The actual service of dedication was held in Wightman Chapel, Scarritt College, located across the street from the "Memorial," in order to accommodate the large assembly. Distinguished representatives of all the agencies of the Brotherhood were present, together with officials and members of the DCHS and members of the Phillips Family. Dr. Lawrence G. Derthick, United States Commissioner of Education, prominent Disciples' layman, delivered the dedicatory address.

No Protestant communion in America has the equal of this magnificent historical library and museum. Since its dedication it has been visited by thousands and used by hundreds of scholars in the pursuit of knowledge of the Restoration Movement.

Mr. Phillips' own use of its facilities in the production of the comprehensive index of the *Christian Standard* constitutes one of DCHS' mose notable contributions to the Brotherhood. Since his father made possible the founding of this journal under the editorship of Isaac Errett, it was most appropriate that the son underwrite this immense project covering all weekly issues of the journal over a period of 100 years. The supervision of the undertaking was in the hands of James DeForest Murch and Rolland L. Ehrman and executed and completed under the expert direction of Claude E. Spencer. Printed volumes of the Index and microfilms of every issue are now available to libraries throughout the world.

Parenthetically to this chapter, it may be well to mention the concern of the Phillips Family for the National City Christian Church in Washington, D. C. It began with the elder Thomas W. Phillips' promotion of and liberal gifts to the Garfield Memorial Church building on Vermont Avenue. Much later, under the ministry of Dr. Earle Wilfley at Garfield Memorial, came the vision of a great cathedral-type structure on Thomas Circle more worthy of the great Movement then over 2,000,000 strong. It happened that Dr. Wilfley had been the well-beloved minister of the First Church, New Castle, the historic Phillips family church. He was especially highly esteemed by Mrs. Grace Phillips Johnson, B. D. Phillips' sister. Mrs. Johnson was from the beginning of the project a generous contributor and enlisted the support of the whole Phillips Family. They made possible the original purchase of the strategic site now occupied by the stately structure—one of the finest "national" church buildings of any Protestant communion in Washington. The man who did more than anyone else to bring the plan to completion was, of course, R. A. Long, of Kansas City, then president of the great Long-Bell Lumber Company. His pledge of a million dollars sparked generous giving all over the nation. When, however, the Great Depression came Mr. Long was threatened with bankruptcy and the Washington Church was saddled with an immense indebtedness which took many years to liquidate. In times of emergency it was Phillips money which often saved the day. Under the ministry of Dr. J. Warren Hastings, Thomas W. Phillips, Jr., and B. D. Phillips became deeply concerned for the loyalty of the Church to the great New Testament principles which brought the Restoration Movement into being. Dr. Hastings cooperated with them in several efforts to indoctrinate the membership. L. N. D. Wells' widely-used tract on the fundamentals of the faith and the "steps into the Kingdom" was placed in the hands of every member and made available for free distribution at all services of the Church. In a building expansion program the beautiful Phillips Chapel, with its rich appointments and fine pipe organ, was presented to the Church and is now one of the most frequently-used portions of the great structure.

This chapter could be doubled in length, should we choose to include Mr. Phillips' gifts to Milligan College, Johnson Bible College, Lincoln Christian College, Manhattan Bible College, Cincinnati Bible Seminary, Pacific Christian College, Ozark Bible College, Emmanuel School of Religion and other such institutions within the orbit of the Restoration Movement. Chapter X will tell the rest of the story, for reasons which will be apparent to the reader.

The day came when Mr. Phillips began to realize that there was a life-or-death struggle going on in the Restoration Movement, a conflict which was changing the picture in higher education. A people who had put so much emphasis on the Scriptural authority and norm in doctrine, ordinance and life and pleading for Christian unity on the Bible and the Bible alone were confronted with a new climate in which to carry on their program. This was not uniquely their problem. Increasingly large areas of Protestantism had come to feel that the Bible might be untrustworthy in cosmology, history, faith, and practice. With the Biblical foundations crumbling, liberal theologians began to talk of a "Christian theology" apart from the Bible. They sneered at those who refused to admit the validity of destructive criticism and who clung to the Scriptures, calling them "bibliolaters." The popular liberal concept of the Bible was that it is in some of its parts a "sign" or "witness" to revelation but not in its Old Testament and New Testament canon "the true Word of God." Some Disciples were beginning to accept the new theories, although the mainstream of the Movement did not. Thus began one of the bitterest controversies in the Christian Churches and Churches of Christ. It was early projected into the schools and colleges, often surreptitiously by those who denied their apostasy. In this situation Mr. Phillips was valiant in the defense of "the faith once for all delivered."

VIII

Valiant for the Faith

1. In Higher Education

L ONG BEFORE THE Christian Churches and Churches of Christ
were forced to confront the issues of theological liberalism,
B. D. Phillips was a "Defender of the Faith." He came naturally
by this role in life, for his father was of the same disposition.

Firmly grounded in the faith revealed in the Holy Scriptures,
they both had that moral courage which could look error and
danger in the face unawed and unafraid. They had no desire to
be "men pleasers." They counted as nothing the possibility that
if they boldly stood for truth and right they might suffer loss of
ease, wealth, friends, or popular acclaim. Neither were they
flamboyant crusaders seeking to enlist an army committed to their
views. They had no desire to "start a riot." They simply stood
quietly, adamantly, smilingly, and intelligently for what they believed, never hesitating to give their open testimony when the issues were clear.

As has been indicated previously, B. D. Phillips had the strong
conviction that higher education, with a distinctly Christian dimension, was the hope of the Restoration Movement. He devoted

117

the major portion of his philanthropy to the support of Christian Church schools and colleges. It was in this field that he first met the challenge of incipient liberalism.

It is natural that Mr. Phillips' first concern in higher education would be Hiram College, his Alma Mater, and the recipient of large gifts from the Phillips Family in early years. Mr. Phillips at first trusted the leadership of the institution and early accepted a place on its Board of Trustees.

Whenever he thought of Hiram he thought of James A. Garfield, B. A. Hinsdale, J. M. Atwater, E. V. Zollars—all bosom friends of his father and noted throughout the Brotherhood for their loyal commitment to the Holy Scriptures, Jesus Christ the Son of God and Saviour of the world, and the movement to restore the New Testament Church in doctrine, ordinances, and life.

And then, there was E. B. Wakefield, whom Mr. Phillips almost worshiped. The impressions he had gained in his classes were more powerful, creative, and worthwhile in shaping his ideals and determining his character than those of any other persons outside his parents. E. B. Wakefield was wholly committed to the Word of God and to what everybody at Hiram called "The Plea."

He was quite unprepared for the declension that had its beginnings in the administration of President Miner Lee Bates (1907-1929). Bates' "ivy league" orientation soon resulted in his bringing into the faculty new men who were of superior academic attainments but weak in their knowledge of the Bible and Restoration principles. They were more concerned with the secular academic standards and ideals of the Eastern universities than with the standards and ideals which had made the existence of Hiram possible. The number of ministerial students declined and the spiritual tone of the institution deteriorated.

Bates' successor was Dr. Kenneth I. Brown, a Baptist, who had been professor of English in Stephens College, a Presbyterian institution, in Columbia, Missouri. Under Brown ten members of the faculty at Hiram left either by resignation or dismissal. Two more were retired because of age. Everything was "different" under the new regime.

The Board of Trustees was persuaded to withdraw Hiram from membership in the Board of Higher Education of the Disciples of Christ and announcement was made that it was no longer a church college. The chairman of the Board gave as a reason for this

118

action that the college did not care to be responsible to any church body for its teaching and that henceforth its chief concern would be to make Hiram the equal of any college in the country in its academic standards. He said that the only relationship it would bear toward the Disciples of Christ would be historical. In this respect it would give "due reverence and respect to its sacred memories and traditions."

The ministerial training phase of the curriculum was scrapped. Young men who had enrolled for the purpose of preparing themselves for the Christian ministry were notified that they would have to seek their Bible courses and other specialized professional training elsewhere. The Christian Church in the Hiram community called a Liberal minister to its pulpit and soon adopted the practice of "open membership."

Hiram was becoming suburban to Cleveland, then claiming to be the "Sixth City" of America. There was money available from community sources if a policy of secularization was adopted. Men of influence in Greater Cleveland were elected to the Board regardless of their relationship to the Christian Churches and Churches of Christ. The chairman of the Board, formerly a member of the Euclid Avenue Christian Church in Cleveland, joined a community "open membership" church at Aurora, near his country home.

With the first intimations of this new trend, B. D. Phillips withdrew from the Hiram board and cut off all financial support of the institution. He was shocked and bitterly disappointed. In the course of his disillusionment, he formed a lasting friendship with P. H. Welshimer, pastor of the First Christian Church at Canton, Ohio. Welshimer was also a Hiram alumnus and strongly opposed to the new policies. The Canton Church was the largest in the nation, with a membership of nearly seven thousand. It had been one of the most generous congregations in its support of Hiram both financially and in sending students.

Dr. Welshimer, in an article in his church paper, *The Canton Christian*, finally (April 4, 1930) publicly repudiated Hiram and announced that the Canton Church would withdraw its support of the institution. He so well expressed Mr. Phillips' views that he clipped the article and preserved it in his files. Said Welshimer:

Hiram began its existence three-quarters of a century ago, through the efforts of some faithful members of the Christian Church in the Western Reserve. It had a long, hard up-hill struggle many years for an existence.

119

James A. Garfield, who graduated at Hiram Eclectic Institute, later became president of the college. B. A. Hinsdale, one of the great educators of America, later was president. In 1888 E. V. Zollars was called to the presidency of Hiram. He found poor equipment, but a fine, consecrated intellectual group of men comprising the faculty, and a small body of serious-minded students. President Zollars stressed the ministerial side of the college. He visited the churches, talked with parents and their children, raised money for endowment and for buildings, brought students to Hiram, prepared many of them for the ministry. He put in a classical ministerial course, that ably fitted men for the ministry. He also gave a shorter course to equip men who could not take the regular classical ministerial course. In his day and the days immediately following, Hiram came to be one of the outstanding schools of the brotherhood. He was surrounded with men whose heart beat in sympathy with the great brotherhood known as the Restoration Movement. There were Dean, and Wakefield, Peckham, Snoddy, Hall, McDermitt, and Pierson. Back in those days a question was never raised concerning the teaching in Hiram. Men went forth to the pastorate, to the missionary and educational fields who have honored their high calling. Out of the many who received their ministerial training at Hiram we present the names of a few. None would dare call these a failure. The list could be greatly multiplied if we had the space: C. R. Scoville, President M. L. Bates, J. E. Lynn, E. E. Snoddy, President H. J. Derthick, John W. Kerns, J. H. Goldner, W. R. Walker, Reed Downs, Willard Mohorter, W. F. Rothenberger, Dr. Elliot I. Osgood, E. C. Davis, H. E. Stafford, Arthur Holmes, I. J. Cahill, C. A. Freer, M. J. Grable, J. J. Tisdall, Scott Cook, A. F. Stahl, Frank Simpson, Mary Lyons, Adelaide Gail Frost, Amos Tovell, Craig Schwartz, Austin Hunter, M. L. Buckley, D. R. Moss, J. P. Allison, and a host of others. With but a half dozen exceptions, this group took no academic work beyond what Hiram gave.

The people of our churches who made Hiram possible gave their money that it might be a church school, where their sons and daughters, along with academic work, would be given Biblical instruction and where young men would be taught and trained for the ministry of our churches. Little did they think the day would ever come when Hiram would not prepare young men for the ministry. But the day has come when the college goes beyond that and ceases to be one of our schools! It ceases to be a church college and is simply—a college. We doubt not the moral atmosphere will be fine and men of Christian character will be the teachers, and a wholesome influence will probably permeate the school, but the same can be said of a score of other Ohio colleges. It still remains true that the best place on earth to educate a boy or girl is in the small church college.

We as a people have a distinctive message: we stand for some things other churches are not standing for. And it still remains true that many of our good church homes prefer to send their children to one of our church colleges, where they will keep in touch with the great onward movement of our brotherhood, and this is not sectarian nor denomina-

120

tional. We ask the question—under the present regime what has Hiram to offer our young people more than can be offered by an other Ohio college?

Canton has sent many students to Hiram. For years we have had one or more in the graduating class every year. But the number has simmered down to three students this year, one in the graduating class. The whole thing makes me sick at heart, and we'll confess we have but little interest and can't have any enthusiasm for the new Hiram. The memories of the old days are most precious; and we cannot help but feel that in listening to voices that are not of us, and in catering to an element which knows us not, and in making an appeal to a student body largely outside our group, the college has departed from the paths unto which she was called.

We wonder what Zollars, Wakefield, Dean, McDermitt, and Pierson think as in the councils of heaven they discuss the situation that now has arisen. And what must be the feelings of the many who through sacrifice and toil gave of their limited means to build a college on the hill that was not for the training of young men for the ministry and others for altruistic Christian service. Verily, "a new generation has arisen that knew not Joseph."

The Hiram debacle made Mr. Phillips wary of possible short-comings, both educational and theological, in other schools of the Christian Churches and Churches of Christ. He had, however, not yet become aware of the fact that there was in the whole of Christendom a movement bent on destroying the biblical and evangelical foundations of the Christian faith, of which the educational phase was a vital part. To him, at this time, the Hiram development seemed to be largely a local affair superinduced by unfortunate local leadership.

Then he heard about the Campbell Institute. It had its origin in the 1890's, in a group of Disciples' graduate students in Yale Divinity School. It had seemingly harmless beginnings, its stated purpose being to promote "a scholarly spirit, . . . quiet self-culture and the development of a higher spirituality," and to make "contributions of permanent value to the liberature and thought of the Disciples." However, since all its members had been duly exposed to the liberal philosophy and theology, it was a natural breeding ground for liberal ecclesiastical action. Joining forces with the extreme liberals of the Divinity School of the University of Chicago, the Campbell Institute soon grew to a membership of several hundred representing most of the colleges of the Disciples and key leaders in the major agencies serving the Brotherhood. Many of the most successful pastors serving notable churches were in its

121

company. Out of its membership came an underground Liberal Establishment which very cleverly proceeded to take over the leadership in the major national agencies of the Christian Churches and Churches of Christ, and, more importantly, the control of all their major colleges and seminaries.

Along with this control of Brotherhood institutions was to come the abandonment of the authority of the New Testament and its normative pattern in all matters of religion. Having undermined this foundation pillar of the Restoration Movement, it naturally followed that a fellowship predicated upon a common body of doctrine would be repudiated. The new school of thought adopted a theology based on expediency and human opinion. It favored the universal practice of "open membership" as a practical demonstration of "Christian unity." It "debunked" the "historic position" of the Restoration Movement, proposed the creation of a denomination with a firmly centralized authority, and moved as rapidly as possible to destroy the freedom of the local churches and deliver the Disciples into an ecumenical superchurch committed to its Liberal principles.

Not long after his introduction to the Campbell Institute, Mr. Phillips heard about the fight for Liberal control of Transylvania University and the College of the Bible. At Hiram in time of crisis the conservatives were so weak and so trusting of their brethren that they could put up little or no resistance. But at Lexington things were different. The conservatives were strongly entrenched and they decided not to give up without a struggle. The conflict centered around the College of the Bible, the ministerial training school.

The Liberal strategy at Lexington was the same as that so successfully employed by Liberal educators of most major Protestant denominations. They insisted that the educational standards of the College needed to be "improved." There were too many students enrolled who had received "improper preparatory training." Some men on the faculty were "beyond the teaching age." Teaching methods in use were "obsolete." Professors were needed who could lecture and conduct "cooperative inquiry" between student and teacher, with much reading and research on "all sides of a question." There ought to be more "freedom of discussion" and stimulation of students to come to "their own conclusions." "Motive and viewpoint" in the study of the Bible had changed and it

122

was time for "a new approach" if the school was not to be "typed" and ostracized by the accrediting agencies. Furthermore, said the raiders, if changes were not made, the graduate ministry would become "negative, obscurantist and defeatist," and make a negligible contribution to "ecumenicity, religious scholarship, art and the culture of our time."

At first, in the name of "academic freedom," the Liberals appealed only for a place or two on the faculty in fairness to a "new theological viewpoint" that had "attained wide acceptance in the religious educational world." Later the "two or three," together with their co-conspirators, declared that there was really no valid viewpoint other than their own which had any "scholarly standing." The Liberal position was buttressed by opinions from the accrediting agencies, which had been taken over by Liberals. These actions did not involve theological doctrine, but they created standards which eliminated much Biblical and doctrinal instruction from the curriculum and disqualified the older, conservative scholars and professors from holding a place on the faculty. In fact the real basic issues of the educational controversy were not allowed to appear. When the conservatives raised such issues, they were branded as "troublemakers" bent on destroying "the peace of the Brotherhood."

Everything would easily have gone in favor of the Liberals had not the *Christian Standard*, a leading journal of the Brotherhood, opened its columns to an expose of what was going on at Lexington. The story of what happened after that is too long to tell here. The incident is cited simply to describe the strategy of the Liberal Establishment. The Liberals were at long last able to win their battle at Lexington. They took over the College of the Bible and the University, but as a result came a "walk out" of enough members of the faculty and the student body to start what is now Cincinnati Bible Seminary and initiate a Brotherhood-wide movement to maintain an effective program of higher education true to the Holy Scriptures and to the principles and ideals of the Restoration Movement.

Mr. Phillips' sympathies were with the conservatives in this battle, though he had never aided the Lexington schools financially. He still had faith in the educational institutions which the Phillips Family had supported through many years. The administrators and faculty members of these schools assured him that they were still true to their original purposes. He believed them and continued to pour millions into their coffers.

From this point on, however, Mr. Phillips began to make a more extensive and intensive study of the new forces at work in Christendom and, more particularly, in the Christian Churches and Churches of Christ. He once told James DeForest Murch, the author of *Christians Only*, "I have known for some time that there was something wrong in some of our Christian Churches, but I never had the situation as clearly and convincingly set forth as in the two chapters in your book, 'The Great Apostasy' and 'The Great Controversy.'" Intelligently alerted to the dangers confronting all that he held dear in his personal faith and his church relations, Mr. Phillips now decided that he would exercise greater care in evaluating all requests for gifts from institutions of higher education. He had no desire to dictate the policies of the colleges requesting his support. But he sought to be a good steward of the wealth with which God had entrusted him and he was resolved that, so far as he was able to determine, henceforth not one penny of his fortune would go to promote apostasy from the "faith once for all delivered."

This decision touched off a tremendously interesting correspondence, portions of which Mr. Phillips' heirs have permitted the author to make available for the first time to the general public. Only his letters are quoted, but the entire correspondence is on file in the family archives.

BETHANY COLLEGE

As we have already seen (page 97), there were many reasons why B. D. Phillips had a warm place in his heart for Bethany College. Its historic background, involving Alexander Campbell and many other great heroes of the Restoration, was unmatched by any of the other colleges of the Brotherhood. Mr. Phillips' father was deeply concerned for its perpetuity and had given sacrificially to save the institution in times of crisis. On the campus are Phillips Hall, the Thomas W. Phillips Library, and the Richardson Hall of Science—all made possible by his philanthropy.

Nevertheless, Mr. Phillips did not allow sentiment to blind him to weaknesses that were becoming evident in Bethany's commitment to the Restoration Plea. When Dr. Perry Gresham became president, he felt that someone thoroughly loyal to the "faith once for all delivered" was in charge—someone who could be trusted to guide the institution in right paths. Gresham's University of Chicago background, and his pastorate of Central Woodward Christian Church, the large and influential congregation in Detroit (where open membership had been practiced), had been explained to Mr. Phillips' satisfaction, and a friendly relationship was established.

It was Dr. Gresham who, after a long correspondence and several visits to Butler, was able to induce the Executive Committee of the College to pass the following resolution clarifying Bethany's commitment to the Restoration Plea:

WHEREAS Bethany College was founded by Alexander Campbell in 1840 as a literary and scientific institution which included courses in Biblical literature and sacred history as a requirement for graduation,

AND WHEREAS Bethany College became known as the "mother of Christian Church colleges" through the influence of Alexander Campbell and Thomas Campbell, who were the most influential pioneers of the Christian Churches (Disciples of Christ) and the Churches of Christ, which represent the largest religious movement indigenous to America with four million adult communicants in its several branches,

AND WHEREAS the site of the famous Brush Run Church founded by Alexander Campbell in 1811, marking the beginnings of the Restoration Movement promulgated by the Campbells and their colleagues, is located only 11 miles from the campus of Bethany College,

AND WHEREAS other important historical landmarks of this movement, including the Campbell Home, the Campbell Cemetery, the Campbell Study, and the famous Old Main Building patterned after the University of Glasgow by Alexander Campbell, are located on the campus,

AND WHEREAS every graduate of the colleges founded and supported by this religious body should, as a part of his or her understanding of contemporary affairs, know the history of and characteristic beliefs of the Restoration Movement which gave rise to the Christian Churches,

BE IT HEREBY RESOLVED that each and every candidate for the baccalaureate degree at Bethany College, including transfer students, must qualify in a required course in Biblical Christianity, a substantial portion of which is devoted to the history and characteristic beliefs of the Restoration Movement, on a parity with any other course which is a requirement for graduation.

THIS RESOLUTION has the specific intent of commending the faculty for modifying the traditional six-hour course in Biblical history and literature in such a manner that every graduate will have, in addition to some knowledge of the Bible, knowledge of the history and characteristic belief of the Restoration Movement, as a part of his or her orientation with regard to contemporary religion and history.

AND FURTHERMORE, this resolution shall be duly recorded on the minutes of the board of trustees of Bethany College this 18th day of November, 1961, and shall continue until rescinded or changed by the board of trustees; and this resolution shall be printed in the Bethany College Bulletin from time to time, and this requirement shall appear in each issue of the Bethany College Catalogue.

Some years later there began to be a weakening of the noble intentions expressed in the Resolution. The course in "Biblical Christianity" was watered down to a point that Mr. Phillips felt was tantamount to a serious weakening of emphasis on the fundamentals of the faith and Restoration principles. In a letter to the Head of the Department of Religion he said:

Your article in the May, 1963, issue of the *Bethany College Bulletin* has just been read with much interest, but with some regret, almost entirely on account of your failure to emphasize to a greater extent the course recently included for "Christian unity and the restoration of New Testament Christianity which gave rise to the college itself." This is very fine, as far as it goes, but like so many of our people you lacked force and emphasis in giving this the prominence it deserved. Your statement is what I might term passive, rather than aggressive.

I believe you are familiar with what I have proposed regarding the Brush Run Church and the Baptismal Site. Now what do you think would be my impelling motive for these proposals, if they could be concluded successfully? Certainly nothing personal, but solely having to do with the location of Bethany College and the location of these two sites nearby, which are of vital importance to our people and of great historical value. By restoring and emphasizing them, my thought is that probably over the next few hundred years and during this present age this historical background in tangible form should have much influence in keeping the teaching at Bethany College sound in doctrine, and prevent the college from following the various vagrancies with which our people are presently plagued.

However, it is very discouraging to me, when a representative of Bethany College does not emphasize our Plea to the fullest extent and does not come out boldly in an article, such as yours, and state a certain course must be taken at Bethany College before a degree is granted, having to do with the history of our church, which the Campbells and our other pioneers sponsored and which has had such a tremendous effect on Protestantism in this country.

126

From the correspondence that ensued, appear the following quotes from Mr. Phillips:

Never overlook the fact that you are the Chairman of the Department of Religion at Bethany College, an honor that should be greatly cherished by you. In many respects you have the most important position of anybody connected with Bethany College, even including Dr. Gresham.

The position occupied by Bethany in the Restoration Plea can and should be of key importance to our people, due to Bethany's location and connection with Alexander Campbell. Unfortunately during much of the past this has been treated in an apathetic manner, taken for granted, and not emphasized or capitalized upon. I hope to have more emphasis placed upon this by restoring the Brush Run Church and indicating in some significant manner the Baptismal Site, and suggesting the course that is now described in the Bethany catalogue, before a degree is granted. . . .

Copies of your article in the *Bulletin* have fallen into the hands of a number of my friends. You might be interested in the comment of one, which coincides with my opinion already expressed to you: "I thought it was watered down so as to 'be pleasing to all men.' It could have been written for any denominational paper, as well as for one of ours. If there ever was a time when we should be letting folks know for what we as a people stand, it is now when in all circles there is so much talk about unity. We are the only people who have a program which will bring unity. Instead of hewing rock, as did the early Christians and the pioneers of our movement, too many are 'singing lullabies'."

In the early days many of those who followed the Restoration Plea came from other communions. Consequently, before a change they were versed in their newly acquired convictions and had some basis for them, but today most of the members of our churches have very little conviction as to why they attend one church, instead of another Protestant church. This is due in part to the preaching in our churches, the lack of constant and persistent emphasis on our Plea, and to articles such as you have spent time and effort in writing, notwithstanding the position of influence you hold. As a result, we have a great many church members who lack convictions and when they move to another community attend any Protestant church located conveniently, or one which some acquaintance attends.

It is up to us and particularly those in positions such as yours to instill more fundamentals in our people. It is the responsibility of the teachers in our colleges, especially in Departments of Religion, to do this to the nth degree. Certainly a man in your position at Bethany should be writing articles that have to do with the historical background of the Restoration Plea, especially dealing with Bethany, its surroundings, and the Campbells. Again, let me say you are the Chairman of the Department of Religion at Bethany College and you would not be occupying that position, and probably there would be no college at Bethany with all its tremendous heritage, if it had not been for the Campbell influence.

Mr. Phillips' rising doubts about the future of Bethany's distinctive testimony were somewhat assuaged by what Dr. Gresham said in a paragraph of his President's Report to the Board in 1964:

(4) The strong heritage of religion bequeathed to us by Alexander Campbell must be clarified and deepened by restoring the landmarks, deepening the interest, increasing the knowledge and creating some substantial support for the college enterprise from the several million communicants of the Christian Churches which have an interest in Bethany College and in the Campbell heritage. Friends of Bethany and the churches must come to realize that Bethany is a college of arts and sciences worthy of dedicated support. At the present time support from the churches is meager in proportion to the vast need. The Christian Churches are in desperate need of a college that will bring great prestige to the Restoration Movement which was intellectual in its orientation.

In 1965 he wrote Dr. Gresham:

We have donated a lot of money to Bethany College since my brother's death, perhaps two or three times the amount given by any other donor. A large portion of this I have contributed individually and my recommendations have been responsible for the balance. As you well know, I have been disappointed. The contributions, however, are now "over the dam."

The question at present is what, if anything, can be done to secure more support from our people? This support must be based on loyalty to our Plea, and not so much support from certain individuals and foundations which have only an impersonal view of the policies of the college, mostly secular, and probably no interest in the Restoration Movement.

I know well that a dollar received from any source has the same potential as any other dollar. However, the management at Bethany College should sense and derive greater satisfaction from funds received from adherents of the Restoration Plea, whose basic incentive is their hope that Bethany College is truly representative of the Restoration Plea, as advocated by our early outstanding pioneers, particularly in the nineteenth century. These were so different from the half-sectarian exemplifications, as pioneered in this century, to mention a few, Willett, Ewers, and Ainslie; and others who you know only too well occupied and presently occupy prominent positions in our churches, educational institutions, and agencies, who on account of their lack of conviction, lack of observation, or lack of analysis, failed to proclaim and propagate the logical Plea that made such tremendous strides in the past century. These should rightly be classified as half-sectarian and neither fish nor fowl.

I cannot help but admire your attitude toward me, as I have been critical of Bethany College and of the administration, but you have been too magnanimous to be offended by any comments I have made. . . .

128

If you think it worth while and if you wish, I shall be pleased to meet with you . . . sometime reasonably soon and discuss in a free and down-to-earth attitude this Bethany situation with you and with anyone else you may wish present.

The results of the meeting were somewhat inconclusive but Phillips' support for Bethany College ceased shortly afterward. Mr. Phillips, telling about his encounter with Dr. Gresham, said, "I told Perry, 'I made you puff pretty hard on that pipe today, didn't I?; to which he replied, 'Puff, Ben? You almost made me swallow it'." Despite their differences, the two men remained warm friends until Mr. Phillips' dying day.

PHILLIPS UNIVERSITY

Since the founding of Phillips University the Phillips Family had been one of its most generous financial supporters. After the death of his brother, Thomas W., Jr., B. D. Phillips as spokesman for the family continued to express this same concern (page 105).

But around 1960 a series of events and informative documents raised doubts in Mr. Phillips' mind about the soundness of the institution. Faculty changes, similar to those that had been made at the College of the Bible at Lexington, were taking place. New educational, administrative, sociological, theological, and ecclesiastical policies were being adopted which indicated a trend toward Liberalism.

The issue of Restructure of the Brotherhood (see Chapter IX) then came to the fore. What would Phillips University do about it? President Hallie G. Gantz gave the impression to Mr. Phillips that he was opposed to it, but subsequent events proved that he was definitely one of Restructure's advocates. This seeming lack of candor irked Mr. Phillips no end and brought the issue of his further support of the institution to a head.

Then, the Board of Trustees of the University voted to join Unified Promotion, the centralized budget and distributing agency of the International Convention of Christian Churches with headquarters at Indianapolis. Mr. Phillips was opposed to Unified Promotion (see letters in Chapter IX) and this further cooled his ardor for the school.

129

Early in March, 1965, Dr. Gantz, faced with the prospect of losing Phillips Family support, made a trip to Butler and spent a weekend seeking to establish more friendly relations. Following that visit Mr. Phillips wrote Dr. Gantz as follows:

It was a real pleasure to have you with us this past weekend and review in person some of the situations concerning which we have had considerable correspondence this past year, and some of which, to state it mildly, have been exceedingly annoying to us.

As explained in one of my previous letters, I encouraged former President Briggs in past years to endeavor to secure from the churches pledges to Phillips University. This was a situation I followed rather closely for some years and finally these solicitations reached a point where they amounted to more than $200,000 per year. This was done with the far-sighted thought in mind, if the churches supported Phillips in a substantial manner, it probably would mean Phillips could be kept very definitely a church-related college, deriving currently considerable support from the churches. Thereby, the University's policies would foster a much greater religious aspect and the University would not drift into largely a secular institution, as has happened with most of the educational institutions in this country which originally were sponsored by individuals on account of their religious beliefs.

When you were here this past year, you stated with pride you were not in Unified Promotion. This was very pleasing and met with our hearty approval. Your pride in this regard you verified this weekend, but for some unknown reason you have embraced Unified Promotion and apparently will largely eliminate solicitations for *direct aid* to Phillips University from the churches. Aid will go to Unified Promotion, perhaps designated for Phillips University, which merely replaces dollars given unpledged which in turn will be used elsewhere. This is a very common misapprehension pertaining to designating funds in all sorts of fund-raising campaigns in which many different institutions participate. This is the so-called "leveling" process, and unless the designations for one purpose exceeded greatly the proposed allotment, in reality there are no designations.

I tried very definitely to learn from you who was responsible for this radical change. Apparently you wished to avoid implication of any individual, or individuals, and stated "we" decided on this. Usually when a drastic move of this kind has been made, changing a policy followed for many years at great effort and expense, very careful consideration is given to it and presumably it is sponsored by an individual, or group of individuals. Who are "we"? I am suspicious this was largely due to the state secretary, or secretaries, in your territory. This would be following the form of the Indianapolis powers, by which state secretaries and state organizations have endeavored to foist changes upon our people.

130

You further stated the State Convention—I assume the Oklahoma State Convention—selects trustees for Phillips. By your action great influence has been given to Unified Promotion and you will find only those trustees will be selected who favor that organization. You countered this thought, however, with the statement certain trustees could be selected at large. This is far-fetched reasoning.

I realize you stated certain promises were made by Unified Promotion, but bear in mind the personnel changes from year to year and may be entirely different ten years from today. I prefer always to look to the future trend, judged by present trends, of various situations, avoiding as far as possible dependency upon human frailties.

You mentioned of all the institutions in our Board of Higher Education, Phillips University and Northwest Christian College were contributing by far the largest number of preachers, more in fact than all other members combined of the Board of Higher Education. We are all seriously concerned about the number of preachers who are recruited for our movement. Many of us are of the opinion the most pressing need we have is recruiting preachers dedicated to the Restoration Plea. The vast majority of those supplied come from institutions in no way connected with and receiving no benefits from Unified Promotion.

Bethany College recently completed an unusually fine Science Building costing well over one million dollars for which there is reason to be proud, but I have raised the point that this places undue emphasis on science at Bethany, probably much to the detriment of religious emphasis. Science has developed to such a point that population centers of the world can be obliterated, but how much emphasis is being devoted to the salvation of the human soul?

Why does Phillips University desire to support Unified Promotion and become a part of it, regardless of promises that may be made currently— promises made verbally and not in writing which are soon forgotten and in a few years can be grossly misinterpreted? The power—and by "power" I mean funds—given to Unified Promotion management undoubtedly are and will be influential and will be used for the benefit of certain individuals, or institutions, perhaps greatly due to favoritism— a political situation described as, "You scratch my back and I'll scratch your back."

Why is it the management at Phillips has not been aroused to this situation, a tendency and a trend of our agencies my brother and I discussed with others in the 1940's? The Phillips board by its action has greatly enhanced the Indianapolis influence, which has increased enormously in recent years. Would or would not the Phillips board favor elimination of this influence, likened to the tremendous influence and favoritism exercised in our Government by such an enormous concentration at Washington?

With Unified Promotion we are building a hierarchical organization which will be subject to pressure—and favoritism will run rampant. Great power and influence can and eventually will be exercised by those who are in charge of the designation of these funds. It seems strange to me you did not realize the terrific influence the distribution of Unified Promotion funds gives to a small group, regardless of whether the board is composed of eight members, or forty-two members. As you know, normally there are nearly always two or three individuals on every board who dominate the policies. Presumably the more representatives on the board the more the dominance by a few individuals is accentuated. Large boards in any organization are objectionable for the simple reason, when an individual is a member of a board consisting of twenty-four he has much less individual responsibility, than if he were a member of a board of six. If only one of the twenty-four, he represents only one-twenty-fourth of the voting power; while if he were one in six, he would represent one-sixth of the voting power—a vast difference. On account of this greater responsibility, the normal person will give his duties as a member of the smaller board much more thought and attention and will follow the activities of the organization much closer.

Judging from your conversation, apparently you went into Unified Promotion partly because you thought it would relieve the University's administration of soliciting vigorously direct support from the churches in your territory, which has been done successfully for many years, this change in part being due to some influence, perhaps by state secretaries. Incidentally, state secretaries for the most part assume too great a prerogative, exercise too much influence, and in many cases are allies of the "powers that be" at Indianapolis. Their influence is exercised to too great an extent in choosing ministers in their respective territories. This has reached a point in some instances where state secretaries are practically "bishops," in the ecclesiastical sense. . . .

The policy just adopted is so inconsistent and you have gotten so far away from the precedent followed for many years that Phillips University's identity will be largely lost. There is neither rhyme nor reason for making this change. . . .

I have made the remark, perhaps to you, that it is only a matter of time until we shall have at Phillips a large and rich institution; and when it reaches that point, unless safeguards are constantly maintained, religion will be relegated to a position of little significance or consequence. This is the case with almost all older institutions in this country, notwithstanding the fact religion was the basis for founding them.

The embracing of Unified Promotion by Phillips University was extremely disappointing to me. Apparently almost everything done, or left undone, recently at Phillips University has a tendency to alienate the support of the Phillips Family.

The foregoing was sent to the twenty-eight Trustees of Phillips University, together with this covering letter:

132

As the only living person who was present, when a student at Hiram College, at the time my father, T. W. Phillips, Sr., made arrangements for E. V. Zollars to canvass the situation in Oklahoma with a view to establishing a college definitely representative of the Restoration Plea, and as I have been largely, perhaps solely, responsible for pledges and most of the payments made to Phillips University since the death of my brother, T. W. Phillips, Jr., in January 1956, amounting to more than $656,000, I am enclosing copy of letter to Hallie G. Gantz, president of Phillips University, dated March 10, 1965. This letter in part, not entirely, is a culmination of voluminous correspondence I have had with Dr. Gantz, and the result of three visits to my home in Butler during the past sixteen months. On one occasion Daniel Joyce accompanied him and on another occasion Carlton Garrison.

I have urged in letters that Phillips University and Seminary, either one or both, publicly and in writing oppose open membership. The administration has avoided this, in fact greatly fears to mention open membership, pro or con, notwithstanding the fact open membership is immoral. If you wish verification of this, kindly advise and I shall forward statement covering this subject in a letter to Dr. Gantz.

I have told Dr. Gantz that by no stretch of imagination do I feel either my father or Dr. Zollars would have taken the passive, neutral, and listless attitude the Phillips management has taken regarding open membership. This in reality undermines the foundation of the Restoration Plea. Had it not been for this Plea, there would have been no Phillips University.

I wrote Dr. Gantz that when the balance on our pledge to the Seminary is paid which will be done this year, amounting to $99,974.00, we will make no more contributions to Phillips University, if the present policies are continued. Of this balance $79,706.00 is to be paid by my brother's Charitable Trust and $20,268.00 by me. Probably I, personally, shall pay both amounts as I am acting as trustee for my brother's Charitable Trust and am satisfied and sure he would not have made a pledge to Phillips University under conditions presently existing. Too many people fail utterly to realize their responsibility when acting as trustees, or in the administration of funds provided by others.

My attitude is strengthened and emphasized due to Phillips University's participation in Unified Promotion, which is dealt with quite fully in the letter enclosed. Because of existing conditions at Phillips University, I have almost completely lost interest.

Since January 1955, I have been responsible for contributions totaling more than $4,106,000 to Bethany College, Culver-Stockton College, Disciples of Christ Historical Society, Johnson Bible College, Lincoln Christian College, Milligan College, Northwest Christian College, and Phillips University. Of this sum more than 59% was donated by me individually. The impelling motive for these donations was the preservation of the Restoration Plea and providing to a considerable extent outstanding buildings. I regret to state in some of these cases I have been greatly disap-

133

pointed and distressed at the half-sectarian attitude some—not all—these institutions have shown.

Under my Will I am leaving a large sum to be administered by certain members of my family, undoubtedly the largest sum ever given or bequeathed by anyone for church and educational purposes having to do with the Restoration Plea. The following is taken literally from my Will:

"The corpus and income of said Charitable Trust shall be held and distributed by my said Trustees for the sole use and benefit of the churches, educational institutions, religious organizations and other institutions of the Disciples of Christ, the Church of Christ and/or the Christian Church, which are advocates in no uncertain terms of the Restoration Plea and are opposed without equivocation to open membership."

In the main, these are the same provisions covering a considerable sum left by my brother, T. W. Phillips, Jr., in his Charitable Trust which it has been my lot and that of other members of the family to administer.

The attitude taken at Phillips has been extremely distressing to many of us. I would be remiss if this letter with enclosure were not sent to each member of the Phillips University board. I realize these communications will not meet with the approval of some of the board members. However, if those not in agreement were as familiar with our people and with the various vicissitudes our movement has passed through during my lifetime and were open-minded, perhaps they would have a different view. I am certain my attitude toward Phillips University under present conditions would be fully countenanced by my father and Dr. Zollars, as well as by my mother and my brother, T. W. Phillips, Jr.

Only one Trustee responded to Mr. Phillips' communication, and he in a non-committal mood. Completely disillusioned about the future of the University, Mr. Phillips did not hesitate to write frankly about his newly-formed attitude, to the many who inquired about the situation. Excerpts from the following letter to Bob Moorehead, then minister of the First Christian Church, Clinton, Oklahoma, are typical of what he said to all:

Since Phillips University has embraced Unified Promotion, "lock, stock and barrel," I have lost all interest in Phillips and never expect to contribute any more funds to it. . . .

I have suggested in letters that the name "Phillips University" be changed. I feel it is a disgrace to the memory of my father and E. V. Zollars, who founded this university, for the institution to pursue the policies that have been followed the past few years and are now being countenanced. . . .

These policies have alienated my interest in Phillips and my decision is unalterable, unless there is a radical change in almost every manner. By "radical" I mean a change such as R. A. Long would make in regard to *The Christian*, if he were to come back and find what the policy is and has

134

been for a number of years. I have written that if he could return and had the power he would clean out the organization from cellar to garret. I share to a large extent the same feeling in regard to Phillips University. . . .

By the lack of foresight, lack of conviction, and lack of dedication to the Restoration Plea, which caused the founding of Phillips University, the management has lost the benefit from my estate alone of some millions of dollars. When the Seminary was started, I was hopeful every precaution would be used to keep it on a safe and sound basis and it would be a champion of the Restoration Plea. We would have gone the limit in making it the outstanding seminary of our people, which we could have done and can do, if it had been blessed with a management dedicated from top to bottom, championing the Restoration Plea without equivocation.

The situation at Phillips University . . . has been terrifically discouraging and disappointing to me and I hate to dwell on it even long enough to write a letter concerning it. How little regard people have for those who have sacrificed, both in time and this world's goods, in building up an institution.

My brother wrote, about a year before his death, to the president of one of our colleges, as follows:

"I have often said that there always seems to be a pack of hyenas ready to seize and subvert an institution that was founded and supported for years by sweat, tears, and blood. Why these hyenas, in human form, never seemed to establish an educational institution with their own efforts, but always tried to appropriate something that someone else has established, is hard to understand. A good illustration is the *Christian Evangelist* or the Christian Board of Publication, which Mr. R. A. Long many years ago at an expenditure of close to half a million dollars purchased, and as I understand it he was unalterably opposed to open membership. Since his death, what has the *Christian Evangelist* ever done to oppose the taking over of churches by open-membership ministers?"

There is nothing secretive about this letter and I am willing, if you deem it desirable, for you to show it to whomever you may wish.

EUREKA COLLEGE

When President Ira W. Langston approached Mr. Phillips hoping to secure Phillips Family support for Eureka, he acknowledged receipt of the brochure, *Eureka College: The President's Report*, and a copy of the 1964 Commencement program. Said Mr. Phillips:

In your report I fail to find any reference whatever to our people or to the Restoration Plea. . . .

I am surprised at the selection of David L. Lawrence, former mayor of

135

Pittsburgh and former governor of Pennsylvania, to make the Commencement address and upon whom an honorary degree was to be conferred by Eureka College. In view of David Lawrence's religion, you certainly have gone far afield in having him make this Commencement address and in conferring an honorary degree.

It seems to me many of our institutions confer degrees or give places of honor to those who are before the public, locally or nationally, and are of no benefit to our communion, have no religious connection with us, and have no interest in the Restoration Plea. In fact if the truth were known, they are far from favorable to it.

If it had not been for the Restoration Plea and those who sponsored it, disregarding criticism and ridicule, we would have no educational institutions and organizations; and those individuals who are heading them would not be so honored. How ungrateful people can be, who attain prominence and standing, but have little or no consideration for those who are responsible for the honor and standing they now have.

It is needless to say that Eureka College received no financial support from Mr. Phillips.

CHRISTIAN THEOLOGICAL SEMINARY

Butler University and its related College of Religion were seldom if ever included in the philanthropic program of the Phillips Family. It was not because of any lack of concern for the welfare and prosperity of these institutions, for they were highly esteemed for many years. They had been well-supported by the strong constituency of Indiana and other Central States brethren so that there was little need for "outside" solicitation.

The Phillipses were friends of the Irwins, Columbus bankers and industrialists, who had richly endowed the Indianapolis institutions. They "saw eye to eye" on the "faith once for all delivered." When the Irwins and their associates set up the Christian Foundation, a multi-million dollar fund for Christian higher education, they contacted Mr. Phillips in the hope that his family would join them in "undergirding the cause for all time to come." Mr. Phillips, never favorable to long-time endowments, declined the invitation and it is well that he did.

In due time Butler became a large secular municipal university and the College of Religion became an ecumenical theological seminary. Their testimony for the evangelical Christian faith and for the ideals of the Restoration Movement was completely lost.

136

During the metamorphosis the authorities of the "Christian Theological Seminary," in a wide search for funds, contacted Mr. Phillips in the hope that he could be persuaded to add millions more to their endowments. In a correspondence with Dr. Bill L. Barnes, director of development, his views were boldly stated.

Two letters written in November, 1963, are excerpted:

It was a pleasure to see you again at Elm Court. Sorry you could not remain for dinner. It is always stimulating to talk with you, although there is quite a difference in our viewpoints. . . .

I regret exceedingly to learn that the total funds of the Christian Foundation are to be given to Christian Theological Seminary for endowment purposes. If my figures are correct the inventory of this fund on September 30, 1963, was $5,652,000. I am informed that over ninety per cent of the income from this fund has been donated to the Seminary for several years, so that your normal income will be but slightly increased by the gift. Knowing the intents and purposes of the original donors, and the radically different policies of CGS, I feel that . . . the Irwins, the Sweeneys, and the Reeves would "turn over in their graves" if they knew their largess were to be so misused. . .

Thank you for sending me the Christian Theological Seminary Bulletin, containing The President's Report 1962-1963. I find in this entire bulletin the Campbells, the Restoration Plea, and our heritage are completely ignored. I further note on Page 6 the following: "Members of the faculty, representing four Protestant denominations, are active in local churches and participate in community programs." What are the four denominations? Do you include our people in that category? As you well know, this is contrary to the viewpoint that has been held by those who were responsible for the inception of the Restoration Plea and have been adherents of it up to the present time.

On top of all this, I see that Ronald E. Osborn is your Dean and Professor of Church History at Christian Theological Seminary. He is the man who edited the volume, *The Reformation of Tradition*, in the notorious three-volume Panel of Scholars Report, *The Renewal of Church*. This publication, if its thesis were followed, would in my estimation ring the death knell of the Restoration Movement.

In the Osborn volume every principle of the Restoration Movement, if not the Movement itself, is ridiculed. He makes clear that the Campbells, Walter Scott and all the early fathers who were responsible for the tremendous growth of our people through the years, were simply "talking through their hats." The book makes it clear that our only hope now is to throw "the rubbish of the past" out the window, start all over, become a responsible denomination and merge with the forces from which we originally emerged.

This book shows a desire, not only to abandon the doctrinal position of the Restoration Movement, but to discredit the congregational autonomy

137

of the churches. Your Dr. Osborn says (page 285), "The presumed New Testament pattern of elders and deacons lingers in public worship as a cultic anachronism from frontier days, but the church is administered through functional committees. . . . Congregational polity is now being modified. . . ." He also indicates that change must be extended to every field of church organization and doctrine (page 278): "Judgement must be pronounced on such central dogmas of the Disciples as restoration, the abolition of the clergy, their particular 'plea,' the wholesale repudiation of creeds and of ecclesiastical organization, their specific program of Christian union, even their doctrine of baptism."

I happened to know "Zach" Sweeney when I was young. I heard him preach and lecture. He was a guest in our home. My brother and I knew Will Irwin and were entertained in his home in Columbus. Not by the widest stretch of imagination could I believe that these men would sanction what you and your associates are now doing with their money.

It is needless to add that Christian Theological Seminary's efforts to add the Phillips Family to its list of donors were entirely futile.

CULVER-STOCKTON COLLEGE

When Mr. Phillips was approached by Culver-Stockton authorities asking for a liberal gift for the erection of the new Alexander Campbell Auditorium, he was given assurances concerning the loyalty of the institution to the Restoration Plea. He was overpersuaded by some of those whom he trusted, but who unfortunately were not in possession of all the facts concerning the beliefs and practices of those who were in control of the institution and responsible for determining its policies and programs.

The Culver-Stockton Board had accepted the "Bethany Resolution" (page 125) and Mr. Phillips thought the situation justified a generous gift to the new Auditorium. It was promised and paid, but with sad aftermath.

When the time came for the dedication of the building (February 3, 1966) he was extended a warm invitation by President Fred Helsabeck to attend and participate in the ceremonies. His answer to that letter tells the rest of the story:

It would afford me almost no gratification to make a trip to Canton, Missouri, and be present at this dedication. I have made many bad business investments during my life and have been terribly disappointed in

138

some donations of considerable size, which I have made or been responsible for; but I have learned in the past to profit from these unfortunate commitments. However, I have also found, other than the fact of the lesson learned which I do not readily overlook, that the sooner I forget about situations of this kind the less irritating they become.

This Culver-Stockton commitment was one I went into without a reasonable amount of inquiry and investigation. I depended entirely too much upon the advice of some whom I highly regard (but who in this instance were not in possession of certain vital facts), and the favorable impression, at least in a casual way, your personality made on me. Consequently, I did not check into the Culver-Stockton situation to the extent that is my custom.

At a later date, I learned that a man favorable to open membership was chairman of your Board, and the church of our people in Canton was open membership—a condition that, regardless of how staunchly the college endorsed the Restoration Plea, was a handicap which almost completely neutralized the Restoration Plea and would foster materially the making of Culver-Stockton a secular institution.

Subsequently, I learned with amazement that you and your associates knew little, if anything, about Lincoln Christian College, located in your area only about one hundred and ten miles distant. This institution the past few years has accomplished in the rehabilitation of our churches in its general area and in the preparation of students for the ministry and Christian work, more than has been accomplished the past few years by any other institution of our people. It has surpassed Culver-Stockton in this respect to such a degree that no reasonable comparison can be made.

Later, I was greatly disappointed with the "on-the-air interview" a radio newscaster had with you, entitled "What a Student Should Look for in College," printed in the June 1964 issue of *Concept*, the college publication. In this interview you completely ignored the Christian church and the Restoration Plea, which were responsible for the very existence of Culver-Stockton College. . . .

According to my records, $200,000 has been contributed to the Alexander Campbell Auditorium, to which I paid $107,695.11 and the T. W. Phillips, Jr., Charitable Trust paid $92,304.89. The contributions paid by the Charitable Trust gave me much grave concern, as in the case of this Trust I am acting as Trustee. I am convinced, if my brother had been living, he would not have sanctioned a contribution to Culver-Stockton by his Trust, because of circumstances pertaining to this institution that were divulged after the commitment was made. . . .

I believe you can readily see from the above, that although we have $200,000 in this building, I would have regretful thoughts, were I to attend the dedication. I could not help but think that the same $200,000 could have been used at several other institutions, where the Restoration Plea is given much greater emphasis and whose support would have been in a favorable environment, which just is not the case at Culver-Stockton.

NORTHWEST CHRISTIAN COLLEGE

For many years the Phillips Family had a deep interest in the welfare of Christian higher education in the Northwest. In a letter sent to the members of the Board of Trustees of Northwest Christian College in August, 1965, Mr. Phillips refers to that concern:

My interest in Northwest Christian College goes back many, many years. As a matter of fact, W. F. Cowden, who was our minister in the 1890's at New Castle, Pennsylvania, where the Phillips Family lived, decided to move to the northwest. As a result, my father, T. W. Phillips, Sr., financed him, I believe solely at first and partially later, in establishing churches of the Restoration Plea in Washington and Oregon. Many churches were started, which in turn led to the inception of Eugene Bible College, now Northwest Christian College.

President Griffeth approached me a few years ago about a donation to this college to which I was favorably inclined, not only on account of my father's connection, but due to the fine record this institution had in the past, as it remained true to the Restoration Plea, evidenced by many sound graduates and the policy prevailing to a large extent in its territory. . . .

Mr. Phillips then called attention to the unfortunate trends toward ecclesiastical centralization in the organizational life of the Brotherhood and indicated that his further support would be conditioned upon the future policies of NCC.

When Dr. Barton A. Dowdy was chosen president of the College he contacted Mr. Phillips about this "donation" and Mr. Phillips replied:

According to my records, I have contributed $24,323.20 to the Chapel at Northwest and an equal amount was to be paid by others; and the pledge I made was to be paid when and as other payments were made. Furthermore, none of the balance of the pledge was to be paid, until we were assured an amount equal to my subscription would be met by others. This pledge was covered in my letter of December 7, 1963. However, probably due to Dr. Griffeth's health and his retirement, which I did not anticipate at that time, and further the example of architecture that was proposed for this building, which I thought was very bad to say the least (I am not an architect, but have had a part in a good many fine buildings), the situation was dropped and, as far as my pledge was concerned, was allowed to lapse. . . .

It is my understanding your situation is somewhat divided between the so-called "cooperatives" and the "independents." The ecclesiastical hierarchy at Indianapolis has entrenched, and is entrenching, itself by the collection of funds from the churches and the apportioning of funds to vari-

140

ous agencies and educational institutions. A tremendous power is being exercised and centered at Indianapolis and it is constantly being fed by those churches, institutions, and agencies embracing Unified Promotion. . . .

I am not inclined to contribute anything to an institution that endorses or is to be a part of Unified Promotion. This, as you realize, will rule out a number of institutions and agencies. . .

If we are to further support Northwest Christian College we shall wish to know, what, if any, solution you may propose to safeguard the policy of the College in this and other respects, in an endeavor to have it remain true to the Restoration Plea and oppose open membership. This should be done publicly in writing. . . .

After a number of personal conferences with Dr. Dowdy and certain members of the Board, the following document was drafted by Dr. Dowdy:

A STATEMENT FROM THE PRESIDENT TO THE BOARD OF TRUSTEES NORTHWEST CHRISTIAN COLLEGE

When an institution comes into being as a corporation it assumes, before the law, the status of a person with both rights and responsibilities. Before such status can be given, the institution must declare clearly the purpose it wishes to serve. Northwest Christian College as a corporation has its purpose for existence clearly set forth in the Articles of Incorporation.

> "To secure, teach, train and send out consecrated men and women of any nationality, to preach and practice the pure New Testament Gospel among all the nations, at home and abroad in harmony with the Divine Commission recorded in Matthew 28:19-20; Mark 16: 15-16; Luke 24: 46-47, as exemplified on the First Pentecost after Christ's resurrection and ascension, and as elsewhere recorded in the New Testament.

> "To stand for the Biblical Doctrine of the Deity of Christ, including His Lordship and Atonement, the Divine Inspiration and Supreme Authority of the Holy Scriptures; the autonomy of the local Churches of Christ, and shall, in every way practicable, promote Christian unity as taught by the Divine Christ and revealed in the inspired and sacred Scriptures."

This statement leaves little doubt concerning the intention of those who founded the school. Their aim was to establish a school which would emphasize the major themes of the Restoration Movement: unity, the restoration of New Testament Christianity, and freedom from ecclesiastical domination. One wonders just a bit that no mention is made of freedom from creeds, but this may be implied. For seventy years, Northwest Christian College and its predecessor schools have endeavored to implement the purpose stated in the Articles of Incorporation.

141

The results of these efforts are apparent throughout the Northwest. Generally speaking, the churches however classified as to method of work hold to a conservative doctrinal position. There is deep commitment to New Testament Christianity. There is dedication to the freedom in Christ of each local congregation of Christians. The age-old difference concerning what is essential and what is opinion, over faith and freedom, does appear but along with it is an equally strong desire to maintain unity in the midst of diversity. Any attempt to read a differing group out of the brotherhood could well be met with rebuff from all sides.

The future course of Northwest Christian College is being plotted to implement this statement of purpose. We intend to continue educating workers for the church who will believe the Gospel, who will accept the authority of Christ and the Holy Scriptures, who will maintain the freedom in Christ that has characterized the local church from the beginning of our brotherhood, who will recognize the church as a divinely given and ordered body rather than merely a human creation subject to man's will, and who will try to practice unity with their Christian brethren as well as preach about it. We hope to fill them with love for Christ, the Gospel, the Church, and their Christian brethren to the extent that they will not stoop to partisan bickering but will exhaust all their energies in promoting the cause of Christ in the world.

These are days of great and rapid change in our brotherhood. Some who have historically objected to organizations larger than the local congregations are developing extra-congregational organizations. Those who have historically believed in the principle of effectiveness through organization and supervision are seeing new dimensions of the church and are attempting to develop new patterns to implement the new concepts. The result has been applause in some sectors and serious misgiving in others. When the new insights are combined with new organizational patterns and a determined drive for denominational merger as the only real evidence of unity, the misgivings begin to gather around two heads: open membership and congregational autonomy. To many in the Northwest, open membership (the receiving into church membership of the unimmersed under whatever plan this may be accomplished) and serious curtailment of local autonomy appear just over the horizon.

What shall be the position of Northwest Christian College in the face of these trends? The guiding light must be our statement of purpose. To wink at it would violate our integrity both as an institution and as individual Christians comprising the institution.

Our desire is to be united with our entire brotherhood. Emerging patterns might stamp this position as anachronistic and untenable but any such conclusion at this time would be premature. On June 4, 1963 the Board of Trustees voted not to participate in Unified Promotion. To date this has not been changed. The future relation of Northwest Christian College to Unified Promotion and other organizational developments will be decided by one simple question—"Will our participation help or hinder the fulfillment of our purpose for existence?"

142

As to open membership, we see our way more clearly. We fail to see how, in the light of our faith and our statement of purpose, we can accept this practice and maintain our integrity. We consider it to be unscriptural, unnecessary, and unwise. Our faith requires that we unequivocally oppose this practice.

In summary, Northwest Christian College has an integrity of its own and intends to maintain it. We know that in times like these we will be subjected to pressures from all sides, as indeed we are at present. In a real sense the pressures are a sincere compliment to us—we do matter. We want to be in fellowship with our entire brotherhood and will be to the extent that this can be done without compromising our integrity. This has characterized us in the past—it will in the future.

In general the statement was satisfactory to Mr. Phillips but he suggested some changes to make clear NCC's position on Unified Promotion and Restructure and to strengthen some vital fundamental assertions. He then stated, in a letter dated January 7, 1966:

If this draft is adopted by a resolution of the Board of Trustees, reciting receipt of the statement from the president and ratifying and confirming the statement as an expression of the belief and policy of the institution, and a duly certified copy of the resolution, as ratified, is forwarded to me; and further provided you are willing to publish this resolution soon in the *NCC Bulletin* (the Northwest Christian College publication, which I understand is widely distributed monthly), and you forward copies of this resolution immediately to the *Christian Standard*, attention of Mr. Edwin V. Hayden, editor, and to *The Christian*, attention of Mr. Howard E. Short, editor, we will reinstate our pledge to Northwest Christian College up to a total of $200,000.00, deducting therefrom $24,323.20 already paid and leaving a balance of $175,676.80.

At this point some static developed. The Board evidently passed the revised statement but decided that it should not be published "at this time." Replying to Dr. Dowdy's letter of January 20, informing him of the Board's action, Mr. Phillips said:

We reviewed with you, on your recent visit to my home, several grievous experiences we have had in the past with certain institutions which we have aided in a very substantial way over a period of many years, and which have now turned their backs on the Restoration Movement.

No individual has unlimited funds to contribute to charitable, religious, or educational institutions. All we can hope is to make our donations where in our judgment they will do the greatest good for the greatest number over the longest period of time. Using these criteria as guide lines, it has been and is our conviction we can more fully accomplish these ends by

143

contributions to institutions which are unequivocally committed to the Restoration Movement, which are its staunch advocates, and which give definite evidence of intending to remain so in the future. If you or the individual members of the Board were guided by the same conviction, I believe you would be derelict in your duty as good stewards if you did not take every reasonable precaution to assure that your own contributions were used in the furtherance of your conviction. . . . .

I am pleased to note, however, that you and your Board believe a proclamation of the school's purpose and position needs to be made and that the Board has authorized you to make such a proclamation in the not too distant future. I will very much appreciate your forwarding me a copy of the same, when and if it has been published and circulated. Provided the article has been published and circulated within the next few weeks, certainly before April 1, and you and your Board are satisfied a sufficient length of time has elapsed thereafter, so there can be no relationship between the publication of the proclamation and any gift which we may later make, we will again take up with you promptly the proposal made in my letter of January 7. However, we do not propose to be obligated for this offer much beyond early spring, as we have other situations in which funds can be used to good advantage by other educational institutions dedicated to the Restoration Movement.

The gift was never made.

HIRAM COLLEGE

Despite the fact that Mr. Phillips had many years ago broken with the policies and programs of Hiram College, his Alma Mater, repeated efforts were made to restore his confidence in the historic Ohio institution and elicit generous gifts for its support and expansion.

In later years when Dr. Paul F. Sharp became president it was widely believed that he was sound in the faith and would initiate new policies which would commit the school openly to New Testament Christianity and the Restoration Plea. Correspondence was opened with Mr. Phillips. After a few exchanges, Mr. Phillips wrote in November, 1959:

I hope conditions are shaping up at Hiram in a satisfactory manner for you. Believe you well know I am interested only in schools of our people that are true to and champions of the Restoration Plea—the New Testament Church. Hiram has strayed so far and so long that I have grave doubts about you or anyone else being able to have it fill the place in our Brotherhood that it occupied at the turn of the century. The only way I see that this possibly can be accomplished is by using the utmost care in choosing trustees who are faithful to and advocates of the New Testament Church, and in turn a faculty and a management of the same type. If this is ever accomplished, it undoubtedly will require several years, as too many of our churches in the Hiram District, particularly in the Cleveland Area, are open membership. While I have not analyzed the Board of Trustees, I suspect some of them have no church affiliation whatever with our Brotherhood, and probably some that do, belong to open membership churches.

In 1962 the correspondence was reopened and Mr. Phillips had this to say:

For a couple of years I have been working vigorously to have established in the colleges supported by our people a course that will instill in the students in no uncertain manner the fundamentals of this plea, making it mandatory that no degree will be granted, even to a transfer student, unless the graduate is qualified in this course. This resolution has now been adopted at Bethany College, Culver-Stockton College, and Phillips University. I happen to have in my possession several copies of the Culver-Stockton College Bulletin for 1962-63, one of which is being sent to you under separate cover; and I wish to call your attention to the resolution which was adopted September 22, 1961 and appears on the inside of the front cover. A similar statement is to be published in future bulletins of Culver-Stockton College, Bethany College, and Phillips University. I am enclosing copy of the resolution that has been adopted by Bethany College (page 125) and recorded in the minutes of November 18, 1961, also a copy of the resolution adopted by Phillips University on February 14, 1962. . . .

Since I wrote you in November, 1957, I would be very much interested in knowing in detail just what progress has been made in this regard, both as to trustees and to faculty members; and what position is taken in Christian training or religious courses in regard to open membership. Also, I would like to know that policy is followed by the Hiram Church, pertaining to open membership. Certainly from my correspondence and my conversations with you, you know my attitude.

It is astonishing to me how many of the Church of Christ colleges, located in California, Texas, Tennessee, and Arkansas, have developed, most of which development has been since the beginning of this century. The only explanation I know for this is the fact they have been sticklers for the plea in which they believe, resulting in every case their trustees are members of the Church of Christ; and for the most part their faculties belong to the Church of Christ.

Suppose some similar policy had been followed at Hiram at the turn of the century, both as to trustees and to faculty. I am certain the development and influence of Hiram would have been many times greater than has taken place, and today Hiram could be the leading educational institution of the Restoration Plea, if a policy had been followed and adhered to, as has been done by the Church of Christ.

Dr. Sharp then wrote delineating some of the new policies he had developed at Hiram and Mr. Phillips replied in November, 1962:

Apparently your viewpoint is entirely that of an educator, the vocation I understand you have followed during your adult years. You disregard completely the theological aspect of an educational institution and the basis for founding the institution. You well know that the church was the cause of the inception of most of the educational institutions in this country, but the vast majority of the older institutions have drifted completely away from the basis on which they were founded. To be church-related, a college does not need to surrender its academic freedom. Most educational institutions were brought into being by the church and therefore have an obligation to the church, involving a doctrinal relationship.

You stated: "The institutions of higher learning in this country that are most successful financially command respect by reason of their academic freedom and intelligent vigor."

Frankly, are you of the opinion this respect is due to "academic freedom and intelligent vigor," or to heritage and present financial standing? Academic freedom has been emphasized many times in the past and educators have always desired it, regardless of the sacrifices that had been made by the founders and contributions made by others to the institutions to maintain them, primarily due to certain policies. Academic freedom, within limits, perhaps is right and proper for state-founded and state-operated institutions, divorced entirely from religion. However, when an educational institution was founded by certain individuals and over a period of many years has been sustained at a great sacrifice by certain individuals in accord with the policies of the founders, academic freedom in a religious sense should play no part; and if those who are administering the affairs of that institution insist upon academic freedom, having to do with religion, a trust is betrayed and a dishonest policy followed.

You realize that the Restoration Plea, if interpreted correctly from the knowledge you should have, cannot be considered sectarian. The church, as founded in the New Testament, was by no means a sectarian institution.

You have stated: "We believe that the wiser policy is to be considered a Christian college and not a sectarian institution."

What do you consider Notre Dame? No doubt the management of Notre Dame considers it a Christian college and not a sectarian institution. Would a graduate of Notre Dame, after spending four years there, have no conception of the Catholic religion, as was the case with a certain Hiram alumnus concerning whom I wrote you under the date of August 26, 1960, who after spending four years at Hiram knew nothing about the Disciples Church, the Church of Christ, or the Restoration Plea?

In 1919, I resigned from the Hiram Board due to the fact the tendency for some years previously had been to make Hiram a higher educational institution—a Williams of the midwest—and ignoring the fundamentals

146

that were emphasized for the previous many, many years of its existence, which had resulted in Hiram having a great influence and being outstanding as a champion of the Restoration Plea. For many decades prior to your administration there was little deviation from this policy. For many years one of your predecessors as president of Hiram, was a member of the Reformed Church; also another president, his successor, was a Methodist at the time of his selection. Either one or both of these men at some later date may have embraced the teachings of the pioneers of the Restoration Plea, but in any event they each had a long tenure of office.

This attitude was extremely distressing to me on account of my ties with Hiram and has been the reason for my lack of support of Hiram; and the letter received from you in regard to "academic freedom and intelligent vigor," certainly was most displeasing to me, because I knew from the time I was ten years old about many of the sacrifices that were made by our people to keep Hiram College and some of our other educational institutions functioning.

You mentioned courses in the curriculum as a consequence of financial aid. From a theological-church standpoint, how can you expect aid for a church-founded institution that insists upon academic freedom and independence, ignoring and placing no emphasis on the fundamental principles that caused the founding of the institution and were responsible for its maintenance up to the early years of this century?

You also mentioned "academic integrity." "Academic integrity" can be quite different from "moral integrity" to which I and others are of the opinion Hiram has had little respect during many years prior to your administration. I am not inclined to contribute to an institution that may be considered Christian, just because it may have some Christian background, well-hidden due to "academic freedom" and "academic integrity." As stated above, Notre Dame perhaps is considered a Christian college, so why not contribute to it?

So Dr. Sharp came and went without any change being made in Hiram's doctrinal views. He came and went without any financial support from the Phillips Family.

Despite his disagreement with Hiram's policies and his determination not to support the school financially, Mr. Phillips had a warm place in his heart for the scenes of his college days. When the fiftieth anniversary of his class was observed on campus, he and Mrs. Phillips (also a graduate of Hiram) returned and enjoyed a fine day of fellowship with old friends. When he was called upon to make a speech, he was felicitous regarding the occasion, but in a brief word courteously told why he could no longer support the College.

Growing out of this contact, an old friend, Ned Hubbell of Bedford, who had recently retired from a successful business career, wrote him a letter urging that he "bury the hatchet," participate in the current fund-raising drive and become an "Annual Giver Forever."

To which Mr. Phillips replied:

With reference to your inquiry as to what I mean by the Restoration Plea, this in short is the restoring of the church founded on Pentecost, described in The Acts and Epistles and nurtured by the Apostles and the Holy Spirit. It is not a Reformation. It is a Restoration, as was advocated by the Campbells, Scott, and Stone; and particularly as advocated by Stone in his later years, after he came in contact with Alexander Campbell.

I note you state: "I believe with Alexander Campbell that while immersion is the most fitting and significant form of baptism, it is not essential to salvation." I believe this can be questioned and with that in view am quoting from James DeForest Murch's *Christians Only* the following from pages 117 and 118:

"Both Stone and Campbell believed that immersion was the Scriptural mode of baptism and that baptism was for the remission of sins. The point at issue with them was whether or not there could be fellowship with the unimmersed in churches of the New Testament pattern.

"Campbell felt that the fate of the unimmersed was in the hands of God; that it is not ours to judge whether or not they will be saved; but that if the testimony of the Restoration was to be pure and undefiled, the unimmersed must not be admitted to local congregations 'after the New Testament pattern. . . .'

"His love and respect for Christians did not go beyond their willingness to investigate and learn the whole truth about baptism, and to comply with the truth as they discovered it. Neither was he willing to call a church a New Testament church that compromised the express teaching of the Scriptures by admitting the unimmersed to membership."

Apparently you liken communion on the first day of each week to the washing of feet. I believe this is a farfetched comparison and does not apply. Communion was a request, bordering on a command: "This do in remembrance of me." In no place in the New Testament is washing of feet commanded, or even requested.

I note with surprise you make the following statement: ". . . we are willing to unite with others in the same way that every other sect is. . . ." The Restoration of the Primitive Church cannot logically be classified as a sect, but this is a mistake so many, many of our people make. If the tenets, teachings, and examples of the early church were followed, as described in The Acts and Epistles, there would be no logical reason for having our own interpretation, as suggested by you.

148

I have never unduly criticized the so-called "Antis," as those opposing music used to be termed. I have admired them greatly for their adherence to the Scriptures. In your letter you speak of the 140th Psalm as "an exhortation to praise God with more than seven different instruments, including an organ." In that day an organ, such as the musical instrument we have today, was not known.

In speaking of Thomas Campbell, you state the Plea he offered "swept through the religious world like a fresh, cleansing breeze." You do not give him credit in any sense for the logicalness of this Plea. Certainly after the man-made creeds the Campbells had encountered all their lives, a Plea based solely on the New Testament, eliminating creeds and dogmas, when logically presented should sweep through the religious world like a fresh, cleansing breeze.

You state this Plea is gradually losing much of its vigor and influence, largely due to lack of enthusiasm and partly because much of its purpose has been accomplished and the need for its message is not quite so great. I disagree with you in this respect, as the Plea has not changed. The Gospel message is just as effective as ever, but there is lack of dedication, zeal and evangelism by those who are endeavoring to proclaim our Plea, but in a listless and halfhearted manner. They have been led astray and overwhelmed by pompous individuals, who due to their standing in various religious bodies are prone in many cases to tear down the Bible, and the New Testament in particular, being what we used to term "higher critics" (that is what they were called in the days when you and I were at Hiram). You well know it is much easier to tear down than to build up. The destructionists far outnumber those of a constructive nature.

You make the statement that times have changed. I have heard this before on more than one occasion. Do you mean by this that the church founded at Pentecost is different today than it was two thousand years ago? Customs have changed, not the church.

You mention the Catholic hierarchy. From the beginning this has been a man-made organization. Many practices are followed for which there is no basis in the New Testament.

In your longhand postscript you state in regard to our way of worshipping God that it is the best, because it does recognize the Bible as the supreme source of authority and inspiration; yet you criticize certain conditions of the Bible, however, in the Old Testament. It seems to me this is somewhat inconsistent. I feel you have fallen into modernistic tendencies that probably would not have been sanctioned by your parents, from what you have said about them and your background.

In any event, I am sending you under separate cover a book that has just been published, entitled *The Free Church*, by James DeForest Murch, which I hope you will read soon—it will not take long. This, I believe, will be one of our outstanding books in future years, having to do with the Restoration Plea; and it is one that should be used as a textbook in any institution of our people that is supported by our churches.

However, we have entirely too many people in our churches and educational institutions, who owe their standing to the Restoration Plea (If it had not been for the Restoration Plea, what standing would they have?) yet in many cases they are intensely critical of our pioneers and are determined to establish a hierarchy. A few people with personal ambitions wish to set up themselves, or himself, as the case may be, with the hope they will be the Presbytery, or the Bishop, speaking for our entire brotherhood; while as a matter of fact, our individual churches are an entity unto themselves. If you will carefully read the book sent under separate cover, I believe you will grasp some thoughts you perhaps overlooked or have forgotten in the past several years.

No doubt you have heard considerably about "restructure of the Brotherhood" proposed by committing our churches to a delegate convention and thereby attempting to obtain power and authority to control our churches and educational institutions. Some of these propagandists apparently feel they are called upon to restructure the divine Church established at Pentecost, which as stated before was guided for many years by the Apostles and by the Holy Spirit. This certainly is most presumptuous on their part and indicates a positive lack of humility, to say the least.

I am sorry you and Lois do not come this way occasionally, as I would like very much to see both of you and have you spend a night with us at Butler.

So ended the long period of interest and support by the Phillips Family of the traditional institutions of higher education among the Disciples of Christ.

150

IX

Valiant for the Faith

2. In the Brotherhood

As Mr. Phillips became conscious of the fact that most of the older colleges and universities of the Disciples had abandoned the Christian educational philosophy and the distinctive biblical testimony of the Restoration Plea, he also began to realize that this blight was widespread in the whole institutional heritage of the Brotherhood of Christian Churches and Churches of Christ.

Mr. Phillips felt no call to enter the lists in any nationwide movement to halt this erosion. He had a distaste for public debate and seldom voiced his views in conventions or general assemblies. But his concern for the church was deep and vital, and whenever opportunity offered he was quick to espouse the cause of truth and right as he saw it, usually in letters addressed to his friends, or to those who solicited his financial support. He wrote literally thousands of letters in defense of the Faith and the Plea, from which the following excerpts have been selected:

OPEN MEMBERSHIP

There was a growing tendency among left-wing theologians, secretaries, and ministers to advocate the reception of unimmersed persons into full membership of the churches. Mr. Phillips believed this practice to be opposed to Scriptural teaching and to the historic practice of the Restoration Movement and opposed it with all his might.

The Phillips Family had over a period of years supported the work of the Park Avenue Christian Church in New York City. The Restoration cause was proverbially weak in the East, so brethren in strong churches throughout the nation underwrote the Park Avenue program as a testimony in the nation's largest city. In 1960 it was proposed that the Phillips Family give $20,000 for the rebuilding of the baptistery. Because of certain rumors concerning the practice of open membership at Park Avenue, Mr. Phillips asked Dr. Hampton Adams to give him assurances on this matter before agreeing to such a gift. Dr. Adams replied:

We do not practice any baptism except immersion. We preach on the importance of that New Testament ordinance. We administer this ordinance in a way to impress its significance on those who see it. We defend, and I believe rightly, the practice of accepting people into our membership who have not come to feel about immersion as we do, but do come with the understanding that we practice and preach the baptism by immersion.

Mr. Phillips then wrote:

For us to donate $20,000 for rebuilding a baptistery in this church under these circumstances, when according to the Year Book you had only five baptisms in 1958 and only five baptisms in 1959, would be placing funds in an apostate church that generally is considered representative of the Restoration Plea in New York City, which is not true as an open membership church is not representative of the Restoration Plea. I am certain that based on the record now of this church neither my father nor my brother would sanction the use of the Phillips name in connection with this baptistery, and I am positive I would not care to have the Phillips name used in this connection. The church just does not measure up to the ideal the Phillips family has had for two generations of a church representative of the Restoration Plea. . . .

I have devoted a large amount of energy and thought, as well as finances, in an endeavor to keep active, as well as aggressive and influential, the Restoration Plea as exemplified by our pioneers. I do not wish to feel that sometime I would have to "apologize," as expressed by my brother in his letter to Mrs. Tangeman under date of May 17, 1955, for contribut-

152

ing to the Park Avenue Christian Church. I shall deem it a privilege, if and when this church adopts a definite policy and becomes a champion of the Restoration Plea without equivocation, to support it in a substantial manner. I am of the opinion that in New York City, the largest city in this country, we should have at least one church well-housed and in a desirable location, as is the case with the Park Avenue Christian Church, that will typify and be an outstanding witness of the Plea. Frankly, I feel chagrined and embarrassed that this is not now so with the Park Avenue Church.

If the policy of the Park Avenue Christian Church were different, I would derive much pleasure and satisfaction in joining with my brother's Charitable Trust in building in this church a beautiful baptistery. But due to your present policy this is impossible.

A few years later, open membership came closer home. A pastor of the Butler, Pennsylvania, church—Mr. Phillips' own congregation—was "soft" on the doctrine. During his ministry Dr. George Earle Owen, liberal Disciple leader, was invited to occupy the pulpit. In his address Dr. Owen strongly advocated the practice. In a letter to his pastor a few days later, Mr. Phillips tells the story:

On March 14 at a Sunday evening service, upon persistent and insistent questioning I finally got George Earle Owen, a member of the Board of Directors of Unified Promotion, to admit he favored open membership. This may have seemed to you and others somewhat tenacious on my part, but I had experiences of this kind before and knew only too well how evasive and indefinite those who advocate open membership may be when questioned, particularly publicly. I fully anticipated this when quizzing Mr. Owen.

When you came to Butler, it was my understanding you were asked very definitely about open membership by the Pulpit Committee and you were positively opposed to open membership. Therefore, I was astonished, after Mr. Owen admitted he was favorable to open membership, to hear you state Barton Stone believed and practiced it and from the time he joined forces with Alexander Campbell in 1830 we have had open membership with us. You referred this to Mr. Owen and he definitely concurred with your statement. It appears you have not given this subject much thought or consideration and I was surprised you would make this statement thoughtlessly, leaving with the audience an impression which was erroneous. . . .

Without getting into details too much, I remember many years ago in our home in New Castle hearing my father discuss David Purviance, who caused a split in our people, and headquarters were set up at Dayton, Ohio. The Christian churches in the East, which were tinctured with Unitarianism and had always practiced open membership, joined with some Ohio,

Indiana and Kentucky Christians in forming the old "Christian Connection." Later on these people merged with the Congregationalists. These "open membership" Christian churches never found any fellowship with the Campbell-Stone movement. To say that the Disciples of Christ, as a distinct communion, ever practiced "open membership" is misrepresenting the facts. That element of the Stone movement that became a part of our Brotherhood was "closed membership."

In the closing paragraphs of Stone's *A Short History of the Life of Barton W. Stone, Written by Himself*, a few short years before his death, he said:

"It is not strange that the prejudices of the Christian Church (the Christian Connection) should be great against us, and that they should unkindly upbraid me especially, and my brethren in Kentucky, for uniting with the Reformers. But what else could we do, the Bible being our directory? Should we command them to leave the foundation on the ground which we stood—the Bible alone—when they had come upon the same? By what authority could we command? Or should we have left this foundation to them and have built another? Or should we have remained and fought with them for the sole possession? They held the name Christian as sacred as we did, they were equally averse from making opinions as a test of fellowship, and equally solicitous for the salvation of souls. The union I view as the noblest act of my life."

In a book entitled *Barton Warren Stone* by Charles C. Ware, the following is quoted from page 338:

"Stone and his co-workers practiced open fellowship at the Lord's Supper. They plead emotionally for the name Christian and quoted some of the approved exegetes of the day in support of it. For a long time after 1807 they observed immersion as a matter of individual privilege and not as an invariable requisite for church membership. Gradually Stone and his associates who were to unite with the Reformers tightened in this, until they were immersing all unimmersed applicants for church membership without exception."

On page 339 is the following:

"However, in the present fellowship of the Disciples are a few exceptions. Historically considered, the practice of these sporadic 'open membership' churches is anomalous. Actually it is a threat to the unity of a communion which for more than a century has idealized a biblical immersion as the inviolable symbol of a participating believer's initial identity with Christ."

Every church Stone served as pastor became a closed membership church, practicing open communion. In his closing years he was never accused of being "soft" on the baptism issue. Too often our people are prone to confuse open membership with open communion—a vast difference.

As a footnote to this early history of the Movement to restore New Testament Christianity, it must be noted that the open-membership Christian Connection (which withdrew from Stone and his followers) united

154

with the open-membership Congregationalists in 1931. The remnant of their churches are now a part of what is known as the "United Church of Christ," which is also an open-membership body. . . .

A minister usually is looked upon as a leader in a community, particularly in the church which he serves. Therefore, he should be very careful in making statements of far-reaching consequences, particularly in our case when voicing the beliefs and policies of one of the pioneers of the Restoration Plea. . . .

The North Street Church has never approved open membership and is not likely to in the future.

When approached by people seeking his views on open membership Mr. Phillips frequently gave them copies of Z. T. Sweeney's tract on the subject, or copies of P. H. Welshimer's published correspondence with A. R. Hamilton.

In his later years when colleges asked for his support he invariably asked their position on open membership. As late as 1964 he insisted that Phillips University make its position clear. He wrote President Gantz:

> . . . Both you and Dr. Garrison have definitely evaded this issue in dealing with me. Dr. Garrison believes that as high as 50% of our churches practice open membership on a nation-wide basis. Your excuse in failing to take a positive stand is that it is not a real problem in Phillips territory, as you estimate that not more than 10% of your churches practice it. . . If there was ever a time to combat this practice, it is in its incipient state and not after 20%, 50%, 75% or more of the churches have succumbed. If your estimate regarding Phillips territory is correct, you *now* have the additional advantage of strong public support for your opposition. If this support is permitted to dwindle away and become ineffective, the task becomes hopeless.

> I have repeatedly urged that the publicity project of Phillips, when used, contain a definite and positive stand against open membership, but the material thus far submitted completely ignores this subject; and as far as we are concerned, it therefore is unacceptable.

> If the decision is that Phillips, meaning you and your board, will not do this, then by the force of our convictions we should withdraw support; and in such case, suggest the name of the institution be changed.

A WEAKENING TESTIMONY

The Phillips Family was one of the main supporters of the Western Pennsylvania Christian Missionary Society and later, after the merger with the Eastern Pennsylvania Society, of the Pennsylvania Society.

155

In a letter to H. A. Denton, the state secretary, in 1944 Mr. Phillips recalled this support and enclosed a check for $600. He indicated that he had been giving around $1,000 a year for the Society's program and would continue to do so if it would give a strong testimony for the Restoration Plea.

He was, however, unhappy about the last state convention. He said:

I believe you now know well my opinion of institutions that were originally started and maintained by our people—at great sacrifices in many instances—and that at the present time, instead of championing our plea, almost ignore it. To have had Dr. Warren Hastings as the principal speaker one year at the annual State Convention, and again have him the following year, as was done this past September, and for the principal speaker at both these Conventions to ignore completely doctrinal subjects, is one of the most astonishing conditions with which I have ever come in contact. It is one that probably would have caused a complete change in the personnel of the society which the Pennsylvania Christian Missionary Society has fallen heir to, if it had occurred early in this century.

Suppose a Convention of the Disciples of Christ were held in a certain province of China or India, and the doctrine which caused money to be given for the sending of representatives of our plea to China or India was completely ignored, what would the reaction be at home? Yet this same situation prevailed at our Convention held in Pennsylvania only a few miles from the cradle of the Restoration Movement.

Frankly, this situation has been so aggravating to me that I thought I would make no contribution whatever to the Pennsylvania Christian Missionary Society this year, or any year in the future, unless an entirely different policy were pursued. However, I have reconsidered this and have decided to go along to the same extent as last year, hoping there will be a very different attitude, and that when the Convention is held this year (believe in Altoona), someone will be selected who will wholeheartedly seize the opportunity to bring out in more than one sermon doctrinal subjects. Many of our preachers need this just as badly as most of our lay members.

I heard about P. H. Welshimer's address at the International Convention at Columbus shortly after it was delivered. Was told it was the outstanding sermon at the Convention, and after delivery a real ovation was given the speaker. After reading this sermon in the *Christian Evangelist* I can well believe the report. If every minister in our Brotherhood, including Dr. Hastings, would just memorize this sermon of Welshimer's and deliver it to his congregation (treating it as his own theme, or giving Welshimer credit for it if he preferred), he could at least have the satisfaction of feeling he had delivered one sermon during the year that he owes it to our Brotherhood to deliver—the Brotherhood that makes it possible for him to minister to a congregation and that is responsible for whatever position of influence he enjoys.

Usually a convention is for the purpose of bringing before those who attend it the best talent the sponsors are able to get, dealing with the particular business or movement the convention represents. How much of our last Convention could qualify?

Nearly twenty years later Mr. Phillips was still pleading for a stronger testimony on the part of the Pennsylvania Society. In a letter to the Secretary he said:

I am disappointed in your rather passive attitude. I believe you realize there is a limit to the amount of time I can spend on situations of this nature—and there are lots of them. I have given a great deal of thought and consideration to our Brotherhood. Letters I have written have required much time and effort and, for the most part, have been painstakingly composed. It has been not only annoying, but aggravating to me, to find the Restoration Plea being ignored and no distinctive doctrinal testimony being given to our people. . . .

You have been with the Pennsylvania Christian Missionary Society long enough to get your bearings, yet you wash your hands completely of the program for the Greensburg Convention, stating this committee was appointed last September. You are the Executive Secretary of the Pennsylvania Society, the only individual in an executive capacity devoting his entire time to this organization. Your position is such that you should review with a very critical eye the program that is proposed for Greensburg this coming May and insist that not one address, but most of the addresses, have to do with the background of our plea. May is approximately three months away and there is plenty of time for you to get into this, if you are so minded. Certainly you will not overstep the bounds of your office, if you care to exercise your prerogative. . . .

Just this morning I received a program from Johnson Bible College entitled, Homecoming and Preaching Rally. The theme is "Let the Word Speak." There were a number of addresses, the topics of which are as follows:

Let the Word Speak Concerning the Church
Let the Word Speak Concerning the Faith
Let the Word Speak Concerning Worship
Let the Word Speak Concerning the Lordship of Jesus Christ
Let the Word Speak Concerning the Ministry
Let the Word Speak Concerning God
Let the Word Speak Concerning the Second Coming of Jesus Christ

I did not hear any of these addresses, but am of the opinion it would be the exception in any of these if the historic plea of our people were not emphasized. If our people are to survive and occupy a position of real influence, it is up to you and others in similar positions to be champions of the principles that caused the inception of the Restoration Plea.

For many years it has been lamentable to me the attitude and the resultant lack of showing our people have had in Pennsylvania, particularly in Western Pennsylvania. I am of the opinion it is time to change this attitude. At every meeting some illustration or reference to our plea should be brought out emphatically in a few words, thereby attempting to attain a better grounding for our people in what is commonly termed "first principles. . . ."

Mr. Phillips read all the Brotherhood periodicals including the *Christian Standard, Firm Foundation, The Gospel Advocate,* and *The Christian.* He detected dangerous trends in the latter and frequently wrote its editor urging him to take a stronger stand for the Plea. One such letter addressed to Dr. Howard Short reads:

For some years I have been desirous of meeting you and regretted greatly that we did not see you when at Bethany this spring. This wish, however, was fulfilled at our meeting with you in St. Louis last week.

This desire was due to several situations: your position as editor of *The Christian,* your having been a professor at Hiram College in the 1940's, and the lack of fundamental restoration policies and quotations having to do therewith in *The Christian;* the undue prominence given to Catholicism, both in writing and in pictures pertaining to Catholics in *The Christian;* the tendency on the part of *The Christian* to become more of a secular paper, pertaining to generalities, and not an emphatic and stalwart publication of the Restoration Plea; and your sponsorship of the so-called "Panel of Scholars," some of whose writings perhaps are the most condemnatory and critical of Alexander Campbell, the pioneers, and the Restoration Plea, that I have ever read.

If it had not been for the Restoration Plea, presumably there would be no publication known as *The Christian,* and of course R. A. Long's purchase of this publication from the Garrisons and donation of same to a non-profit organization would not have taken place. . . . Mr. Long was a very rugged individual in his attitude toward the Restoration Plea; and I am of the opinion he would be tremendously disappointed, if he knew the trend this publication has followed in recent years; and furthermore, that a considerable donation has been made yearly to the Park Avenue Christian Church, New York City, an avowed open membership church. . . .

When some questions were asked concerning policies, I was very much surprised that you, as editor of *The Christian,* "passed the buck" to your boss and your board of trustees. With your age, experience, and background, it was surprising you used this excuse and alibi. . . . Many individuals are prone to accept the trusteeship, as a member of a board, due to the standing it may accord them. Others of some standing and influence accept a trusteeship, as a member of a board, and grossly neglect their responsibilities, permitting one or two officers to dictate policies without interference. As a matter of fact, this is exactly what is desired

158

and sanctioned by one or two in the active management of many corporations, whether of a business, religious, or educational nature. I do not know the situation in Saint Louis but someone is very much to blame for your compromising policies. . . .

However, be that as it may, I was glad to get some thoughts across to you and hope our paths may cross again in the near future. I shall be very happy to have lunch or dinner with you, if you happen to be in Pittsburgh sometime; or you will be a very welcome guest at our home some evening, if you are passing through Butler.

One of Mr. Phillips' favorite ministers through the years at the North Street Church in Butler was N. Quentin Grey. Under his leadership the congregation prospered and became one of the most influential in the state. After Mr. Grey's acceptance of the pulpit of First Church, Fort Worth, Texas, Mr. Phillips struck up a considerable correspondence with him about Brotherhood affairs. A few excerpts will be informative:

Apparently you are very much engrossed in the work you are doing and are meeting with much success. According to this report, there have been 194 additions your first year, 11 have moved, and 6 have removed membership. Very good.

In one of your sermons at Butler, I remember you quoted some figures showing the growth of the church on a nation-wide basis during a five or ten year period. Analyzing these figures, one would have thought we were making quite a showing, but you failed to state the increase in population in the period covered. When this was taken into consideration, our showing was very poor. You perhaps will remember I called your attention to the figures you quoted.

The growth of our church membership the country over has been very disappointing to me. I hope with the new life you brought into the Fort Worth Church and the way you have been stressing our Plea that your second year, ending this coming September, will be a record one. It has always seemed to me our growth in the Southwest should be much easier to attain than growth in the section of the country in which I happen to reside, notwithstanding the fact Western Pennsylvania sometimes is considered almost the Cradle of the Restoration Plea.

I have just about finished reading Richardson's *Memoirs of Alexander Campbell.* In reading this carefully, I have not found many things that I did not have reasonable knowledge of, but it brings to light with emphasis the historical position of our Plea and the struggle some of our pioneers had, particularly the Campbells, in breaking away from ecclesiasticism and hidebound policies that the Baptists and the Presbyterian Churches were adherents of.

Furthermore, I got the idea that many sermons could be preached which would be most interesting and instructive, if the basis of sermon after sermon consisted of incidents from the lives of the Campbells and their problems, having to do particularly with the establishment of the Brush Run Church—sermons in fact that would adhere to the subject without too many ramifications and which should be short, concise and to the point.

In a recent issue of the *Christian Standard* an article was published, written by Emerson G. Hess. The following is quoted from this article:

"Most ministers prepare their sermons well and convey helpful concepts, especially if they confine their discussions to religious matters. It is deplorable, however, when they digress to controversial subjects like politics, philosophy, or reviews of books they have found interesting. The church was not built for a lecture hall. The audience is there to worship and not to listen to a talk on a subject that would be appropriate in a lecture series. The minister has only one product to sell, and when he digresses to other lines of salesmanship he is perhaps among superior competitors!"

The average intelligent person going to church desires to have a discourse on the minister's specialty. The minister is a specialist in religious matters and his efforts should be confined to religious subjects, and not with matters with which for the most part he is not conversant, is not living with from day to day, and concerning which he is not a specialist and not recognized as competent to discuss. We have so many, many subjects that should be emphasized persistently at nearly every opportunity, which have to do with our background and are of an historical nature. People in all lines of endeavor are inclined to overlook the past and lack its beneficial effects. We have a wonderful heritage, one of which we can be justly proud, but unfortunately too many of our people, especially ministers, wish to digress into fields in which they are not specialists.

I am thoroughly convinced our people would be very much larger numerically and have much greater influence, if they avoided the various vagrancies that have developed in many cases by those who had little respect for or realization of the principles that caused the Campbells, Stone and Scott to break away from ecclesiasticism and to take the New Testament as the basis for their faith and practice and to follow the precept, "Where the New Testament speaks, we speak; and where the New Testament is silent, we are silent." This is as essential for their guidance as the north star and the sun are essential in navigation.

Later Mr. Phillips wrote:

I just happened to glance at the headlines of your church paper, *First Christian*, dated December 2. Two things are very noticeable to me: (1) "Rev. Wright to be Installed This Sunday." (2) "Parent-Baby Dedication, December 5."

I have never liked the word "Reverend" used in the appellation of a minister of one of our churches. I always think that if we use "Reverend," why not go the full length of the Catholics and use the title "Right Reverend Bishop," or some other such unscriptural terminology?

160

Dedication of babies so often is mistaken for baptism. It is a very dangerous procedure. Unless very definitely explained, it can readily be confused with immersion; and even when very definitely stated or explained, people may have the distorted idea in years hence, and the victim himself perhaps will get the implication, that by being dedicated the subject has been baptized.

We are inclined to follow entirely too much a half-sectarian policy and one that was entirely foreign to our pioneers. In any event, in this day and age it behooves us to be less "broad" and more "narrow." When writing a letter recently, I said that I admired the Church of Christ (non-instrument) people in many respects and some of their so-called "narrow-ness" to me is far better than the so-called "broadness" endorsed by many of our people. Certainly a half-sectarian policy is sanctioned by the powers —and I mean "powers" of an ecclesiastical nature—that I suspect you and many others are wholeheartedly endorsing at Indianapolis. This has reached the point which T. W. and I told you many years ago would happen, where many of our ministers fear to take an independent stand, which in many cases to some extent may be a "bread and butter" situation.

These are just a few thoughts expressed to you, which I know for the most part will not coincide with your views; but nevertheless it ought to be refreshing to you to have someone bring out some of these points in writing, not verbally, when the present trend is to get away from the moorings of the church established at Pentecost and described in The Acts and the Epistles. The claim has been made that many of the innovations are based on expediency.

UNIFIED PROMOTION

As early as 1909 the service agencies of the Christian Churches and Churches of Christ related to the national convention began to confer on ways and means by which there could be a unification of appeals for funds. One of the results was the organization of the United Christian Missionary Society. Some agencies refused to join the UCMS, with the result that Unified Promotion came into being, eventually exercising fiscal controls of various sorts over some sixty agencies.

Early in this development Mr. Phillips sensed grave dangers to the freedom not only of the agencies involved but the local churches as well. Unified Promotion moved beyond the unification of appeals to limiting the budgets of its constituent members, centralizing the total giving of the churches, and designating the percentages of this total which each agency could receive. Eventually local churches were told how much and for what purpose they should give.

Writing to a Unified Promotion official in Indianapolis he said:

The agencies you "serve" have definitely lost the control of their future and have surrendered to the whims and caprices of Unified Promotion. . . .

The personnel of your Board indicates that the controls you exercise will be Liberal-oriented. Two examples: Dr. Beauford A. Norris who, when in my home last September, made the astounding statement he was of the opinion our people as a brotherhood should go out of existence and combine, or be amalgamated, with some sort of universal church. This would mean, of course, the repudiation of the distinctive principles that brought the Restoration Movement into existence—an astonishing theory for a man in his position to advocate. The other man to whom I would refer is Willard M. Wickhiser. I heard him speak at our annual convention of the Pennsylvania Christian Churches recently and of all the "fuddy-duddying" I ever heard about Our Plea he took the prize. You could not tell whether he was in or out of it, whether he was fish or fowl. A study of the men on your Board would indicate that you would be willing to sell the cause down the river whenever opportunity offered. . . .

There has been set up at Indianapolis a hierarchy and form of ecclesiasticism that are unbelievable, and the rank and file of our people do not realize this. This has been brought about by the fact certain individuals connected with the International Convention wish to be able to meet with representatives of other religious bodies and present credentials showing they are acting for several thousand churches, the inception of which was the restoration of the church founded at Pentecost. We, as a people, cannot set up any body of this kind. The fact this has been done by other religious bodies has caused an enormous amount of doctrinal differences in churches and the chaotic state which prevails in the church, as a whole, resulting in all sorts of human interpretations not found in the New Testament. Apparently the hierarchy at Indianapolis desires to combine with certain religious communions, establish a universal church, and attempt to improve on the church divinely established at Pentecost. Whom do we have who can lay claim to any such prerogative? Certainly not the man who, as secretary of the International Convention, was ordained at your last Assembly with a considerable show of ceremony, reminding one of the installation of a Pope.

To his friend Quentin Grey, in Fort Worth, Mr. Phillips wrote:

As to Unified Promotion: believe you will remember some of the conversations T. W. and I had with you, probably in the 1940's, regarding this hierarchical and ecclesiastical domination which was under way years ago, but some of you were not in accord with our views and were not farsighted enough to share them.

The dominance at Indianapolis and its power to distribute funds are entirely out of proportion to the churches represented. Most of our people fail to recognize the tremendous influence that has on many of our ministers and state secretaries, particularly in the case of ministers who fear the

162

consequences if they fail to wholeheartedly support Unified Promotion, or even if they recognize in any manner independent work. The independent work, both foreign and domestic, is several times bigger than what is being done by Unified Promotion. How many people know this? How quiet do you keep about this?

When Unified Promotion extended its octopus-like tentacles into the colleges Mr. Phillips determined that none of his philanthropy would go to any institution involved in it. His stand kept several colleges outside the system for a number of years but hierarchical pressures—state, regional, and national—became so strong that practically all of them eventually succumbed. Phillips University was one of the last to enter Unified Promotion. Mr. Phillips' files were filled with correspondence in which he argued with and pleaded with the administration during the years of its hesitancy in making the final decision.

When he finally withdrew support from Phillips, the institution suffered a severe loss. Some indication of its proportions may be gained from the following figures from the records of his gifts to Phillips for 1962-64:

	1962	1963	1964	Total
B. D. Phillips	106,600.00	69,872.00	59,438.00	235,910.00
T. W. Phillips, Jr. Charitable Trust		28,915.38		28,915.38
T. W. Phillips Gas and Oil Company	4,680.00	47,112.00	20,588.00	72,380.00
	111,280.00	145,899.38	80,026.00	337,205.38

Mr. Phillips lived to see all his predictions about Unified Promotion come true, it being one of the chief instruments by which Restructure of the Brotherhood was achieved and by which the freedom of the agencies and the local churches submitting to it was destroyed.

INTER-CHURCH COOPERATION

Mr. Phillips had a deep concern for the unity of all Christians in the Christ of the Scriptures and lent his influence to all interdenominational movements which did not compromise the Plea for the restoration of the New Testament Church.

From the beginnings of the Federal Council of Churches and later of the National Council of Churches he had his doubts about their loyalty to the fundamentals of the Christian faith and their socio-political policies.

When the National Council erected its headquarters building near the United Nations in New York City, Mr. Phillips was approached by Dr. Gaines M. Cook, executive secretary of the International Convention of Christian Churches, asking him to make a generous gift toward furnishing the administrative offices and the main conference room. There was a special appeal to Disciples because one of its own leaders, Dr. Roy G. Ross, had been chosen as the Council's chief administrator. After considerable investigation of the proposal, Mr. Phillips wrote to Dr. Cook:

> Frankly, I cannot become enthusiastic over this project. I am of the opinion it will be an enormously expensive enterprise to maintain. It is a very serious question whether we, as a people, will benefit in joining this movement to an extent comparable with the commitment made. In nearly all undertakings of this kind, our people who become affiliated with the movement almost invariably lose sight of our historical background, the Restoration Plea, and the fundamentals that brought our movement into being. Somehow when our people become associated in a program with leaders of other communions, our people lose all sense of balance and are carried off their feet.

> I am of the opinion in this category you are not immune. This was brought to light very definitely in the article that appeared in the July 29, 1957 issue of *The Christian Evangelist*, which told of your participation in the ceremonies creating the "United Church of Christ" (Congregational and Evangelical and Reformed). Shortly after this was published, I received a letter from one of our prominent people, pertaining to your article, and the following is quoted from the letter:

> "In many respects it is one of the most amazing documents which I have read in a number of years. Basically, this document is an out and out avowal of the open membership position taken by the denominational world. Paragraph two on page two is a complete denial of the historic position which the Disciples of Christ have occupied for the last century and a half. What we have concerned ourselves about as a people is not an amalgamation, but a restoration. The closing sentence of the last paragraph on page three is a remarkable statement, 'Those of us who were privileged to be present as guests felt that we had already been inducted and accepted as members of the United Church.' It would appear from that statement that Dr. Cook is perfectly willing to leave the Restoration Movement and to get into some other movement which is not a movement of restoration but which is a movement for consolidation. . . .

> "This article to me is a most disturbing one for the simple reason that it has been broadcast throughout the entire Brotherhood of the Disciples of Christ and was written by one who is recognized as one of the leaders in

164

our movement. However, this is just an indication of what is happening in the Brotherhood today. There is a very strong movement toward open membership and I am of the opinion that we here in the cradle of the Restoration Movement should do something about this situation."

If your article is an example of what this Interchurch movement has done to you, the question is what has it done to Dr. Roy G. Ross? Due to the position you hold in our Brotherhood, it seems to me you should exercise the utmost care in the articles you have published. On the other hand, I am of the opinion *The Christian Evangelist* was greatly at fault for not having in the same issue in which your article appeared, an editorial showing just where the propaganda, which you apparently have endorsed, will lead our people.

My brother often stated we should "give up the ship," if we do not have a distinctive plea and one that justifies maintaining, and join with some of the other communions, many of which greatly antedate our beginning and therefore are much larger and have better locations and facilities. One is led to believe you are willing to "give up the ship" and disregard the Restoration Plea.

The day came when Mr. Phillips refused to contribute in any way to the work of the Councils of Churches. In fact he took every opportunity offered him to disseminate information exposing the dangers inherent in them. He was instrumental in distributing many copies of James DeForest Murch's critiques of the Councils and also his book, *The Protestant Revolt*.

RESTRUCTURE OF THE BROTHERHOOD

In 1960 the Indianapolis Establishment announced a "Decade of Decision" through which Leftist elements within the Restoration Movement planned to create a connectional, centralized denominational power structure that would take over the Christian Churches and Churches of Christ and deliver them into an Ecumenical World Church.

Mr. Phillips immediately recognized the plan as a venture which, if not opposed, would destroy the Restoration Movement or result in a schism of Gargantuan proportions. He was not unprepared for this development for he had watched with great trepidation the steps toward it over many years.

Before World War I the Campbell Institute envisioned such a move. In 1919 the major national service agencies of the Brotherhood were merged into the United Christian Missionary Society. He saw the Society assume semi-official advisory and/or supervisory authority over functional aspects of regional, state, and

165

local corporative associations. Its tentacles penetrated women's work and men's work in many local congregations.

Then came Unified Promotion (page 161) in which almost all agencies of the Brotherhood, including its schools and colleges, accepted a united fiscal, promotional, and strategic operational program. Mr. Phillips fought Unified Promotion with all his might. He realized that it was a power structure which could eliminate free and independent initiative, force reorganization, create new structures, and eventually achieve complete ecclesiastical unification and coordination.

Mr. Phillips watched theological liberalism penetrate the changing ecclesiasticism. He heard its leaders deny the credibility, inspiration, and authority of the Holy Scriptures and try to laugh the Restoration principle out of existence. He saw an incipient hierarchy developing as "secretaries" assumed the role of "bishops" enlisting the ministry and the churches in dramatic "crusades" without foundation in the Word of God. He saw these liberal leaders, without doctrinal or traditional inhibitions, seeking ecclesiastical status in the denominational world and making concession after concession for the promotion of ecumenical church union. Along with all this, Mr. Phillips saw a local church leadership Biblically ignorant and without knowledge of the origins and principles of the Restoration Movement, obsessed with the desire to better their social status and "be all things to all men" for the sake of "universal brotherhood, peace and prosperity."

When a "Committee on Brotherhood Restructure" reported at the Louisville assembly of the International Convention of Christian Churches (Disciples of Christ), Mr. Phillips was shocked at its findings and proposals for the future, but he was fully prepared to assess it and realize its implications for the future.

The Louisville Report proposed that the Disciples of Christ develop a completely new theology of the nature and mission of the Church and proceed to restructure for bigger and broader "involvement" in keeping with an "over-all master plan which will relate each part to the whole." The new structure should extend beyond our own borders, including our "historic concern for Christian unity." The time has come, the Report said, to "quit tinkering with the machinery" and seek a new design "rooted in a new Christian conviction concerning the Church." It boldly stated that *every level* in the Brotherhood should be involved in a new

166

denominational structure including "its church members, its ministry, its function, its authority, city unions, district and state conventions and organizations, its International Convention and all agencies reporting to it, colleges, seminaries, benevolent homes, national planning bodies, and involvement in all ecumenical bodies." The words "autonomy" and "self-government" should be scrapped, said the Committee, and replaced by "inter-dependence" and "responsibility." The freedom of the local church should be impregnated with a new sense of obligation to proper official authority. At Louisville it was evident that the Establishment had embarked upon a ruthless policy, determined to achieve Restructure with all due speed regardless of the costs involved. Dr. Loren E. Lair, who was president of the International Convention that year, made the statement that "we must have an organization that can move together if we are to have an effective witness. This needs to be achieved, even if it means a breaking away of the anti-organization wing of the Christian Churches, a possible loss of 2,700 churches and 650,000 members." Similar expressions were heard in night sessions of the Campbell Institute, where many leaders of the Restructure spoke. The Louisville Assembly approved the Report of the Committee and authorized the appointment of a Commission on Brotherhood Restructure and Restructure of the Brotherhood in depth and breadth.

The brethren assembled at Louisville seemed unaware of the fact that Restructure was already being realized in many ways under supervision of the Establishment. A Panel of Scholars had been at work since 1956 drafting the tentative blueprint. Their findings were now published in three volumes under the general title, *The Renewal of Church:* (1) *The Reformation of Tradition,* (2) *Reconstruction of Theology,* and (3) *Revival of the Churches.* Many other volumes designed to prepare church leaders for the abandonment of the Restoration tradition, including the Free Church idea, had long been in circulation and were now promoted with new enthusiasm. Actual restructuring of state and regional "missionary societies" and "associations" was already proceeding step by step as rapidly as the opposition would permit. National agencies were being persuaded to change their constitutions and by-laws so that all legal barriers to complete involvement with the new centralized ecclesiastical structure would be removed. In fact, more was being accomplished in Restructure behind the scenes by pressures from the Establishment than in the much-publicized "open," "democratic actions" of the Convention.

Mr. Phillips was now ready to mount some kind of effective opposition to Restructure and invest time, effort, and money in it. It so happened that about this time James DeForest Murch was concluding a series of meetings in First Christian Church, Canton, Ohio, and had proposed to a group of brethren there that they organize for action. Upon his return to his home in Washington, D. C., he wrote an "Open Letter to Christian Churches and Churches of Christ" under the title *Freedom or Restructure?* for Brotherhood-wide distribution. Called to Elm Court to confer with Mr. and Mrs. Phillips about other matters, he mentioned the manuscript. Mr. Phillips immediately said, "Do you have a copy with you?" Providentially he did, and Mr. Phillips asked to read it. He took it into his private office and after more than an hour, he emerged waving the manuscript and saying, "This must be sent out to the whole Brotherhood right away. I shall be glad to underwrite the cost. When can we get things moving?"

Almost immediately a meeting of the Canton brethren and others that Mr. Phillips invited was held in First Church, Canton, at which a "Committee for the Preservation of the Brotherhood" was organized* and plans were laid for printing and distributing *Freedom or Restructure?*

The brochure was mailed to every church in the Brotherhood, four copies to each congregation. Immediately there was an overwhelming response from the Establishment. Meetings were called by state and area secretaries all over the nation, to which ministers, elders, and deacons were invited. The brochure was vehemently condemned, and plans were laid to discredit the "Committee." There was little attempt made to answer the arguments made against Restructure. The strategy was to disparage the whole "Letter" because it had been issued anonymously.

---

*The personnel of the "Committee for the Preservation of the Brotherhood," when created, was as follows: B. D. Phillips, Butler, Pa., Chairman; James DeForest Murch, Washington, D. C., Vice-Chairman; Sherrill E. Storey, Canton, Ohio, Secretary-Treasurer; Mrs. Phillips; Dean E. Walker, Milligan College, Tenn.; Murhl H. Rogers, Indianapolis, Ind.; Rolland L. Ehrman, Hershey, Pa.; and Harold E. Davis, Canton, Ohio. At that time, as individuals, half were members of "cooperative" churches and half of "independent" churches.

The Committee issued to the Brotherhood the following apologetic for its method of approach:

We wished to have the facts, principles and issues, concerning Restructure considered strictly on their own merits. It has been our observation that, in similar situations in the past, principles were forgotten in a welter of personal diatribe and organizational bias. We will not be parties to a repetition of such debacles. After careful and prayerful consideration, we came to the conclusion that the issues would receive far wider attention if the authors and sponsors were not disclosed. Our position has been amply justified. Not in fifty years has there been a response comparable to that received by this pamphlet. The reaction of state and national leaders, in itself, demonstrated the wisdom of our decision. Orders for extra copies have forced us to reprint the pamphlet three times and new orders continue to arrive every day.

Anonymity, alone without further knowledge, should not be condemned. One of the greatest and most influential books ever written on the Restoration Plea was *The Church of Christ*, "By a Layman." It received a far wider reading and had a much greater acceptance because there was no prejudice or preconceived disposition in favor of or against the author. Our Lord, at times, desired anonymity. He charged certain persons, whom He healed, to "tell no man of this." After the Good Confession by Peter, He charged His disciples "that they should tell no man that He was Jesus the Christ." Even following His resurrection, on the road to Emmaus, He saw fit, temporarily, to withhold His identity. The book of Hebrews in the New Testament is credited to no author.

We may say, however, the Committee is a voluntary group composed of brethren whose ancestors, in some cases, were champions of the Restoration Plea before the beginning of the present century. The project has been financed from sources which have long contributed generously to so-called "official" and "responsible" agencies and institutions of the brotherhood.

Interest in the booklet did not flag. New developments in Restructure called for another "Open Letter." It was entitled, *The Truth About Restructure*. It called forth from the leaders of Restructure for the first time public recognition of the opposition. Dr. Stephen J. England, president of the International Convention, wrote an "Open Letter" answering the brochures. An issue of *World Call*, the official journal of the Establishment, gave four full pages to *The Truth About Restructure*, including an editorial, "Has the Break Really Come?" All state and area papers joined in publishing condemnatory articles. Following this the CPB issued a *Restructure Report* from time to time keeping the Brotherhood informed concerning developments.

To summarize its position, the Committee opposed Restructure because:

1. It would change the Brotherhood from a voluntary fellowship of individual Christian and local churches, accepting the supreme authority of Christ and seeking to serve Him according to the teaching of the New Testament, into an official, connectional, centralized denomination acknowledging the authority of a liberal Super-Church hierarchy.

2. It would require as a test of Christian fellowship, not only the acceptance of Jesus Christ as Lord and Saviour, but also support of specific official denominational agencies and conventions.

3. It would no longer accept the Bible as sole and ultimate authority in matters of faith and practice.

4. It would permit open membership and condone sprinkling, pouring, and infant baptism.

5. It would reject the free-church polity of the New Testament and replace it with a "modified presbyterian" or "controlled congregational" system in a denominational Super-Church.

6. It would exercise money-raising and money-spending powers over local churches and endanger their right to hold property without regard for any extra-congregational authority.

7. It would require ministers to get extra-congregational authority for ordination, installation, choice, and release.

8. It would create a whole new category of general ministers —national, state, and area (similar to bishops) outranking local ministers and exercising a species of unscriptural authority—over local churches.

9. It would limit the local churches in their support of extra-congregational agencies and conventions. Approved agencies and conventions would have to be recognized as parts of "the whole church."

10. Colleges and seminaries would have to be denominationally related. Boards of trustees and administrative policies would be required to have Super-Church approval.

11. Christian unity would be sought, not through the Restoration of the New Testament Church in doctrine, ordinances, and life, but through ecumenical discussion, negotiation, compromise, denominational mergers, and eventual extinction of the Restora-

170

tion Movement in an Ecumenical World Church similar to the Roman Catholic Church.

12. Local churches could be compelled by extra-congregational authority to enter mergers, close their doors, or change their policies and practices in the interest of ecumenical progress.

It soon became evident that the crucial issue in Restructure was church polity and the freedom of the local church. Mr. Phillips commissioned Dr. Murch to write a scholarly and definitive treatise on *The Free Church* for the enlightenment of ministers and lay leaders. Mr. Phillips sent out one thousand copies of the book to key churches free of charge. Two editions of the book were printed and it still has a wide circulation. It had a tremendous impact on the churches.

Others were encouraged by Mr. Phillips to disseminate information about the dangers of Restructure: Dr. R. M. Bell, president of Johnson Bible College, through the college paper, *The Blue and White*, published effective critiques of Restructure. Judge B. D. Sartain, noted layman in Central Church, Dallas, Texas, circulated his "Restructure is Unwise, Undemocratic and Unscriptural." Attorney Rolland L. Ehrman, business associate of Mr. Phillips, answered President England's "Open Letter" in a brilliant and comprehensive defense of the Restoration Plea. Dr. Robert W. Burns, pastor of the great Peachtree Christian Church, Atlanta, Georgia, inspired a trenchant document, *The Atlanta Declaration*, and led in setting up The Atlanta Declaration Committee, opposing Restructure. W. F. Lown and Dean Walker wrote thoughtful and incisive critiques. Mr. Phillips' correspondence files during this period were filled with letters indicating his appreciation of the efforts of many leading brethren who were brave enough to take their stand for the right, regardless of the cost.

There were also scores of letters exchanged with distinguished advocates of Restructure in which Mr. Phillips revealed his keen understanding of the issues involved. The "Bible" of Restructure was "The Provisional Design." He read it, analyzed it, and interpreted it, until he understood it better than many men on the Commission. An excerpt from his correspondence with Dr. Hallie G. Gantz, president of Phillips University, is an example of this:

You are astonishingly naive in not appreciating and foreseeing the dangers inherent in Restructure and in not recognizing the motivation

171

impelling at least most of the leaders sponsoring it. I am aware that you have been a member of the "Commission on Restructure of the Brotherhood" since its inception and you apparently are "sold" on it. Here again, your position seems perplexing.

In the fourth paragraph on Page 2 of your last letter you stated: "I do not favor the loss of our valid Christian witness *as a Brotherhood*, or the dissolution of our Brotherhood into some ecumenical ecclesiastical machine."

In the light of your advocacy of Restructure, compare this with the following taken from the "Statement of Principles" adopted and submitted by the Commission:

"(6) *The Brotherhood seeks to be ecumenical.* Maybe this deserves reading. The Christian Churches and Disciples of Christ will continue their whole hearted participation in the ecumenical movement in every way including the local, state, area, national, and world Council of Churches. . .

"(8) The Brotherhood seeks *to lose itself in the life of the whole church* of Christ on earth. The Christian Churches must always be ready to enter into vital conversation with other bodies where it seems that conversations looking toward larger unities might be fruitful in relation to the nature and mission and unity of the churches in the world. . . ."

Is it any wonder we are perplexed and disillusioned, when at one moment you express concern and disappointment over "the loss of our valid Christian witness *as a Brotherhood*, or the dissolution of our Brotherhood," and at the next you devote time and energy and your support to the nurture and advancement of a cause which expressly has as its ultimate goal the accomplishment of these very ends? There is no doubt whatever in my mind that the three-volume report of the Panel of Scholars (of which your Dr. England was a member) was designed and intended to have a direct effect on Restructure; and one has only to read this report to realize just where we are headed if we follow its lead—a repudiation of the Scriptures, abandonment of the Restoration Plea, and merger into some larger unit with the inevitable submission in time to a world-wide ecumenical ecclesiastical hierarchy.

(See also correspondence with the Disciples of Christ Historical Society, page 173.)

Mr. Phillips followed in great detail all the developments in the national service agencies, the area conventions, and the International Convention, leading up to the final vote on "The Provisional Design" at Kansas City in 1968. He knew that adoption was inevitable because of the tight control exercised by the Indianapolis hierarchy over every channel of parliamentary action. When the new "Christian Church (Disciples of Christ)" was established, he cast his lot with the continuing Brotherhood with the knowledge and satisfaction that he had done all an individual Christian could do to "preserve and perpetuate the faith once for all delivered."

He lived to know that 4,600 churches (including his own North Street Church in Butler), 4,038 ministers, and 1,018,912 members had refused to enter the ranks of the new denomination and that their number was growing rapidly in all parts of the nation. The cause he so greatly loved would go marching on!

DISCIPLES HISTORICAL SOCIETY

The magnificent building of the Disciples of Christ Historical Society at Nashville, made possible by the generous giving of the Phillips Family, was to B. D. Phillips for many years "the apple of his eye." He was deeply interested in the work of the Society and kept up a lively correspondence with its officials seeking to make its services broader and more effective.

Mr. Phillips was particularly concerned that the Society should not be limited in any way to any particular sector of the Restoration Movement. He advocated a trusteeship made up of both "cooperative" and "independent" brethren, and even irenic friends in the Churches of Christ (non-instrument). He rejoiced to know all three groups made growing use of its facilities and services.

When Restructure threatened to take over the Society, Mr. Phillips saw new dangers to this broad concept of policy and operative procedures, and warned against it. The ensuing controversy over Restructure constituted one of the most tragic chapters in the history of his philanthropies.

In an "Open Letter to the Board of Trustees of the Disciples of Christ Historical Society," published in the *Christian Standard* for May 18, 1968, after he had exhausted every other means of making his opposition to Restructure known to the Society, Mr. Phillips said:

Mrs. Phillips has shown me a copy of the minutes of a meeting of the Board of Trustees of the Disciples of Christ Historical Society, held November 7, 1967, in the Board Room of the T. W. Phillips Memorial Building

I note with particular interest the motion presented by Dr. Howard E. Short to have the Board approve the Provisional Design for the Christian Church as recommended by the St. Louis Assembly of the International Convention of Christian Churches (Disciples of Christ) and Dr. Short's statement that the Board's acceptance of the Provisional Design "... would in no sense commit the Board to any changes in its structure or operation, and in the future, when and if any changes are proposed, they could be effected only by mutual consent of the Disciples of Christ Historical Society Board."

Dr. Short's assurance is directly contrary to the provisions of paragraph 52 of the Provisional Design as recommended at St. Louis. The first sentence of paragraph 52 reads as follows:

"Upon adoption of this design, all general agencies, associations, institutions and societies which report to the International Convention of Christian Churches (Disciples of Christ) shall be recognized as provisional units of the Christian Church. Wherever *appropriate* the provisional units will be called upon to bring their *constitutions and bylaws into harmony with this design.*" (Italics supplied.)

This language clearly indicates that an agency which has approved the design will be obligated to change its constitution and bylaws when called upon to do so. Contrary to Dr. Short's assertion, consent of the agency is neither expressed nor implied. Who is to determine what changes are *appropriate* and what changes are required for an agency to bring its constitution and bylaws *into harmony with the design?* What is or what is not *in harmony with the design?* Obviously, the agency itself will not be permitted freedom in the determination of policy. The third sentence of paragraph 52 states:

"The General Board shall initiate procedures for establishing administrative units of the Christian Church *under policies to be approved by the General Assembly* in keeping with the principles set forth in this article." (Italics supplied.)

Dr. Short's statement that future changes in structure or operation can only be effected by "mutual consent" is not borne out by paragraph 52. The final sentence of paragraph 52 reads as follows:

"During the period of interim coordination as well as in development of the administrative units of the Christian Church all existing agencies, associations, institutions and societies remain intact, subject to modification by mutual consent of the agencies, associations, institutions and societies involved, in the light of the corporate judgment of the Christian Church as expressed through the General Assembly." (Italics supplied.)

You will note, however, that it is the *existence* of the agencies which is to remain intact "subject to modification by mutual consent," but there is no assurance whatever that an agency's *constitution and bylaws* will remain intact.

Furthermore, Dr. Short's assurance entirely overlooks paragraph 102 of the Provisional Design, which provides for revisions and amendments of the Provisional Design which might well remove any security an existing agency has in the preservation of its present constitution and bylaws.

It is the common experience of history that a central authority, such as is envisioned in the Provisional Design, continuously strives to (and most often succeeds in) usurping to itself powers beyond the original powers with which it was invested. No better example need be given than that of our Federal Government which today exercises power and authority over the states and over individuals far in excess of the powers contemplated by the framers of the Constitution.

Mrs. Phillips correctly expressed my unequivocal opposition to the Provisional Design, and I am especially concerned as it affects the Disciples of Christ Historical Society. The Charitable Trust of my late brother, T. W. Phillips, Jr., the T. W. Phillips Gas and Oil Company, and I contributed a total of $1,020,304.75 toward the purchase of the real estate and the erection of the T. W. Phillips Memorial Building which now houses the Disciples of Christ Historical Society, and of this amount the writer individually contributed some $700,000.00. Our attraction to this project was the fact that the constitution of the Society provides that it is to serve all segments of the Restoration Movement, including the cooperative group, the independent group, and the Churches of Christ (noninstrumental). It was our hope that the erection of an adequate and an attractive building at a desirable location would enhance the ability of the Society to exert a unifying influence throughout the entire Brotherhood. If it had been our thought that at some future date one segment of the Brotherhood would insist upon the Society's alliance with it, which would or could impair its service to the Brotherhood at large, the contribution would never have been made. The approval by the Board of Provisional Design under which an authority beyond the Board itself is empowered to force a change in the Society's constitution and bylaws would be an abdication by the Board of the responsibilities vested in it and would be a breach of the trust placed in it by all who have contributed to the Society in reliance upon its constitutional provisions.

The Provisional Design creates an exclusive structure as only those ". . . congregations listed in the latest *Year Book of Christian Churches (Disciples of Christ)* . . . shall be recognized congregations of the Christian Church" (paragraph 86). Under the first sentence of paragraph 52 quoted above, the Society upon adoption of the Provisional Design would become a "provisional unit" of this exclusive church, and would no longer be an institution of the Brotherhood at large. In other words, the Society would be placed in a status directly contrary to the very purposes for which it was founded, as specifically stated in its constitution.

After Mrs. Phillips had indicated my opposition to the Provisional Design, the minutes indicate that Dr. Short spoke of his contact with me over several years, with the implication that in view of his assertion that I knew the operating funds of the Society had been contributed in large measure by the International Convention, I should have no objection to the Provisional Design. A diligent review of my files covering a period of some years does not support this implication and his assumption that I would not oppose the Provisional Design is entirely unwarranted and erroneous.

175

I have also received from the Society a copy of an address by Dr. Granville T. Walker, chairman of the Commission on Brotherhood Restructure, delivered at the Tenth Annual Dinner of the Society held in St. Louis during the Assembly of the International Convention. Dr. Walker endeavors to justify the structure created by the Provisional Design on the basis of a need for an efficient and coordinated effort by various agencies; but he carefully avoids any reference to the controls which will be exercised over these agencies, as well as over congregations and the ministers. At one point he states:

"In Detroit, the venerable and greatly honored Dr. W. E. Garrison spoke of our present situation as a 'fork in the road.' This is an apt description of where we are, for we have reached a moment of truth."

I am astonished that Dr. Walker in endeavoring to support the Provisional Design refers to "the venerable and greatly honored Dr. W. E. Garrison," for Dr. Walker well knows that Dr. Garrison is unequivocally opposed to the Provisional Design. In a letter dated July 21, 1967, Dr. Garrison in writing of the Provisional Design states in specific reference to his "fork in the road" speech in Detroit:

"I find I was more prophetic than I then realized. The Commission has taken what I think is the wrong fork."

At another point Dr. Walker refers to Paul's letter to the Corinthians and to one of Aesop's Fables, both of which stress the interdependency of all parts of the body in order that the body may effectively function as a unit and as a whole. In the portion of Paul's letter quoted by Dr. Walker, Paul says:

"The eye cannot say to the hand, 'I have no need of you,' nor again the head to the feet, 'I have no need of you.' "

Dr. Walker, however, makes no reference to the above mentioned paragraph 86 of the Provisional Design, which provides that *only* churches listed in the latest *Year Book* shall be "recognized congregations of the Christian Church." Dr. Walker and the Provisional Design, therefore, are arrogantly and presumptuously saying to the congregations not listed in the *Year Book:* "I have no need of you."

This is a declaration of divisiveness and exclusiveness which the Society cannot constitutionally adopt or endorse.

I am forwarding a copy of this letter to all members of the Board of Trustees of the Disciples of Christ Historical Society and would strongly urge that the Board reject the Provisional Design.

Despite Mr. Phillips' strong objections, the Board of Trustees of the Society voted May 14, 1968, to endorse Restructure and commit the Society to a corporative relationship with the new denomination.

In a letter to President Willis R. Jones, dated May 31, 1968, Mr. Phillips said:

176

I have read your report made to the Board of Trustees of the Disciples of Christ Historical Society of the meeting of the Board held on May 14, 1968. Also, I have a written report from Dr. Robert W. Burns and a written report from Mrs. Phillips, the latter having been written the day after the above meeting, and both of which set forth their respective versions of the events and discussions which occurred at the meeting.

There are two things that are astonishing to me, namely: (1) The scant consideration shown Dr. Burns, particularly to a man of his maturity, standing, and leadership among our people for many decades. (2) The lack of consideration and discussion at this meeting in regard to the resolution I proposed in my letter to the members of the Board dated April 19, 1968. This was particularly uncalled for, as a majority of the Board owe the positions they occupy to the Restoration Plea. True, if it had not been for the Restoration Plea, many of them might have been in other positions of influence and standing; nevertheless, they might not have had similar opportunities to have positions such as many of them occupy, be it in the ministry, in education, or in business categories, if it had not been for the Restoration Movement.

However, in taking the action the Board did and putting the Disciples of Christ Historical Society and its assets under the jurisdiction of a Delegate Convention, and committing the operation of this institution to a hierarchy or synod, the Board is reverting to the very type of organization from which our pioneers withdrew. It may be said that certain of the controls established in the Provisional Design may never be exercised, but nevertheless the mechanics are set up for them to be enforced; and there are very few organizations the leadership of which in time will not exert power to further their own aims, if they have authority to do so.

The perspicacity and analytical ability of those who voted for the resolution that was passed are most questionable and definitely show no perceptiveness, and I believe in many cases indicate a woeful lack of interest and total indifference to the funds, which probably none of them had any part whatever in donating; "for where your treasure is, there will your heart be also" certainly applies in this case. The action approved by nearly all members of this Board indicates that there is no significant appreciation of values by an individual, unless such values are the product of his own time and effort.

Your building bears the name of my sainted father. My father's worldly possessions were greatly overrated, due to his unusual liberality. However, my father and mother owed a great deal to the Restoration Plea, as there were times when they were very heavily burdened, but from early life they had from a logical viewpoint very great reverence for the Plea of our pioneers; and there is no question but that this sustained my father in keeping faith with this Plea during his lifetime. This has been definitely reflected in me. If he had been a member of some other religious body, he could not well have arrived at certain logical views which he held pertaining to religious matters. Now his testimony to "the faith once for all delivered" is marred if not completely distorted.

My experience with the Disciples of Christ Historical Society has utterly destroyed any incentive to pursue similar benevolences with other institutions of the Disciples which as a matter of fact I have done in at least two other instances and with which I have been grievously disappointed, as I am now with the situation at Nashville. These experiences show the frailties of human nature, when put to the test, and how little consideration is given by those who assume responsibility and accept positions of trust, but shirk their responsibility when the showdown comes.

The members of the Board of the Disciples of Christ Historical Society should have analyzed the problem as a personal situation and applied it to themselves individually, as though it were their own property for which they had provided the funds, in which case I am sure an entirely different action would have been taken. . . .

Regardless of the interpretation by some, that the Board of the Society will not be interferred with by the organization created by the Provisional Design; if the Disciples of Christ Historical Society could be considered the domicile of certain individuals on this Board, how many of them would be willing to do as they did, that is, turn the ultimate administration over to a much larger and less intimate Board, elected as proposed in the Provisional Design? It seems to me it is preposterous for any body of individuals to set up a hierarchy-devised organization for the divinely-created church founded in the first century.

The Provisional Design is, of course, a definite step toward the ultimate merger of the Brotherhood into the Ecumenical Church contemplated by the Consultation on Church Union. The *Principles of Church Union*, already approved by the delegates to the Consultation and unanimously accepted by the nine Disciple representatives to the Consultation, *requires* the use of both the Nicene and Apostles' Creeds, accepts the Doctrine of Apostolic Succession, as well as infant baptism and believer's baptism in *any form*.

I do not propose to contribute to or support in any way a church committed to these doctrines so alien to the faith and practice of the church established at Pentecost. In order that none of the assets of my estate following my demise may be so used, I have established by my Will a Charitable Trust, the principal of which will represent the largest sum by far ever given up to this time by anyone connected with the Restoration Movement. The assets of this Trust will be distributed by my Trustees: ". . . for the sole use and benefit of the churches, educational institutions, religious organizations and other institutions of the Disciples of Christ, the Church of Christ, and/or the Christian Church, which are advocates in no uncertain terms of the Restoration Plea and are opposed without equivocation to open membership."

THE CHURCHES OF CHRIST

One of Mr. Phillips' closest friends in the business world was Clinton Davidson, an investment banker in New York City. He

178

was often a guest at Elm Court. Mr. Davidson was a member of the Church of Christ, that particular branch of the Restoration Movement that prefers to worship without the use of instrumental music.

Mr. Davidson had studied, in Abilene Christian College, to be a minister when Dr. George A. Klingman was dean of its Bible school. Certain circumstances had changed the course of his life, but he maintained until his death his ardent commitment to the Restoration Plea. He and Mr. Phillips often discussed their common faith and they came to have a very close fellowship in religious matters of common concern.

Mr. Davidson greatly admired the book, *The Church of Christ*, written by Mr. Phillips' father. On one occasion Mr. Davidson wrote:

> How unfortunate it is that your Park Avenue Christian Church here, which claims to have inherited Alexander Campbell's "mantle" and whose building was largely financed by more loyal churches throughout the United States, could not have followed the clear and explicit writings of your father.

When Manhattan Church of Christ decided to build a house of worship in New York City, Mr. Davidson approached Mr. Phillips asking whether he would be willing to have fellowship in the project. Mr. Phillips immediately responded with a pledge of $50,000 and thereafter manifested a deep interest in the work of the congregation. When he and Mrs. Phillips visited New York City they often attended services there in preference to the Park Avenue Christian Church.

In writing to Dr. Lawrence V. Kirkpatrick, general secretary of the World Convention of Churches of Christ, about this time, Mr. Phillips said:

> We enjoyed having you with us at Elm Court Monday night and going over with you the work of the World Convention of Churches of Christ.
>
> I was glad to mention the pledge of $50,000 made just last week to the Manhattan Church of Christ to be located at Madison Avenue and 80th Street. Do make a point of contacting and spending a little time with Burton Coffman, pastor of this church, who has done a wonderful work the past ten or twelve years. It is almost unbelievable this church now owns free of debt the property of considerable size and frontage on Madison Avenue and 80th Street, costing $525,000; and this is not all, as there is a little over $500,000 in savings accounts in three different New York banks, which is to be used for a new church building. I am informed

this will be the first church to be erected in thirty years or more in a very large area centrally located in New York City. I made my pledge in order to get this building started, which is designed by a well-known New York architectural firm and the estimated cost of which will be $1,500,000. This pledge is an incentive for raising another $200,000 immediately, making a total of $750,000 which will make possible the starting of one-half of the proposed building in the next couple months.

Just compare this with the record made at our Park Avenue Church, which I understand has an indebtedness today of about $800,000. This church has been fiddling along with open membership for years and has gotten nowhere. As mentioned to you, the growing churches and institutions of our people are those which almost invariably are remaining true to the Restoration Plea and not countenancing open membership. Others which are not growing are in many cases embracing Unified Promotion, thereby enhancing and entrenching more than ever the hierarchical ecclesiasticism which has been notorious for many years, and which my brother and I seriously objected to before his death in January 1956. This has been nourished and nurtured at Indianapolis by people who owe their positions and standing to the efforts and sacrifices of our pioneers. However, many of these propagandists are doing their utmost to undermine the Restoration Plea and have us classified as merely another denomination or sect.

The pledge I have made probably will be paid this year and will give me a great deal of satisfaction, as for sometime I have felt the so-called "Church of Christ" branch deserves encouragement. It has so far outstripped us in membership in many parts of the country, in aggressiveness in new congregations, and in educational institutions, that we can hardly be seen for their dust. Some claim they are narrow and in many instances this probably is true, but their narrowness is far superior to our broadness. Their adherence to the New Testament has been most effective, as evidenced by the funds raised for the Manhattan Church of Christ.

It is high time for our people to wake up and realize that what is needed is Gospel preaching and evangelism, which is sadly missing in many of the churches, particularly those supporting Unified Promotion. This also applies to missionary work of our free churches, which is several times larger than that supported by Unified Promotion.

In a letter to Mr. Davidson, November 12, 1966, Mr. Phillips said:

For a long time I have felt there should be more cooperation between the Church of Christ, with which you are affiliated, and the conservative group in our Brotherhood. As a matter of fact, I am largely responsible for the Disciples of Christ Historical Society building at Nashville and to some extent the location at Nashville for this building. Frankly, when this was decided after I made a trip to Nashville, I felt that on account of the large membership of the Church of Christ in Nashville it was very desirable to have this building there; and in the future there would be much more cooperation with the Church of Christ. This had much to do in my willingness to underwrite this building at Nashville.

Furthermore, it was due not only to our personal acquaintanceship with you, but to certain other personal reasons, that both T. W., Jr., and I were, and I have been, interested in Camp Shiloh. Of course over and above all this is the way you conducted it, the type of campers you have had, and the Christian personnel of the camp.

Camp Shiloh was a unique Church of Christ project of considerable proportions which Mr. Davidson generously supported financially and to which he gave many hours of his time. It was located on a beautiful wooded tract of land near Mendham, New Jersey, surrounding a large lake. It was designed to minister especially to underprivileged children from the crowded ghettos of the great city.

Mr. Phillips visited Camp Shiloh on occasion and supported it generously, as witness the following excerpt from a letter to "Dear Clinton":

Confirming my conversation with you this morning, I will be pleased to contribute to the Mendham-Bernardsville Church of Christ $10,000 before the end of this year, $1,000 of which is to be used for expenses incurred in operating Camp Shiloh during the present year; and of the balance of $9,000, approximately $5,000 is to be used for scholarships to Harding College of the type you mentioned today, and the remainder of $4,000 is to be used for Camp Shiloh next year. Whether this is exactly $5,000 in one case and $4,000 in the other is a matter I will leave entirely to your judgment.

It may be necessary to furnish something more than merely scholarships for these students. In this day and age they should be at least reasonably well-outfitted with wearing apparel, even if they are attending Harding College by means of scholarships. In any event, I know you will use good judgment in this respect.

Through the years Mr. Phillips' philanthropic program often included other Church of Christ concerns. He at various times contributed to Harding College and other schools of these brethren. He was a liberal supporter of *The Voice of Freedom*, a periodical edited by L. R. Wilson, dedicated to informing the public about developments in the Roman Catholic world and inspiring his brethren to active support of the doctrine of separation of Church and State.

He looked forward to the day when divisive beliefs and practices he considered to be of secondary importance would be forgotten and when all those in the Restoration Movement committed to the great fundamental truths of the Scriptures would cooperate in carrying out the educational and evangelistic directives given the church by our Lord in the Great Commission. This he often made a matter of prayer.

X

Building for Tomorrow

Thoroughly disillusioned by the departures from original Restoration ideals on the part of Leftist elements in the Movement, B. D. Phillips came to a new awareness of the importance and significance of developments at its Center.

For many years he had put great faith in the leadership of the traditional agencies of the Movement—its conventions, its colleges, and its service institutions—but now that faith had been shattered. He did not, however, succumb to bitter pessimism or cynicism. He did not fall into the pit of classifying everybody as either openly bad or secretly bad or believing that all virtue and generosity and disinterestedness are merely the appearance of good, but selfish at heart. He was not indiscriminately critical of everybody and everything, voicing his views as a destructive frost on a garden of flowers. It would be folly, however, to pretend that Mr. Phillips ever fully recovered from the disappointments of his misplaced faith. Such wounds leave a scar. There were faces he could not look upon without emotion. There were names he could not hear spoken without starting up as from a bad dream. But he blamed himself more than others for having been misled into what he considered, in his later years, somewhat futile philanthropies. As he wrote to one college president, "When I make a mistake, I try not to make that same mistake twice."

As he resurveyed the Restoration Movement a new optimism was born in his heart. The conviction he had concerning the glorious future of the cause to which he had committed his life found new certainty as he became better acquainted with the leadership of the Center of the Movement. In the midst of widespread doubt and apostasy they were giving new emphasis to the Biblical principles set forth in Thomas Campbell's *Declaration and Address* and Isaac Errett's *Our Position*. They were advocating stronger commitment to the Holy Scriptures as divinely inspired, alone and all-sufficient as the revelation of the will of God for mankind and of Christ and His Gospel. They were boldly asserting that the basic pattern for the Church is revealed in the New Testament and that it is the duty of every faithful follower of Christ to restore and maintain that pattern. In the midst of a divided Christendom they were expressing a new concern for the unity of all Christians as one body in Christ. In this company there was no equivocation, no compromise; new churches were being organized, new conventions were being developed, new institutions were being created, new missions were being established around the world. Forgetting those things that were behind and trusting in the eternal promises of God, these brethren were pressing forward with new zeal to the things which are before and getting things done at an amazing rate. All this had a tremendous appeal to Mr. Phillips.

One of the first institutions of higher education to attract Mr. Phillips' special attention in this new era of his philanthropy was Milligan College. He had known of Milligan for many years and often recalled an occasion when he and his mother visited the school while Henry J. Derthick was its president. The roads to the campus were tortuous and muddy and the aspects of the institution that impressed him were its ministries to the mountain youth of east Tennessee and western North Carolina. The Phillips Family gave Milligan some support at that time, but nothing comparable to that given Bethany and Phillips.

With the changes taking place in Brotherhood life Mr. Phillips came to see Milligan in a new light. The institution was founded in 1882 by Josephus Hopwood, noted Southern educator, and had a long and distinguished regional history. Under Henry J. Derthick Milligan became nationally known, new buildings were constructed and the student body was enlarged. Hopwood and Derthick accounted for fifty-two years of its administrative guidance, a somewhat remarkable record for educational stability among the Disciples. For many years Milligan was noted for its loyalty to the evangelical, Biblical faith and the principles of the Restoration Movement. It did not succumb to the humanistic cultural trends so noticeable in the other liberal arts colleges and finally came to stand almost alone in its testimony in the higher educational life of the Brotherhood.

Then a new era came to Milligan. Dr. Dean E. Walker, who had served for years with marked distinction as professor of Church History in the College of Religion, at Butler University, became conscious of the liberal blight slowly but surely impregnating its faculty. He came to see that there was no future at Butler for an educator thoroughly committed to the authority of the Holy Scriptures and the divine plan for Christian unity. Providentially, at this time Dr. Walker was called to the presidency of Milligan College. He saw the call as an open door to the realization of his life-long dream of giving leadership to a new day of truly Christian higher education among the Disciples and accepted.

Dr. Walker's inaugural address stressed anew the well-nigh forgotten Campbellian educational ideas in the context of the modern world. So significant were his pronouncements for future policy at Milligan and in the enlistment of Mr. Phillips' interest, that we quote at length:

After a few remarks of definition, I shall attempt to develop a three-fold thesis. First, that Christian higher education has a distinct mission in the process of teaching and of curricula. Secondly, that a Christian College is the custodian of learning which possesses distinctive character and values. And thirdly, that these processes and this learning may be embodied in a program adequate for the danger and the opportunity we face.

Higher education today is undertaken through the university, through technical and professional schools, through research foundations, and through the college. All are essential. As distinct from the others, the college—product of a definite American idea—aims to qualify people for practical life in all occupations by teaching things basic to proficiency therein; and at the same time to provide people with ground for common understanding by teaching arts and sciences contributory to mental curiosity and sympathy. The college looks upon a man as educated when he knows how to do some useful work, provided that he distinguish the same

185

ability in others. He who works usefully, and senses a comradeship with others similarly engaged, is an educated man. The college exists to extend and intensify such knowledge. . . .

Now a Christian college accepts this aim. It adds another element, however, to the ends so defined. For the Christian college would add to education the facilities of becoming acquainted with God. Hence we arrive at a definition of Christian higher education as that process of equipping people with not only the knowledge necessary to be and to do, but the knowledge also to be constant and to act consistently in regard to truth, and to fraternity, under the judgment of God. This definition is neither narrow nor broad. It is rather foundational.

The service rendered to the State and to Society by a college operating under these aims is thus unique without being partial or sectarian. It is impartial, in that it includes the study of religion along with the study of the world and of mankind. It is non-sectarian, in that it imposes no religious disabilities upon its students, nor does it screen them on the basis of the religious experience and affiliation of their choice. The Christian college rejoices to see a Christian profession by its students. But it desires this profession to be the result of considered decision—a personal choice freely made upon the confrontation of the student with the Word of God. . . .

Dr. Walker next dealt with teaching and curricula. The studies to be offered were grouped under "liberal arts and sciences," pre-professional subjects, and religion. Of the latter he said:

In the third phase of the curricula, that related to religion, the Christian college makes its contribution not only in a manner unique, but in a field of learning largely un-considered by other institutions of higher education. This fact grows out of the practice of European universities. There the individual is not called upon to judge moral issues for himself, nor to arrive at his own faith. These things are done for him by the churches by law established, and furnished with police powers by the state. Study of the Bible is accordingly without point. The tragedy of American culture is that our schools have followed the European example without possessing a similar environment of control. Religion in America is free —and by "free" we mean that every man may avow or disavow faith without external pressures guiding his decision. So it has come about that higher education in America has regarded the data of religion as scarcely worth investigation except occasionally as a phase of curious human behavior.

The Christian college holds this to be a grave omission from the proper heritage belonging to the student. Not that the college is the Church. The Church propagates the faith. The college studies the faith. What are the grounds of faith? Has God spoken to men? If so, by whom? And to what purpose? Is there such a thing as Revelation as distinct from Discovery? Is God a Person, desiring to reconcile men to

Himself? And if a man refuse to hear God, what consequences issue from the refusal? If a man be a spirit, as Christians affirm, goes he alone into the abyss of death? Or is God his Companion familiar with the unseen land? Is spiritual life as real as economic or political life? These questions are not only practical, they are academic—they are subject to observation, investigation, analysis, organization and synthesis. They respond to intellectual scrutiny just as do the other aspects of learning with which education may concern itself.

Again let me illustrate my meaning by taking the example of the study of the Bible itself. It is good to study this collection of Scripture merely as literature, or as a datum of moral idealism, or as a record of one phase of human history. But such studies are peripheral, superficial, and in themselves without central value in education. They disclose much material of some use. They are not determinative of personality. Even the widely popular study of the Bible's possible origins in an earth-bound evolution contributes nothing to the rise of mankind—even if it could be shown that such theories may probably be true. For, you see, not even the most learned demonstrator of the human origin of the Bible has demonstrated his power to add another book or chapter to that ancient collection! Such learning is sterile.

Suppose, however, you study the Bible for its own message. What does it say? The message is really simple in its enveloping profundity. God loved, and lost; He grieves, and seeks His beloved; in that search God spared not His own Son, but freely gave Him up for us; and in the deliverance of His Son to the death of the Cross, God has spoken the last Word to a lost world—and that Word has found men and has turned men back to love God and to serve Him. In short, God has sought men by revealing Himself to men in the stream of human history. The man who has looked into the face of Jesus has seen God. Now as one reads this drama of human redemption in the Bible, a strange thing happens. The power of God leaps from the printed page into the heart of the student. For the moment there are no persons in the world but God and the student himself. As the intensity of this convention deepens, and its meaning clarifies, the shadows of life take form as realities. The world is peopled with other spirits—as precious to God as that of the student himself. Then the grace and truth of God are brought to light in the Presence of the beloved Son of God. And in the company of Jesus of Nazareth the student learns to love the least, and the last, and the lost. He becomes himself a son by adoption, and a brother to all the adopted.

You ask for peace and justice and righteousness and democracy on this earth? You will never see them until you heed the plea and example of the Christian college, and make the Bible a field of study. In this study one comes to grips with reality. This realm of experience called religion is the one in which the last battle against danger, ignorance, and superstition is being fought. . . . .

187

This was Mr. Phillips' philosophy of higher education and he reacted favorably and enthusiastically.

One of the first crucial problems faced by the new administration at Milligan was the provision of adequate library facilities. Accreditation in the South Central Association was at stake. The solution of this problem came about providentially. Mr. Phillips had been contemplating some kind of a suitable memorial to his longtime friend, Dr. P. H. Welshimer, pastor of the largest Christian Church in America, who had recently passed to his reward. He invited Mildred Welshimer, his daughter, then Dean of Women at Milligan, to visit Elm Court and discuss the matter with him. Mr. Phillips was impressed by the fact that the Welshimer family planned to give Dr. Welshimer's books to Milligan. He asked whether the library of the college was adequate to take care of all of them. He was told that they might have to be stored for a while. Then he suggested that he would like to have President Walker get in touch with him the next time he was in the Pittsburgh area. He said, "I am interested in doing something about that library." Entirely on his own initiative Mr. Phillips proposed financing the erection of a thoroughly adequate library building provided it be named "The P. H. Welshimer Memorial Library." Needless to say, his proposition was joyfully accepted by the college authorities.

The P. H. Welshimer Memorial Library, worth today more than a million dollars, provides open-stack services for over 100,000 books and more than 200 periodicals. Study stations for students are scattered liberally throughout the building. Individual carrels for reference work line the walls in the stack rooms. Special study rooms are provided for faculty members currently engaged in research and professional writing. There is a language laboratory with thirty listening stations. Audio-visual rooms provide use of motion pictures, slides, film strips, television, tape recordings, and radio. Soundproof listening rooms enable students to study music as recorded by the masters. Equipment for micro-card and microfilm study of rare books, original manuscripts, documents, and periodicals vastly expands the services rendered by the library. As this is written there are plans in the making for extensive additions to its facilities.

One feature of the building is that portion specifically dedicated to the memory of Dr. Welshimer. Ralph and Mildred Welshimer gave their father's personal library, his desk, his chair, and the furnishings of his office to be preserved for future generations. This area of the building is truly "holy ground" for those who knew this great Restoration leader. Mr. Phillips depended almost wholly upon Mildred for assembling and planning this feature of the building. During the construction period the two came to a realization that their beliefs, their hopes and fears for the Restoration Movement were one. Shortly after the dedication date they were married. Thus began a companionship which brought new joy and happiness to Elm Court and new hope and anticipation for the cause of higher education among Christian Churches and Churches of Christ. If ever a marriage was "born in Heaven," this was one, for God blessed their union in many ways to His glory.

When dedication day arrived Mr. Phillips consented to speak briefly, an unusual concession from a long-established habit of quiescence. He said:

In this day of so many distractions, we are prone to overlook those to whom we are indebted for many of the fundamental principles and influences of this remarkable country in which we live. Many of us credit England with most of our institutions. We are greatly indebted to the Netherlands for many institutions upon which the United States was founded and exists. The Netherlands and its influence brought about our Declaration of Independence, federal constitution, state constitutions, freedom of religion, freedom of press, public schools and equal education for boys and girls, the written ballot, town and country systems of government, system of recording deeds and mortgages, the common practice of allowing prisoners the free services of lawyers for their defense, and the custom of equal distribution of property among the children of a person dying intestate.

We overlook the fact that the early influences which fashioned American life were largely brought direct from the Netherlands in the lives of the early settlers. The men who founded New York were chiefly from the Netherlands. The Pilgrims who settled Plymouth had lived eleven years in the Netherlands. The Puritans who also settled in Massachusetts had all their lives been exposed to the Dutch influence. New Jersey, as well as New York, was settled by the Dutch West India Company. Roger Williams was a Dutch scholar.

These are a few of the facts that influenced the development of this country. The English are commonly given credit for many of these institutions. I have often thought that if in this country the universal language were Dutch, instead of English, we would recognize the Netherlands' influences in this country to a much greater extent.

Now turning to religious influences, many of us are prone to overlook the tremendous influence the Restoration Plea has had on Protestantism in this country. The Campbells, through the Declaration and Address, and the subsequent rise of our movement, established throughout the Protestant world the idea that the Church of Christ on earth is essentially, intentionally, and constitutionally one. There was only one church in the Mind of Christ and in the records of the New Testament. Our Restoration Movement has been unique in proposing a union of Christian people on the basis of the New Testament, rather than a union of sovereign denominations.

American Protestant bodies have been greatly influenced by the Restoration Plea idea that the theological agreement stated in some creed is not essential for cooperation. This derives from our maxim, "In essentials, unity—in non-essentials, liberty—in all things, charity."

Our Movement has greatly reduced the magical idea of infant baptism as essential to the salvation of innocent children, and our strong witness for immersion baptism has carried substantial weight and brought a new interpretation which American Protestantism has otherwise overlooked.

We of this great country owe a great deal to the advances that were initiated by the Netherlands; just as Protestantism is greatly indebted to the Restoration Plea and to the Campbells, Scott, and Stone, who were the pioneers in our Movement.

I am pleased to represent the Phillips Family in the dedication of this library today. Especially are we honored to have housed in this library the books and manuscripts of P. H. Welshimer, who richly deserved having this building named for him; and who, I believe, was without question the leader of the Restoration Plea for the many years when at the peak of his ministry in Canton, Ohio.

Our hope is that this building with the name it bears will be used to the utmost in fostering the New Testament Church that was established on Pentecost, and in getting back to First Principles, as advocated by the Campbells, Scott, and Stone; and subsequently by P. H. Welshimer in one of the most effective, perhaps the most effective, ministry of any of the Restoration advocates, since the days of the four pioneers mentioned.

Mr. Phillips' growing interest in the future of Milligan College is best symbolized in the great Chapel which his generosity made possible. It is today worth some two million dollars and is said to be the finest chapel building ever erected for any college or university of the Restoration Movement. It does not bear his name but his concern marks every stone, every brick, and every window. Since it was the last of all such gifts made and completed in his lifetime, it seems fitting to describe it in some detail.

In size, in design, in materials, in workmanship, and in function the Memorial Chapel is a building of excellence.

190

In size the Chapel is the largest structure of its kind in East Tennessee with 31,000 square feet of floor space. Its dimensions are 177 feet in length and 76 feet in width. At the roof ridge it is 57 feet above the ground level; at the top of the spire it is 169 feet above the ground level.

The two auditoriums are spacious: the auditorium-sanctuary will accommodate 1,300 persons; the auditorium in the undercroft will seat 350.

On the first level the entrance floors are of natural slate; the base is of marble (Vermont Verde Antique); the treads and risers for the stairways are of marble (Lido, quarried in Morocco); the stair railings are of bronze and steel; and, the doors, frames, and trim are of Appalachian white oak.

In the auditorium-sanctuary the Appalachian white oak has again been used in the base, wainscoting, and trim. Red oak plank flooring—with wooden pegs—are used in the sanctuary floor and the stage floor. The pews are of white oak with padded opera chair seats. Marble (Ozark Rouge) has been used in the window stools. Marble (Lido) with inlaid carpet runner has been used in the treads and risers of the spiral stairs to the balcony.

The baptistery facing is of Rose Espanel marble. The interior of the baptistery employs two grades of marble: Italian Creme and Alabama Creme A.

The lighting is unique. The sanctuary chandeliers are of imported Flemish brass—antique brass finish—imported from Belgium. They are of original design following the Georgian colonial pattern. The chandelier in the tower vestibule is an authentic Williamsburg reproduction. All of the bracket lights and chandeliers used elsewhere in the building are designed to be compatible with the sanctuary chandeliers.

The tower and spire are a thing of beauty and can be seen for several miles from the campus. It is of steel frame construction with brick and limestone facing. The tower houses one section of the air conditioning system equipment and has provision for a future 50-unit, cast bell carillon and the installation of a manual clavier. The tower also supports a twelve-foot high bronze cross —weighing approximately one ton—designed on a Celtic cross theme.

A distinctive feature of the Chapel is that symbolic art has been successfully employed in the Colonial design of the building.

Circling the main auditorium—where the main wall meets the ceiling—is an endless golden cord, symbolizing the eternal wisdom, goodness, and love of God. The upper windows on the East portray events from the era of the patriarchs and the law; on the West representative events from the New Testament are recorded. Each window below the balcony designates one of the twelve Apostles.

The Chapel has many functions and serves many purposes—worship, lecture, concerts, drama, and instruction.

The architects have designed with an eye for both beauty and function. The contractors and sub-contractors have displayed the finest skill in their workmanship. A building of excellence, it will stand for centuries.

At the dedication of the Chapel Mr. Phillips again consented to make some extended remarks. He said:

I appear on this program today with a keen sense of honor, combined with gratitude and responsibility.

Honor on account of this Chapel to be used by both Milligan College and Emmanuel School of Religion;

Gratitude due to the fact there is at this location a building that is worthy of the name it bears and which represents the Movement of our pioneers who had to do with the restoration of the church founded at Pentecost and described in the Book of Acts and the Epistles;

Responsibility due to the participation of the Phillips Family for over a hundred years in perpetuating the Plea of the pioneers of the Movement.

There never has been a time in the history of our people, when an institution, such as is represented at Milligan College and Emmanuel School of Religion, has had more opportunity, so to speak, "to hold the fort" and remain free from human-made organizations and ecclesiasticisms that presently are tempting many of our churches.

These two institutions have an opportunity that occurs not in a lifetime, but in a century, to make their influence felt to a much greater degree in the restoration of the first century church than has ever before occurred to a similar extent in the lifetime of anyone present. A graduate of either one of these institutions should be looked upon as one bearing the hallmark of the Restoration Plea that was propounded and proclaimed by Thomas and Alexander Campbell, Walter Scott, and Barton W. Stone, whose teachings were continued so outstandingly by Isaac Errett, P. H. Welshimer, and W. R. Walker, and now by Dean E. Walker.

These institutions should be supported at this time and under present conditions to a greater extent than the followers of the Restoration Movement have ever done with any other educational institution. These two institutions are considered by many to be two of the outstanding exponents of the Restoration Plea, and I believe funds can be raised promptly in

192

P. H. Welshimer Memorial Library, Milligan College

Memorial Chapel, Milligan College

Memorial Library, Johnson Bible College

Alexander Campbell Auditorium, Culver-Stockton College

College Chapel, Lincoln Christian College

Restoration Hall, Lincoln Christian College

Mountain Mission School, Grundy, Virginia

Entrance to Restoration Hall, Lincoln Christian College

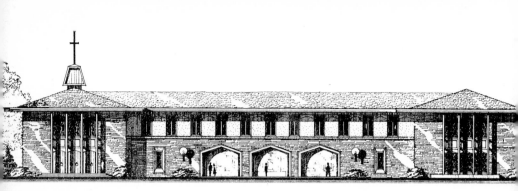

Tentative Architect's Sketch, B. D. Phillips Memorial Quadrangle
Emmanuel School of Religion

Crouch Memorial Library, Cincinnati Bible Seminary

(Left) Dr. and Mrs. J. D. Murch, (Right) Mr. and Mrs. B. D. Phillips and Dr. Perry Gresham
Services Commemorating the 100th Anniversary of the Death of Alexander Campbell

Site of Brush Run Church, Near Bethany College

Site of Baptismal Pool, Brush Run Church

T.W. PHILLIPS GAS AND OIL COMPANY

BUTLER, PA.

B. D. PHILLIPS
PRESIDENT
B. D. PHILLIPS, JR.
VICE PRESIDENT
V. K. PHILLIPS
VICE PRESIDENT
L. J. CHAMBERLAIN
SECRETARY
D. C. PHILLIPS
TREASURER

March 29, 1966

Dr. James DeForest Murch
4711 Trent Court
Chevy Chase 15, Maryland

Dear Dr. Murch:

I have your letter of March 25 and wish to thank you for the summary you have given, touching upon several topics.

I note with much interest the influence you have exerted regarding some of the foreign conferences.

I am particularly pleased with the progress that apparently is being made at Nashville in connection with the Christian Standard Indexing Project. In many respects I believe this is the most significant situation and is of more far-reaching effect than perhaps anything else we have underwritten the past few years.

I am very willing for you and Rollie to work out whatever you think desirable in connection with visits to Nashville from time to time in regard to the indexing. Any time you have suggestions to make, please feel free to do so, but send to Rollie copies of whatever letters you write to me.

With kind regards to both you and Mrs. Murch, I remain

Sincerely,

B. D. Phillips

hk

cc: Rolland L. Ehrman

Facsimile Copy of a Typical B. D. Phillips Letter

sufficient amount to place Milligan College and Emmanuel School of Religion in such sound financial condition that their standing will be maintained and they will be looked upon as beacon lights of the Restoration Plea.

However, this will be true only if the greatest care is given to selecting board members who, without exception, will place those of like belief in all executive positions. Furthermore, when an individual is to become a member of the faculty, it will be an extremely exceptional case, if he is not thoroughly in accord with our Plea and with the board and the other faculty members.

My hope and prayer are that in the next 25, 50, or 100 years, no one will have cause to look back at the record established here and question the integrity of those responsible for this record, or their strict adherence to the principles that brought about the beginning of our Movement. I am of the opinion that very few of those within the sound of my voice realize the tremendous possibilities thrust upon us by these institutions.

Through the changing years Milligan has found itself in an increasingly cosmopolitan industrial and cultural area in Eastern Tennessee. Indeed, the "Tri-City" complex of Bristol, Kingsport, and Johnson City together with numerous suburban towns is a center of growing importance not only to Tennessee, but Virginia and North Carolina. As far as Christian Churches and Churches of Christ are concerned the area includes many large and influential churches. Milligan's importance to them is shared with hundreds of other churches in states from the Mississippi River to the Atlantic Coast. The institution now has a strategic position from which its ever-enlarging influence radiates to the whole Brotherhood.

Out of the new era at Milligan came the dream of a fully-accredited graduate theological seminary. There was a strong "Bible Department" in the college and had been for years. Over a considerable period of time courses had been offered in Old Testament, New Testament, Life and Teachings of Jesus, Church History, the Restoration Movement, Psychology of Religion and Religious Education. Such courses presented a practical approach to religion but the curriculum was not designed specifically to train young men for the ministry. There was a growing need for a graduate school of religion that would be fully accredited and produce a ministry fully qualified according to the highest standards of excellence. Exploratory studies were undertaken under the direction of President Walker, following the accepted patterns

193

of the American Association of Theological Schools, with the result that the "Emmanuel School of Religion" was organized in 1961, becoming operative in 1965. Some of the most outstanding scholars in the Brotherhood were called to the faculty. It was found that such an institution could not be an integral part of Milligan College because of strict rules of accreditation, but by special dispensation of the accrediting associations the use of some members of the Milligan faculty and its classroom facilities was permitted for a limited time.

Mr. Phillips was interested in this development from the beginning and gave it his generous support. So favorable was the reception accorded the school that the projected student enrollment for the first few years was greatly exceeded. As the time approached for complete separation from Milligan, many serious problems arose. A new campus, new buildings, and additional full-time professors had to be provided if accreditation was to be assured. One of the last acts of Mr. Phillips was to promise the underwriting of this immense undertaking. Without his favorable decision the dream of Emmanuel School of Religion would never have been realized.

Now the spacious Hopwood Campus has been acquired, architectural plans for the first building are on the boards and construction will start soon. By decision of the Board of Trustees and with the consent of the Phillips Family this structure will bear the name of Benjamin Dwight Phillips—the first building of the many he has given to be so designated. Other structures are planned for what will eventually be one of the best-equipped seminaries of the Christian Churches and Churches of Christ for the graduate training of men and women for full-time Christian ministries. Preministerial undergraduate work can be done at Milligan College or other accredited colleges, and specialized courses leading to master's and doctor's degrees will be offered in Emmanuel.

Also in Eastern Tennessee there is another school which refused to follow the liberal, humanistic trends in Disciples' higher education. It was founded in 1893 by Ashley S. Johnson at Kimberlin Heights (suburban to Knoxville) under the nomen "School of the Evangelists." It was intended to be a training center where capable young men could earn their own way while learning to be ministers of Christ. It laid great stress on the necessity of a practical knowledge and use of the Bible in an evangelistic

194

ministry. The Phillips Family had encouraged the institution, later named Johnson Bible College, with gifts from time to time. Under the presidency of R. M. Bell, JBC had achieved high attainments in scholarship, new buildings and equipment, and in favor with the loyal churches of the Brotherhood. B. D. Phillips was intrigued with the possibilities of further development, visited the campus on a number of occasions and began to give generously to various projects. His largest gift was to a new library. Though it bears the name of another it was his philanthropy which made possible its erection and the quality of its service.

One of the most important reactions against the liberal take-over of Disciples' colleges was the "Bible College" movement. In Chapters VII and VIII allusions have been made to this signifi-cant development. At first, it did not have much of an appeal to Mr. Phillips because of its break with the old liberal-arts-college traditions. But as he studied the movement he began to see it as essential if the Brotherhood educational emergency were to be met speedily and pragmatically.

Cincinnati Bible Seminary early assumed leadership (1924) in the movement, followed by Minnesota Bible College, Manhattan Bible College, Atlanta Christian College, Pacific Christian College, San Jose Bible College, Ozark Bible College, Lincoln Christian College, Kentucky Christian College, and many others, until today there are some thirty institutions of varying size and quality serving in this field. They have an enrollment of over 4,000 young men and women studying to fit themselves for full-time Christian service. If it had not been for this development loyal churches would have experienced a generation gap without a committed leadership true to the Bible and to the Restoration Plea.

The leading Bible colleges, members of the Accrediting Association of Bible Colleges (AABC), have certain minimum educational requirements. Thirty to forty hours of Bible and theology constitute the core of the curriculum. Basic subjects in English, history, and natural sciences, generally included in liberal arts college courses, are required. Other subjects from the human-ities and social sciences are recommended. These include intro-ductory and historical studies in philosophy, logic, ethics, psychol-ogy, sociology, economics, political science, and ancient and mod-ern languages. In the fine arts, music is a requirement in all the

195

schools.   Professional studies and activities fit students for specialized services.

Back of this program is a very definite philosophy of education, something that is almost totally absent from the modern secular church-related colleges.   The final criterion for a unifying philosophy must be revealed biblical Christian truth, not expediency.   It allows for breadth by cultural studies in the humanities and has room for both the social and natural sciences.   It seeks to orient the student theistically in the important areas of human knowledge. It seeks to coordinate history and science with revealed truth and thus to bridge the gap between secular and sacred learning.   In a word, general education in the Bible college makes for orientation, integration, and unity.   Finally, the Bible college puts its main emphasis on direct Bible study.   Believing that the first-hand study of the Holy Scriptures is the most effective means of teaching the Christian view, the Bible college holds that in the total scale of educational values, such study is the most rewarding.

Most of the graduates from the Bible colleges go immediately into service in the special field for which they have been trained— the local-church ministry, evangelism, teaching, Christian education, missions, and social work.   Others continue their studies in graduate schools.   Two institutions have graduate schools of their own.   Despite the problems involved they are not essentially different from those which are being successfully met by teachers colleges where both undergraduate and graduate education are offered in a special field.

It was not long before Mr. Phillips became enthusiastic about the tremendous accomplishments of the Bible colleges and their immense potential for the future of the Restoration Movement. Elm Court extended its hospitality to many Bible college presidents and professors as he sought to learn more about the institutions they represented.   He and Mrs. Phillips journeyed from coast to coast to see for themselves the quality of the educational work being done, the business and administrative methods employed, the service being rendered the churches, and the prospects for future development.

Mr. Phillips was greatly impressed by the work being done by President Earl C. Hargrove and his associates at Lincoln Christian College at Lincoln, Illinois. Illinois had been one of the leading states in the growth of the Restoration Movement but in the 1940's losses in churches and membership indicated that all was not well. Liberal influences from the Disciples' Divinity School at the University of Chicago had spread like a blight to Eureka College which had for many years produced most of the ministers occupying Illinois pulpits. Earl Hargrove was minister of First Church, Lincoln, one of the largest in the state. He saw the situation and attempted to help the cause by training young men along lines similar to those employed in the old Phillips Bible Institute in Canton. "Lincoln Bible Institute" was organized "on a shoestring" but with great faith in the promises of God. The school soon outgrew its quarters. Hargrove resigned his pulpit to give full time to the presidency. A large acreage was purchased at the edge of the city, several functional buildings were erected, the vision grew. "Lincoln Christian College" came into being with an outstanding faculty. Soon a new sound, well-prepared ministry was bringing new life to Illinois churches. The institution was becoming national in character. Enrollment moved up to nearly 800. When Mr. Phillips saw what had been done he equated the accomplishment of Hargrove with that of his old friend P. H. Welshimer of Canton and was ready to render generous aid.

A $500,000 home for the graduate school, Restoration Hall, was largely the gift of Mr. Phillips. Its functional edifice houses a library, assembly hall, classrooms, offices, and conference rooms. Then came a generous contribution which is making possible the erection of a million-dollar Chapel which will house the spiritual life center of the college.

Mr. Phillips became greatly interested in the work of Cincinnati Bible Seminary when he visited its campus and the sessions of its annual Conference on Evangelism at the invitation of President Woodrow Perry. He saw the thousands of ministers and church leaders with their deep concern for the advance of "the faith once for all delivered" and rejoiced in this manifestation of hope for the future of the Restoration. At this time the officials of the Seminary were engaged in raising the necessary funds to start construction on the new Edwin G. Crouch Memorial Library and Graduate School building. He was shown the site, on Price Hill overlooking the Mill Creek Valley in the heart of Cincinnati, and immediately indicated that he would be glad to have fellowship in the $500,000 project. His decision became the turning point in construction plans. Dr. R. C. Foster in his dedication address one and one-half years later said, "The $50,000 gift of B. D. Phillips and his insistence that work on this building be begun immediately gave the impetus to the start of its erection. The soundness of his business judgment has been fully established. It was his gift and his insistence on an immediate beginning of the work which enabled us to edge in ahead of a new inflation spiral which would have cost us a great deal more in construction expense." This incident is but one example of the new spirit of encouragement he was able to inject into the life and program of many educational institutions across the nation.

Manhattan Bible College, located ideally on a campus contiguous to that of the great Kansas State University at Manhattan, Kansas, impressed Mr. Phillips because of the high quality of instruction maintained and the uniqueness of its curricular structure. Under the leadership of President W. F. Lown, a frequent visitor to Elm Court, close relationships were established with the University which made it possible for students in MBC to do extra years' work in the University and receive accredited degrees. Thus all Christian youth, whether preparing for full-time Christian service or not, might have the benefits of a thorough Christian education. While special emphasis is given to preparation for the preaching and educational ministries, the curriculum is such as to provide basic instruction for business and the professions. Many MBC graduates go forth from its halls to become lay leaders in local churches. Mr. Phillips made several generous gifts to Manhattan and took a deep interest in its future development.

He visited Ozark Bible College, Joplin, Missouri, during the transfer of operations from a limited downtown location to a broad and beautiful acreage at the edge of the city. This expansion program delighted his heart. Again he had a feeling that a new day was dawning in the educational life of the Brotherhood. But the muddy roads and the debris of construction irked him. He impulsively turned to President Don Earl Boatman and said, "Build the necessary campus roads and I will pay the bill." On seeing the great new Auditorium, he asked about plans for the organ. Learning that the installation of this feature of the structure would have to be provided much later on account of the expense, he arranged for one of the finest pipe organs in any of the colleges to be built at Ozark. His interest in this school, now enrolling around

198

800 students studying for full-time Christian service, continued to his dying day.

In 1967 the Phillipses visited the Pacific coastal area. It was the first time in many years that Mr. Phillips had seen the western country which had such an appeal to him as a boy (page 16). He was greatly impressed with California which was fast assuming leadership of all the states of the nation in population, political influence, and industrial and economic development. He rejoiced to see rapid growth of the so-called "independent" Christian Churches and Churches of Christ. Pacific Christian College at Long Beach gave him a testimonial dinner. He was inspired by the quality of its faculty and student body, and particularly by its loyalty to the Restoration Movement. As a result of his visit he made a generous contribution toward the purchase of additional property to secure PCC's ideal location fronting the Long Beach Municipal Golf Course and within a short distance of the campus of burgeoning Long Beach State College. Mr. Phillips also expressed great interest in the work being done by Pepperdine College, an institution serving the Churches of Christ (non-instrument) in the Los Angeles area.

In the center of Appalachia Mr. Phillips found a new appeal to his philanthropic heart—the Mountain Mission School at Grundy, Virginia. This institution was established because of the vision and concern of Sam Hurley, a lay preacher among the Christian Churches of Virginia who saw hundreds of orphans, in abandoned coal-mining communities and under-privileged areas of the mountains, left without homes, moral and religious disciplines and the opportunity to get adequate education. He began a combination children's home and school largely on faith. Response and support from the churches were meager, but gradually the social conscience of churches in many states was aroused and the work began to prosper. Mrs. Phillips' mother, Mrs. P. H. Welshimer, was one of Grundy's most enthusiastic supporters. It was this personal concern that caused Mr. and Mrs. Phillips to undertake a journey to Appalachia. Theirs was a unique experience. They saw conditions that stirred their hearts. Mr. Phillips immediately promised to help provide what the directors of the institution had long desired—a thoroughly modern and adequate school facility. Today its splendid chapel, classrooms, and administrative offices are a great blessing. Grundy is now one of the finest private benevolent and educational agencies operating in this area. Its future is assured.

As B. D. Phillips contemplated the future of higher education among the reborn Christian Churches and Churches of Christ he determined that he would make a gift larger than any he had ever made to underwrite the development of their schools and colleges. As he confided this decision to his family and intimate friends they were amazed at this evidence of his high sense of Christian stewardship. When he indicated something of the size of the immense sum he had in mind, it was evident that this would constitute the largest gift ever made by any person or group of persons in the entire history of the Restoration Movement. He immediately went into consultation with his attorneys and proceeded to set up what is now known as the B. D. Phillips Charitable Trust to become operative at his death. His will specifies its use in no uncertain terms:

> The income of the Charitable Trust shall be held and distributed by the trustees for the sole use and benefit of the churches, educational institutions, and religious organizations of the Christian Churches and for Churches of Christ which are advocates in no uncertain terms of the Restoration plea and are opposed without equivocation to open-membership.

Mr. Phillips' concern for the future of the Restoration Movement extended beyond its schools and colleges. For example, he became greatly interested in the North American Christian Convention. It had its beginnings in 1926 when many brethren felt they could no longer endorse the leftward theological and ecclesiastical tendencies of the old International Convention and the United Christian Missionary Society. The gathering proposed to be a mass-meeting of "believers in Christ," not a denominational assembly. No form of rationalism, unitarianism, or unbelief was to be expressed from the platform. Principles, rather than causes or agencies, would be represented. It would provide conferences for elders and deacons, Bible school officers and teachers, and workshops where the best methods of doing church work would be discussed. Great sermons would be heard on the deity of Christ, the integrity of the Scriptures, the Church, Christian evangelism, Christian education, the Restoration Movement, and Christian unity. There would be no resolutions, no business sessions, no agency or convention promotion, no bitterness, no wrangling, or protesting.

200

Its constituents would go back to their homes and their churches pledged to greater loyalty to Christ, His Gospel, and His Church.

The NACC has grown through the years until it is now probably the largest religious convention in America. Today it will number around twenty to twenty-five thousand in registrations. When Mr. Phillips attended his first "North American" in 1964, he was thrilled by its magnitude, simplicity, loyalty, and power. He never missed one thereafter. Here he saw tremendous potential for the future of "the Plea." He was offered the presidency of the Convention but declined it because he felt someone else with more physical energy and free time should be in leadership. In 1968, however, he consented to become Vice-President. That year he never missed a meeting of the Executive Committee or the Committee of One Hundred and took an active part in all the proceedings. His advice was always well received to the profit of all concerned. He presided at one of the major sessions in the great new Cincinnati Convention Center and conducted it with such businesslike precision and keen understanding of its purpose that it was the subject of wide and favorable comment. He said of the experience, "It was one of the mountaintop moments of my religious experience." In Cincinnati, as well as at every other NACC convention, he engaged a suite of rooms with a parlor where friends could come and talk and where small groups could meet for dialogue on Brotherhood matters of importance. As he was packing in his Netherland-Hilton hotel suite, getting ready to go back to Butler, he remarked to Mrs. Phillips, "I wish the next convention would be in six months from now instead of a year." One wonders whether he then had a premonition that he would not be physically able to be present for the next great gathering in Cobo Hall, Detroit, in 1969.

Many hours of his precious time were devoted to conferences with leaders on ways and means of extending the Restoration cause. He was interested in the possibilities of developing a world fellowship through the instrumentality of the World Convention of Churches of Christ. He attended the 1965 convention in San Juan, Puerto Rico, but came home before it ended because he was distressed with certain trends. He spent many hours with men like M. Norvel Young and William S. Banowsky of the Churches of Christ (non-instrument) in the hope that eventual unity would come among all those who are committed to the Restoration ideal.

He sought to be helpful in improving the journalism of the Brotherhood and was deeply interested in the project for indexing the *Christian Standard* (page 114). He saw the value of preserving the classic literature of the Restoration Movement and disseminating it in areas where it would do the most good. At one time he was ready to underwrite such a program. Elm Court's doors were wide open to all who sought unselfishly to promote the Restoration cause. There was no subject on which he liked more to think and to talk. Whenever he felt a proposition was worthy and of real importance he was glad to participate in a practical way.

October 23, 1968 was a day like other days at Elm Court. There were prayers and breakfast. The day's agenda was agreed upon. On the agenda this day was an annual event. For years Mr. Phillips had made it a point to visit his sister, Grace Phillips Johnson, at her home in New Castle and bid her a fond farewell before she left for her winter's stay at her Orlando, Florida, estate. Otherwise, there was "business as usual." This involved his vigorous morning "constitutional." Despite Mr. Phillips' 82 years he thoroughly enjoyed the long, brisk walk from Elm Court to his downtown office, weather permitting. This morning he negotiated the considerable distance without fatigue. He went through his mail with his secretary. He surveyed the boards which told him the status of his two thousand gas wells and dealt with the problems involved. He conferred with his key men and made important decisions in a number of important matters. Then after lunch he got out his trusty Studebaker, called for his wife and they set forth for New Castle. He drove the considerable distance as usual without incident. As was his custom when visiting New Castle on week-days he stopped for a few minutes at the Citizen's National Bank, on whose board he had served for so many years.

When he arrived at his sister's he complained about an uneasiness in his stomach and asked to lie down for awhile. Later he seemed to be his usual self, and joined in discussion of domestic matters and, of course, considerable conversation about the Church and his latest projects for the extension of the cause of Christian education. Meanwhile Mrs. Phillips had phoned the Ehrmans at Butler and suggested they better come to New Castle so someone could drive the Studebaker back home. When they arrived, Mr. Phillips said he was feeling so much better that this was not really necessary. After fond farewells and brotherly admonitions he drove to Butler.

Arriving at Elm Court the Phillipses ate a light dinner. They read the evening paper in the sun room and talked a bit. Mrs. Phillips told her husband that she had decided not to go to Milligan College for the meeting of the Board of Trustees next day. He protested that he was feeling much better and that she should wait until morning before making her final decision. She replied, "No, I would not even think of going. You are worth more to me than all the college board meetings in the world." Then he walked to a couch, took off his coat, carefully hung it on the back of a chair and laid down. In two minutes, without warning, he breathed deeply and all was quiet. Mildred was shocked, immediately came to his aid, called physicians and his children, but it was too late. After a day of "business as usual" Benjamin Dwight Phillips had passed to his reward.

With apologies to William Cullen Bryant, we can say:

He had "so lived that, when his summons came to join
    The innumerable caravan which moves
To that mysterious realm where each of us must go. . . ."
    He was "sustained by an unfaltering trust" and
Went to his reward "like one who wraps the drapery of his couch
    About him and lies down to pleasant dreams."

We can appropriately imagine his confrontation with his Lord in the context of what happened to another successful businessman called to give an accounting:

So he that received the five talents came and brought other five talents, saying, Lord, thou deliveredst unto me five talents: behold I have gained beside them five talents more. And his Lord said unto him, Well done, thou good and faithful servant: thou hast been faithful over a few things, I will make thee ruler over many things: enter thou into the joy of thy Lord. (The Parable of the Talents, Matthew 25:20, 21.)

MEMORABILIA

Memorial Services

THE MEMORIAL SERVICE
BENJAMIN DWIGHT PHILLIPS

NORTH STREET CHRISTIAN CHURCH
BUTLER, PENNSYLVANIA

Saturday Afternoon, October 26, 1968

As hundreds of Mr. Phillips' Family, relatives, friends, and associates gathered in the beautiful sanctuary to pay their last respects, the organist played a repertoire of the Christian hymns he loved.

At the appointed hour, Dr. Wilbur A. Reid, minister of the North Street Church, made the following introductory statement:

We have gathered here today as members of the family and friends to pay our tribute of respect to Mr. Benjamin D. Phillips, Sr., known familiarly to most of us as "B. D." His humility allowed his many friends to speak to him in this very familiar manner.

Mr. Phillips shared generously of his wealth with many of our educational institutions. Sharing with me in this service is Dr. Wilfred Lown, President of Manhattan Bible College. He will speak his word of tribute for Mr. Phillips in behalf of the schools Mr. Phillips has helped. Sitting before me are most of the presidents of the colleges that Mr. Phillips has helped. They are honorary pallbearers.

One of Mr. Phillips' grandsons, Phil Weigand, will speak for the family, their words of appreciation for him.

Dr. Perry Gresham, for many years President of Bethany College, will lead our hearts before the throne of God in prayer.

Following these appearances I shall bring the message of the hour.

209

DR. W. F. LOWN

I *knew* a man—resolute and kind, severe and warm. The sun of many summers he had known. The snows of many winters had his forelock turned to snowy white, and with the richness had deposited the loam of wisdom's fertile potent, so that paths of many sought his sage injunction.

Of good stock he came, and good stock was he, and good stock did he beget. His dear ones gave him reverence, and their love.

Disciplined—twice disciplined, by self and Holy Writ. His fellows' best was his anticipation. Of himself, no less was his commitment. And determined. Self he gave unstintingly to task till all was done, then quickly slipped away through corridor of "sleep" to readied palace where anticipates the King.

He spoke of death, that leveler of all breeds, and stern of jaw he faced into its wintry blast—but not alone! In cadence strict he marched beside Another.

I *know* a man—in recollection's pensiveness, yet more, for he beside me shares the pilgrimage. From "serried ranks" he beams encouragement, probes with maxim past recited. His reason chides me, and in the controversy I am enriched—and bettered.

He bemingled caution and philanthropy on yestermorn, and now above it, though dead, still speaks in endless Godsend through the Cause of Christ.

Insistent on my ear his allegiance to antiquity. "Restore," he cries to us who carry on, "Restore His sacred body. Have patience with no alternate nor substitute. The body's His, and He will have His way in those who bear a part. Hold high the Guide!"

I know that man today.

I *shall know* a man—tomorrow, and tomorrow, and tomorrow. And we shall roam the plains of glory, changed you may be sure, and like to Him who is the Lord. And we shall see Him! Hallelujah, we shall see Him! And then recall our days of talk on earth where little things then said and done composed a portion of the great mosaic now displayed.

We may recount that time then was, but now has given way to endless ecstasy. That sin and death beset the sons of men, but now the cheers of victory shunt them back into the shadows.

Yes, I shall know him. And we shall know HIM! And other loves, and other worlds shall dim away.

210

MR. PHILLIPS WEIGAND

On behalf of the children and grandchildren of B. D. Phillips, my grandfather, I now speak. The *Bible* tells us in Psalm 127, verse 3: "Lo, children are an heritage of the Lord." Children are a gift of God. As one looks at the wonderful family of my grandfather, he sees that he was richly blessed by the Lord. He has left behind his beloved wife, Mildred. He has left behind his three sons and his three daughters and many of us, his grandchildren. Surely, his memory will not die while we remain in this world.

Grandfather Phillips successfully started and carried on both business and Christian Church endeavors, and in both of these he was highly successful. What an example he has set for us!

He honored his mother and father, and he honored his God by carrying on their spiritual heritage. This is the heritage that has been left to us, his grandchildren and his children, both earthly and spiritual. It is up to us since each of us is individually responsible for carrying on in a way that will be pleasing in the sight of our Lord. This is not the end; this actually is a beginning. It is a new beginning—the beginning of a new era and a continuation of a great work that was started by our grandfather and father.

Much on the mind of our grandfather was the spiritual condition of the souls of his children and his grandchildren. Each one of us has been so richly blessed in every way, and we are responsible—we are individually responsible—to serve our Lord and Saviour, Jesus Christ, with everything that we have.

Of major concern to my grandfather was that each one of us should come to have a saving and believing knowledge of the Lord Jesus Christ in our hearts and to establish a relationship—a living relationship—with our Lord and Saviour, for without this there is no eternal salvation for our souls. This is the way we prepare for death.

This was grandfather's great hope and prayer for each one of us. This is the most wonderful heritage that he could leave to each of us. As grandchildren and children, we owe so much to a very great man. Let us honor him and his memory in the days ahead by continuing in the great and wonderful works that he has started and left to us.

Let us pray. Father in Heaven, in the days ahead help each one of us, the children and grandchildren of B. D. Phillips, to spiritually discern what Your will is for us. In the name of Jesus Christ we pray. Amen.

DR. PERRY E. GRESHAM

Let us pray. God of all generations, be Thou our fixed star when the heavens are shaken and the earth is consumed by fire. We praise and honor Thee for both life and death. We thank Thee for the days of our lives when we know changing seasons and rose golden sunsets. We thank Thee with heavy hearts that night must fall reminding us that all men are mortal and that nothing abides —neither wealth nor power, nations nor institutions, people nor places.

We remember before Thee Benjamin Dwight Phillips whose long life links generation with generation and leaves a noble heritage which lives on in his children. We remember him for his quiet courage which assumed the awesome responsibilities of wealth and power. We honor his memory for his tireless efforts to fulfill the tasks that were set before him. We honor his strength which we regarded as indestructible. We remember his loyalty which refused to yield. He fulfilled the commandment to honor his father and mother and exemplified heritage to his children's children. His convictions were enormous. His generosity was an object of wonder.

We remember his love for the Church of Christ on earth. Etched in our memories is his determination to set right the errors which he felt had possessed the Restoration Movement. We remember his relentless efforts to defend the faith against all adversaries. His impatience with those who shared not his opinions derived from his devotion and loyalty to the faith once delivered to the saints.

Help us who walked with him in the fret and jar of life to cover his faults with the mantle of charity that we may honor him for what he was—diligent in business, formidable in controversy, fierce in loyalty, steadfast in his convictions.

We ask, O God, Thy blessing upon Grace, his wise and venerable sister; upon Mildred, bride of his golden years; upon Stella,

212

Clarinda, and Undine, his lovely daughters; upon Ben, Victor, and Don, his stalwart sons. Bless, O God, all of us who worked with him and who cherish his memory. May his noblest qualities live on in us.

In the name of Jesus Christ, our Lord, who has touched our fleeting years with immortality and has redeemed us from sin and destruction. Amen.

The Sermon Delivered by
DR. WILBUR A. REID

When Jesus met the funeral procession at the gate at the city of Nain, He stopped the funeral procession and brought back to life again the young man who was being carried forth for burial; and His message to the weeping mother was simple, "Weep not," he said. And the people who saw it exclaimed: "God hath visited his people" (Luke 7:13, 16).

If Mr. Phillips had been invited to visit the king of some important country, we would have rejoiced greatly and shared the joy which he would have in accepting such an invitation. Today he has been summoned into the courts of the King of kings, our Lord of lords.

I wonder if you knew that in addition to his being the president of the T. W. Phillips Gas and Oil Company, Mr. Phillips was also quite a student of the Bible. It was his custom to spend as much as two hours in the evening reading from the Bible. Recently he talked to me about a book that he was reading, *The Flood*. He had some comments about it, most of them very favorable. This morning, as I passed his favorite chair, I noticed a copy of this book lying on the stand beside it.

Now and then he would comment on my sermons. He would say to me: "You thought I was sleeping this morning, but I heard you." He was a careful student, always seeking more information from the Word of God.

Mildred told me this morning that after they would return from a long trip and retire at night, very frequently he would burst out —she would think he was asleep—he would just begin to pray and his prayer was a prayer of thanksgiving for the protection of the Lord, as they traveled, and giving thanks for their safe journey home.

213

One of the fine citizens of our community only yesterday spoke to me about his humility in making the generous contributions that he had made to many causes. Some of the contributions that were made to folk in this community are not known to the folk to whom he made them. They are known only to the ministers who served this congregation, and perhaps occasionally to members of his immediate family.

Every one of you here today could bring a personal testimony, if you were called upon to do it. I am the one who has been called upon to bring the message this afternoon. I could say more, but I want to confine the rest of my remarks to the Word of God, which Word he revered, studied, and searched, and to share with you some of the things that I think he would like to have shared on this occasion. If you were to bring a testimony this afternoon of what Mr. Phillips meant to you, it might be that you would recall some of the things in which you were not in agreement with each other; but you would respect him for his position, for his faith in Jesus Christ, for his faith in the position of the New Testament Church. He was a friend at large. If he believed in a cause, he would support it quickly. If he was not sure of the cause, he would quickly reject it. He loved the Church of Christ. He loved the institutions training men for the ministry of the church.

He's gone, yet he isn't gone, not as long as there are memories. I read from the twenty-third chapter of Numbers in the tenth verse of that chapter—a verse of Scripture which I think is helpful to us at a time like this and let me share it with you. It's a covetousness about which the Bible does not condemn us. Covetousness is condemned. It's forbidden in the Bible, but here is a sort of holy covetousness that is not forbidden: "Let me die the death of the righteous, and let my last end be like his!" And so this afternoon we have a perfect right, even as our brother had a perfect right, to covet love, to covet sympathy and wisdom and holiness and usefulness, and to "die the death of the righteous" and inherit eternal life.

As I think of this word "death," there isn't anything very pleasant about it for any of us here this afternoon, for no one of us on this side of eternity can see one redeeming feature about this word "death." It means separation to us, but I would like to ask you to look at it from a different point of view. Mr. Phillips lived beyond the threescore years and ten, even beyond the fourscore years. Many things could have happened to his body that would have made him miserable for many months or even years to come, but it didn't happen that way. Death came quickly to him and it came without suffering. He had his house in order. He had spoken to some of us about death, not that he was going to die last Wednesday night, not that he was going to die next week, but he was constantly aware of the possibility of death before too many years had passed. He stepped out into eternity without very much pain, at least. All of a sudden he was released from the limitations of his body of clay, and he stepped out into eternity.

We shrink from the idea of death, because our finite minds cannot understand the infinite mind of God; but out there is God and out there is Jesus Christ to welcome and to receive the redeemed ones who have been born into His Kingdom. Hear the Word of the Lord, as He spoke to His disciples on that occasion when He was about ready to depart from them, and He said to them: "Let not your heart be troubled: ye believe in God, believe also in me. In my Father's house are many mansions: if it were not so, I would have told you. I go to prepare a place for you. If I go and prepare a place for you, I will come again, and receive you unto myself; that where I am, there ye may be also." "I am the way," said He, "the truth, and the life: no one cometh unto the Father, but by me" (John 14:1-3, 6).

This brings me to say that the death of a righteous person is not to be compared with the death of a wicked person. With the wicked and the unbelieving death is the end of all Gospel opportunities, it is the farewell of all holy companionships and all opportunities. Loved ones in Christ can never be with the wicked unredeemed ones after death. To such as these death is a plunge over a precipice into the starless night of suffering and sorrow. But to the Christian, death is moving out into the eternal daylight of God where the Son of God is the light. And so we, who are Christians, cannot compare the death of a Christian loved one to the sad things of this earth.

As I was preparing to speak to you this afternoon, I couldn't help but bring into this message the words of Paul to a young son in the Gospel, Timothy. He said to him: "I am reminded of your sincere faith, a faith that dwelt first in your grandmother Lois, in your mother Eunice, and now I am sure dwells in you" (II Timothy 1:5 R.S.V.).

Mr. Phillips in my presence a number of times in the last two years or so had talked to me and he had talked to other friends and the family about his mother. He spoke of her with such genuine affection, such warmth and consideration. And all of you here this afternoon know something of his father, well known among all the brethren of the Restoration heritage. His book, *The Church of Christ*, went out at first anonymously. Later it became known that it was from the pen of T. W. Phillips, Sr. It has been made required reading for the students in many of our colleges. I am told that Mr. Phillips often would ask, as he contemplated an investment in some institution of Christian education, "Would my father or mother approve of this?" So, this faith that was in his father, and I am persuaded even in his grandfather and mother and grandmother, has come down to us through him this afternoon.

Thinking of death, I am certain that it does not take away the conscious being. Our spiritual parts are imperishable: "Dust thou art to dust returneth was not spoken of the soul." Jesus said: "Whosoever liveth and believeth in me shall never die" (John 11:26). Death then does not destroy us. We have this on the authority of Jesus Christ himself. Death only takes down the house in which we live: "For we know that if our earthly house of this tabernacle were dissolved, we have a building of God, an house not made with hands, eternal in the heavens" (II Corinthians 5:1). "So when this corruptible shall have put on incorruption, and this mortal shall have put on immortality, then shall be brought to pass the saying that is written: Death is swallowed up in victory" (I Corinthians 15:54).

We are confident this afternoon that, as Christians, we are sure of the Resurrection. Jesus assured us, saying: "I am the resurrection and the life. He that believeth on me, though he were dead, yet shall he live" (John 11:25). When God breathed into man the breath of life, man became a living soul, and that immortal soul shall live forever. Those who have done the will of God shall rejoice forever more. They shall live in the presence of the Lord. Those who have done evil shall arise, but to a resurrection of damnation. Death is the highway to the betterment of the Christian's estate. It is the gateway of life, the vestibule of heaven. Death is the soul's release from handicaps and limitations of life on the earth, and it opens the door to larger opportunities.

Paul, caught up into heaven, seemed to sense this and tried, I think, to say it to us, but he could not. There weren't words that were quite acceptable to use. There wasn't wisdom quite so that he could express it and reveal to us what he had seen there. Surely heaven must be like moving from the poorhouse into the king's palace. Death to the Christian is the last battle that is fought, before the victory and the crown are won. "Thanks be to God who giveth us the victory through our Lord Jesus Christ!" (I Corinthians 15:57).

Edward Payson said: "The battle is fought, the victory is won." Paul said: "I have fought a good fight, I have finished my course, I have kept the faith." And it seems to me that he must have leaned back and with confidence said: "and not to me only, but to all them also who have loved his appearing" (II Timothy 4:7, 8). This I reach out and grasp with confidence this afternoon, as my hope in Christ:

> Servant of God, well done,
> Thy glorious warfare past,
> The battle fought, the victory won,
> And thou art crowned at last!

Sometime ago one of our ministers lost a daughter. She was in the prime of her life and it was a blow to them, but a friend of theirs sent this note; and I pass it along to you, as I close this afternoon, quoting exactly as the note came to them. It says:

> "I am standing on the seashore. A ship at my side spreads her white sails to the morning breeze and starts for the blue ocean. She is an object of beauty and strength and I stand and watch her until at length she hangs like a speck of white cloud, just where the sea and the sky come down to mingle with each other. Then someone at my side says: 'There, she is gone!' Gone where? Gone away from my sight, that's all. She is just as large in the mast and hull and spar as she was when she left my side, and just as able to bear her load of living freight to the place of destination. Her diminished sight is in me, not in her, and just at the moment when someone at my side breathes, 'There, she is gone!' there are other

eyes watching her coming and other voices ready to take up the glad shout, 'There she comes!'"

"Weep not." .... "God has visited his people" (Luke 7:13, 16).

THE BENEDICTION

Let us pray. Our Eternal Father, we come this afternoon, reaching out to Thee in the darkness of this hour and in the uncertainty of all that is before us, reaching out to Thee with calm confidence and hope in Jesus Christ. Wilt Thou be our Companion just now, as we go from here to the silent city of the dead. Wilt Thou be the Strength of our lives, as we look through the mist of tears that clouds our eyes this day. Give us Thy Peace and Thy Companionship. And our Father, we ask a special blessing upon the bosom companion, who has stood by him these few years, upon each of the children and grandchildren, and upon each one of us, as we share the additional responsibility which we must share. As we reach out and carry on in Christ, may Thy Grace be sufficient for our needs. It is our prayer in Jesus' precious name. Amen.

BETHANY COLLEGE MEMORIAL SERVICE
October 28, 1968

WITNESS TO THE RESURRECTION

A SERVICE DEDICATED TO THE
GLORY OF GOD AND REMEMBERING
BENJAMIN DWIGHT PHILLIPS, SR.

OPENING SENTENCES
I am the resurrection and the life.

INVOCATION   Mr. Barton R. Updike
AND LORD'S PRAYER
    Chaplain of the College

THE PSALMS
Psalm 90
Psalm 121

THE NEW TESTAMENT
John 11:17-27
John 14:1-6
I Corinthians 15

REMEMBERING THE GIFTS   Mr. John J. Clopine
    Director of the Library

MEMORIAL ADDRESS   Dr. Perry E. Gresham
    President of the College

MEMORIAL PRAYER   Dr. Richard B. Kenney
    Associate Professor of Religion

BENEDICTION

MR. JOHN J. CLOPINE

To a librarian, it was only fitting and just that the first new academic building to be constructed at Bethany College during the current era should be a library. The T. W. Phillips Memorial Library is one of the most beautiful buildings in this country. The foresight and taste of Benjamin Dwight Phillips are shown in the location and design of this building. His devotion to his church is further emphasized by this chapel in which we are gathered this morning.

This great benefactor of Bethany College has built a living memorial on this campus. Not only is this library a storehouse for the wisdom of the past, but let us hope that it shall help to provide the necessary knowledge for future Bethanians.

Truly, no man is dead, who has used so much foresight in providing for the future.

DR. PERRY E. GRESHAM

We meet to remember Benjamin Dwight Phillips, scion of the Phillips Family, whose benefactions created this handsome library building which bears the name of his father and his brother. It was a deep autumn day when we said good-bye to him at Elm Court, his home, and at North Street Christian Church, his place of worship. Occasional snow flurries turning to rain on autumn leaves reminded us of summer past and harvest ended. Members of the Phillips Family were there from all over the world to express their respect, affection and sorrow.

B. D. Phillips was a remarkable industrialist and businessman. His intimate knowledge of every phase of the T. W. Phillips Gas and Oil Company of which he was president was without parallel in modern America. He was proud of the fact that he was able to supply his patrons with excellent service for very little money. He was shrewd in investments, loyal to his colleagues, and a paragon of financial integrity.

He knew how to play. He was an avid hunter and had considerable interest in baseball in which he excelled as a college student at Hiram. His stamp collection was one of the foremost in the nation. He was fiercely dedicated to the Restoration Movement. He believed in controversy and was a formidable opponent in conversational debate. He expected his colleagues of the Christian Church to be forceful in the presentation of doctrine and aggressive in promoting and defending their positions. He felt every man should take a stand.

His benefactions were truly wonderful and awe inspiring. Notable among them are T. W. Phillips Memorial Library, gifts toward Robert Richardson Hall of Science, and the restoration of historical landmarks at Brush Run Church and the baptismal site. He and his family built the handsome Disciples of Christ Historical Society building at Nashville, Tennessee.

His strong identification with his father, T. W. Phillips, Sr., who wrote *The Church of Christ* by a Layman, appears to have been a major motivation of his interest in and contributions toward the institutions that serve the Restoration Movement. He carried the awesome responsibility of wealth and power with humility and quiet dignity as did his parents before him, his siblings with him, and his children after him.

The death of B. D. Phillips marks the end of an era. The strong man in complete command of a vast enterprise is passing with the autumn leaves. Change in the world, in the church, and in his family and friends suggests another springtime.

We join this day in remembering a great, noble, strong, and controversial friend and benefactor whose memory will be long in this land and on this campus. Without his family this school would probably not have survived. With the help of him and his family it is the academic dream of Alexander Campbell exemplified.

DR. RICHARD B. KENNEY

O God, our Father, from whom we come, unto whom we return, and in whom we live and move and have our being, we praise Thy name for the gift of life, for its wonder and mystery, its interests and joys, its friendships and fellowships. We thank Thee for the ties that bind us one to another. We bless Thee for Thy loving and patient dealings with us, whereby Thou dost ever teach us Thy truth, by the varied experiences through which we pass, and for the meanings in life so often hidden from us.

This day especially we give Thee thanks for Thy servant Benjamin Phillips. We remember his steadfastness in the faith and the courage with which he held to his own personal convictions. We praise Thy name for the opportunities which he and his family have provided for us here at Bethany College. May we ever be worthy wisely to use what others have given us.

Our Father, we pray that Thou will renew ever within us the gifts of faith and love. Help us to walk amid the things of this world with eyes open to the beauty and glory of the eternal, that our hearts may always be fixed where true joys are to be found.

In the name of Christ our Saviour. Amen.

Resolutions

MILLIGAN COLLEGE
Benjamin Dwight Phillips

The Board of Trustees of Milligan College and the Advisory Board of Trustees being in joint session on this October 25, 1968, there was presented the following Resolution, prepared by Dr. James DeForest Murch, Dr. Robert W. Shaw, and Dr. Robert O. Fife.

RESOLUTION

WHEREAS, it has pleased Almighty God to call His servant, Mr. B. D. Phillips, of Butler, Pennsylvania, our trusted friend and beloved brother in the Gospel, to enter into his eternal reward on October 23, 1968.

The Board of Trustees and the Board of Advisers of Milligan College do express their profound regret and great sorrow in his passing, and express their deep sense of indebtedness to his nobleness, and his Christian witness, and their great loss in the passing of B. D. Phillips.

The Board of Trustees and Board of Advisers give thanks to our Heavenly Father for Mr. Phillips' years of fruitful service in the Phillips family tradition, first expressed by his revered father, T. W. Phillips, Sr.

We give our thanks also for Mr. Phillips' faithfulness to the Gospel of our Saviour, Jesus Christ, as recorded in the Scriptures.

We give thanks for Mr. Phillips' stewardship of the financial means committed to him by his Creator, for his sustained support in behalf of Christian education, and especially as expressed in Milligan College.

The two Boards desire to express their profound sympathy to his family, and our appreciation for his participation in Milligan College, and his great influence for noble Christian vocation in the lives of the students and graduates of Milligan College.

The Board of Trustees and the Board of Advisers resolve and pledge to keep the faith and trust which B. D. Phillips' purposeful Christian life of faith and stewardship exemplified, and which he greatly committed of his time and talents to Milligan College.

Copies of this Resolution shall be transmitted to Mildred Phillips and to the family of Mr. B. D. Phillips by Dr. Johnson, President,

225

and Robert E. Banks, Secretary of the Board of Trustees, and a copy shall be placed in the permanent minutes of both Boards.

The foregoing Resolution having been presented to the Board of Trustees and the Board of Advisers, was upon motion by Robert E. Banks, seconded by Wade Patrick, unanimously adopted this October 25, 1968.

Jess W. Johnson
President of Milligan College

Robert E. Banks
Secretary of the Board of Trustees

DISCIPLES OF CHRIST HISTORICAL SOCIETY

Benjamin Dwight Phillips

MEMORIAL RESOLUTION

By action of the Executive Committee of the Disciples of Christ Historical Society taken in Saint Louis, Missouri, November 13, 1968.

The Executive Committee of the Board of Trustees of the Disciples of Christ Historical Society pauses in this moment of sorrow at the passing of Benjamin Dwight Phillips to express deep sympathy to Mrs. Phillips and to the immediate family. It is for us, as for his many friends, associates and acquaintances, a time of regret. Since he was older than we, he has always been present and active in our work as in many other Christian philanthropic endeavors since we can remember.

Yet, for us, as we hope for those nearest and dearest to him, the regret turns easily to rejoicing that we have had the privilege of knowing him and working with him to accomplish one particular project and to bring one dream to realization.

We shall always remember how Mr. Phillips almost literally picked up the shovel, the trowel and the hammer where his brother, Thomas W. Phillips, Jr., had laid them down at his death, and how diligently he worked to ready our magnificent Phillips Memorial for dedication day. In order to give the Brotherhood and the city of Nashville a building of outstanding architectural design, he spared no expense, to the extent that he added

226

several hundred thousand dollars of his personal funds to those previously allocated.

Mr. Phillips was concerned about the service the Disciples of Christ Historical Society renders and the use it makes of the Phillips Memorial which houses it. His concern was not for an historical museum to the past but for a place the present and future generations might come to, to find the witness of the past. His last generous contribution to the program of the Society was to underwrite the heavy expense of a professional index of the *Christian Standard*. This work, when completed, will serve as a permanent reminder that Mr. Phillips wanted us to have every tool possible for the operation of this Brotherhood research center.

Like all of us, Mr. Phillips was pained by the divisions within the Brotherhood. He had his favorite theological and ecclesiological positions and "took sides," just as all of us do. So far as the Society is concerned he had one interest—he wanted this place and these materials to be available always for persons of all persuasions in the brotherhood. This is exactly our position.

To this end we pledge ourselves to take whatever steps we deem necessary for the preservation of the Society and for enlarging its holdings and its services. And we believe no more fitting sign of our appreciation for his life and work among us can be made than to keep our stacks open for materials and our doors open to all who would use them and learn their lessons.

BUTLER Y.M.C.A.

Benjamin Dwight Phillips

A RESOLUTION

WHEREAS: God in His Infinite Wisdom has removed from our midst our fellow citizen and co-worker, Mr. Benjamin D. Phillips, Sr., and

WHEREAS: Mr. Phillips was an outstanding citizen and an influence for good in this community and beyond; and

WHEREAS: Mr. Phillips used his time, many talents, and possessions for the upbuilding of the educational and cultural improvements of colleges and other worthy institutions over a wide area of our country; and

227

WHEREAS: Mr. Phillips served faithfully and well on the Board of Directors and the Board of Trustees of the Butler Y.M.C.A. in which capacity his wisdom and guidance were of inestimable value:

THEREFORE: Be it resolved that we, the Board of Directors of the Butler Y.M.C.A. acknowledge the constructive help and service Mr. Phillips has rendered to the growth and progress of the Butler Y.M.C.A. and the loss sustained by his sudden death; and

THAT Memorial tributes be paid to his memory by individual gifts to the Y.M.C.A. Building Fund, the General Fund, or the Endowment Fund in accordance with previously adopted Board action and established policy; and

THAT this resolution be made a part of the permanent minutes and records of the Board of Directors of the Butler Y.M.C.A., and a copy of this resolution be sent to the bereaved family.

Adopted unanimously by the Board of Directors of the Butler Y.M.C.A. in regular meeting—November 1968.

Loyal R. Mitchell
President

George A. Braun
Secretary

THE CITIZENS NATIONAL BANK
OF NEW CASTLE
Benjamin Dwight Phillips

RESOLUTION

It is fitting that our Board of Directors record in its minutes our feeling of sorrow and loss in the death of our fellow director, Benjamin D. Phillips, on October 23, 1968, at his home in Butler, Pennsylvania.

Mr. Phillips was the son of Thomas W. Phillips, one of the organizers and the first president of our bank, so it was most natural that Mr. Phillips would become at an early age in 1915 a director in our institution. He continuously served as such director until his death, a period of 53 years.

During that period he gave generously of his time and experience in furthering the interests of the bank. Mr. Phillips had broad and active business associations, yet he was one of the most regular attendants at directors' meetings and we who observed him closely somehow had the feeling that The Citizens National Bank was one of his very special interests. We would hardly classify him as a perfectionist, yet he was keenly interested and aware of small items of business income and expense which go to building a profitable operation. On the other hand, in policy decisions which involved a special knowledge of the local New Castle situation, Mr. Phillips often said that he deferred to and would be guided by the judgment of his fellow New Castle directors. Without attempting to detail his other business activities and his philanthropic interests, we pay tribute to a very fine friend.

We will miss Mr. Phillips in our meetings and our personal associations.

Certified from the minutes of the Board of Directors of The Citizens National Bank of New Castle at its meeting held November 13, 1968.

William D. Coban
Secretary to the Board of Directors

Tributes

TRIBUTE DINNER
BENJAMIN DWIGHT PHILLIPS
FRIENDSHIP HALL
PEPPERDINE COLLEGE
LOS ANGELES, CALIFORNIA

April 19, 1969

Some two hundred leaders in the life of the Christian Churches and Churches of Christ of southern California, invited by the officials of Pepperdine College, gathered on this occasion to hear the following program and witness the presentation of a bas-relief plaque to the Phillips Family:

Master of Ceremonies ....Dr. William S. Banowsky
Executive Vice President

Invocation ....Dr. J. P. Sanders
Dean of the College

Dinner

Pepperdine Chorus ....Norman B. Hatch
Director
    "If We Believe That Jesus Died"
    "The Lord's Prayer"
    "Good Tidings to the Meek"

Address ....Dr. James DeForest Murch
    "B. D. Phillips—Indomitable Advocate of the
      Restoration of New Testament Christianity"

Tribute ....Dr. M. Norvel Young
President

Response ....Mr. Rolland L. Ehrman

Benediction ....Dr. Kenneth Stewart
President
Pacific Christian College

233

CHRISTIAN STANDARD
Edwin V. Hayden, Editor

RESTORATIONIST

The death of B. D. Phillips, Sr., of Butler, Pennsylvania, on Wednesday evening, October 23, removes from our present scene one of the most knowledgeable and enthusiastic restorationists we have ever known. The business world knew him as president of the T. W. Phillips Gas and Oil Company, with substantial interests in various other enterprises; but among readers of *Christian Standard* he will be remembered for his vigorous promotion and generous support of the movement to restore New Testament Christianity, its doctrine, its ordinances, and its fruits.

Born at New Castle, Pennsylvania, eighty-two years ago, Benjamin Dwight Phillips was the son of T. W. Phillips, Sr., who was himself perhaps best known among our readers as the "layman" who wrote the widely read book, *The Church of Christ.* The Phillips home was the scene of the December 22, 1865, meeting of seven men to lay plans for the beginning of *Christian Standard.* B. D. Phillips never faltered in his admiration for these men and their notable colleagues and successors among churches of Christ and Christian churches. More importantly, he retained a lifelong zeal for the cause they promoted. An avid reader in the fields of biography, history, and doctrine, he knew why he believed as he did.

B. D. Phillips backed up his beliefs with his personal and financial resources—and both of these were considerable. His principal interests outside the local church were in colleges established to prepare ministers in the Restoration Movement. A prolific writer of forceful and forthright letters, he expressed himself with vigorous logic, always to the purpose that present and future generations should not be allowed to forget the men and the Movement that meant so much to him. His older brother, T. W. Phillips, Jr., established the T. W. Phillips, Jr., Charitable Trust, through which, along with Mr. Phillips' personal donations, he made substantial gifts to many institutions.

There was a large and lasting quality about the Phillips gifts, which most often took the form of substantial buildings for institutions that had already proved their worth. The Phillips Memorial Library, housing the Disciples of Christ Historical Society at Nashville, Tennessee, is a notable example. Another is the sanctuary of the North Street Christian Church in Butler, Pennsylvania, which he and T. W. Phillips, Jr., built in memory of their father.

Especially in the later years, Mr. Phillips became acutely aware that men and institutions do not always continue in their original courses. He therefore sought to diversify his educational, as well as his business interests, seeking always those investments that gave best promise of remaining true to the cause he loved. The campuses of Bethany College, Milligan College, Johnson Bible College, Lincoln Christian College, the Cincinnati Bible Seminary, Ozark Bible College, Manhattan Bible College, Minnesota Bible College, Pacific Christian College, and the Mountain Mission School at Grundy, Virginia, bear notable marks of his generosity in recent years. . . .

Close to his heart were his home and family in and around Butler, Pennsylvania. On his last day he was at work in his office downtown, then visited his sister, Grace (Phillips) Johnson in New Castle, where he became ill and returned to his Elm Court home for a light supper and a few minutes with the daily paper. He lay down to rest on a couch on the sun porch where he and Mrs. Phillips were accustomed to spend hours in reading and conversation, and died almost immediately.

Memorial services were conducted Saturday, October 26, at the Butler North Street Church where he served as a trustee. Mrs. (Mildred Welshimer) Phillips survives, as do his three sons and three daughters, twenty-two grandchildren, and eight great-grandchildren. The sons—B. D., Jr., Donald, and Victor—live at Butler, as does one of the daughters, Mrs. Rolland Ehrman. The other daughters—Mrs. Frank Weigand and Mrs. Joseph Sprankle —are in nearby Pittsburgh.

In B. D. Phillips we found a latter-day Nathanael, "an Israelite indeed, in whom is no guile!" His passing removes a strong link with the past. We could wish most fervently that all who have benefited from his faith, his friendship, and his provision might employ that inheritance as faithfully as he employed what he accepted so gladly from his fathers in the Restoration.

THE LOOKOUT

Jay Sheffield, *Editor*

A FRIEND OF CHRISTIAN EDUCATION

B. D. Phillips' life ended as it was lived—in orderliness and confidence. After having visited his sister, Grace Phillips Johnson, in New Castle, Pennsylvania, he returned to his beloved home, Elm Court, in Butler, Pennsylvania, Wednesday evening, October 23, where he fell asleep quietly and peacefully.

In the passing of Benjamin Dwight Phillips, Christian educators and institutions of Christian education have lost a faithful friend. In the business world he was recognized as the president of the T. W. Phillips Gas and Oil Company, with substantial interests in many other enterprises. But on Christian College campuses across the nation he will be remembered for his genuine interest in and generous support of Christian education. The campuses of Bethany College, Milligan College, Johnson Bible College, Lincoln Christian College, The Cincinnati Bible Seminary, Ozark Bible College, Manhattan Bible College, Minnesota Bible College, Pacific Christian College, and Mountain Mission School at Grundy, Virginia, are among the schools that were recipients of his generous gifts. Other institutions are Phillips Memorial Library, housing the Disciples of Christ Historical Society, Nashville, Tennessee, and the sanctuary of the North Street Christian Church in Butler, Pennsylvania, which he and T. W. Phillips, Jr., built in memory of their father. His benefactions were truly wonderful and awe-inspiring.

This publication felt a close kinship to B. D. Phillips, not only because of his interest in Christian education, but also because of his relationship to the family of P. H. Welshimer, long-time writer of our weekly Bible-school lesson. His wife, Mildred Welshimer Phillips, survives, as do his three sons and three daughters, twenty-two grandchildren, and eight great-grandchildren. The P. H. Welshimer Memorial Library on the campus of Milligan College will be a lasting reminder of the friendship of two great men— B. D. Phillips and P. H. Welshimer.

B. D. Phillips' life was long, whether it is measured in terms of years or in terms of service. "He has gone—like the sun that drops behind the western hills on a quiet autumn evening when the light lingers, as if loath to go, and bathes with life-giving qualities the things of earth." So he has gone behind the western hills, but the light lingers, a benediction to all who knew and loved him.

THE CHRISTIAN

Howard E. Short, *Editor*

PHILANTHROPIST BACKED HIS BELIEFS

Benjamin Dwight Phillips, Sr., 82, died suddenly at his home in Butler, Pennsylvania, October 23, after an afternoon visit with his sister, Mrs. Grace Phillips Johnson in New Castle, Pennsylvania.

A trustee of North Street Christian Church in Butler, Mr. Phillips was a member of the Phillips family which has played a large part in the history of the Christian Church over a century. He was well known as a church philanthropist.

He was president of the T. W. Phillips Gas and Oil Company in Butler.

A memorial service for Mr. Phillips was held October 26 at North Street Church. Wilbur A. Reid, Sr., minister, delivered the message. He was assisted by Wilfred Lown, president of Manhattan Bible College; Perry E. Gresham, president of Bethany College; and Phillips Weigand, a grandson of Mr. Phillips.

He was the son of the late T. W. Phillips, Sr.

B. D. Phillips, Sr., was an avid reader of biography, history, and church doctrine.

He backed his beliefs with large gifts of money, most of which went to institutions of higher education. Among these were a library at Bethany College, Campbell Hall at Culver-Stockton College, the Thomas W. Phillips Memorial building of the Disciples of Christ Historical Society, the P. H. Welshimer Memorial Library at Milligan College and, in recent years, substantial gifts to several independent Bible colleges.

In another memorial service held at Bethany College in the chapel which Mr. Phillips helped to build, President Gresham said:

"The death of B. D. Phillips marks the end of an era. The strong man in complete command of a vast enterprise is passing with the autumn leaves. Change in the world, in the church, and in his family and friends suggests another springtime. We join this day in remembering a great, noble, strong, and controversial friend and benefactor whose memory will be long in this land and on this campus."

Mr. Phillips is survived by his widow, Mrs. Mildred Welshimer Phillips; three daughters, Mrs. Rolland Ehrman of Butler, and Mrs. Frank Weigand and Mrs. Joseph Sprankle, both of Pittsburgh, Pennsylvania; and three sons, B. D. Phillips, Jr., Donald, and Victor Phillips, all of Butler.

TWENTIETH CENTURY CHRISTIAN
William S. Banowsky, *Associate Editor*

B. D. PHILLIPS—A LEADER IN
THE RESTORATION MOVEMENT

One of the truly important families in the history of the American Restoration Movement is the remarkable Phillips family of Pennsylvania. A few months ago that family lost its most vital leader of this generation, Benjamin Dwight Phillips, Sr.

B. D. Phillips was the son of T. W. Phillips, Sr., and the key to understanding the faith and vision of the son is to know the distinctive life of the father. T. W. Phillips, Sr. (1835-1912) was a highly successful Christian businessman. Along with his three brothers, he built, by the 1880's, one of the largest independent oil producing companies in the United States. A close personal friend of James A. Garfield, T. W. Phillips was the originator of *The Campaign Text Book* which greatly assisted in Garfield's election as President in 1881. In 1892, T. W. himself was elected to the United States Congress where he served with special distinction. He was responsible for the bill which ultimately created the Industrial Commission of America.

The first interest of T. W. Phillips' life, however, was a burning zeal to restore New Testament Christianity—its faith and its fruits. He was the "layman" who almost a century ago wrote one of the classic books of the American Restoration Movement, *The Church of Christ*. Throughout his lifetime the profits from his business interests were used for philanthropy—to build churches,

238

endow colleges, help the poor, and to support preachers and teachers. When they were still young and Bible-centered, Bethany College in West Virginia, Hiram College in Ohio, and Phillips University in Oklahoma especially benefited from T. W. Phillips' generosity.

B. D. Phillips followed very closely in his illustrious father's footsteps. He was born in New Castle, Pennsylvania, November 20, 1895. His mother was Pamphila (Hardman) Phillips. With his older brother, T. W. Phillips, Jr., who also served as a United States congressman, B. D. was active in the formation of the T. W. Phillips Gas and Oil Company. In the Pennsylvania business and financial community he was known as the president of the firm.

But to those who knew him well, Mr. Phillips was a resolute but kind, decisive but warm, human being whose first commitment was to God and the Scriptures.

A man of unusual energy and intellectual vitality, B. D. Phillips held deep religious convictions. He read constantly in the fields of history, biography, and religion. He knew what he believed—and why. One of his deepest beliefs was that Christ's church on earth is undenominational and indivisible, and that all believers should be drawn into it by taking the Scriptures as their only guide. Following in his family's tradition, he added to his faith the works of philanthropy, and generously supporting the causes and institutions which embodied the ideals to which he was committed. He had a passion for quality—for doing things right —and this passion was displayed in the Phillips' gifts, which usually took the form of substantial buildings for institutions of higher learning that had already proved their worth.

He was the largest single contributor to the drive to construct a Church of Christ building in New York City because he could see the need of penetrating the great metropolitan centers of the world. He also contributed the funds for the Phillips Memorial Library which houses the important Disciples of Christ Historical Society at Nashville. In recent years he made substantial investments for capital expansion at eleven Bible colleges. His concern for quality led him to take a keen personal interest in the architectural and constructional developments of the buildings he sponsored. He wanted anything he participated in to be well done.

Mr. Phillips is survived by three daughters, Mrs. Rolland Ehrman of Butler, Pennsylvania, and Mrs. Frank Weigand and Mrs. Joseph Sprankle, both of Pittsburgh; by three sons, B. D., Jr., Victor, and Donald, all of Butler; and by his widow, Mildred Welshimer Phillips. Daughter of the nationally-known preacher, P. H. Welshimer, and sister of the respected poet-essayist, Helen Welshimer, Mrs. Phillips has herself achieved a distinguished reputation in the field of education, lecturing and writing. A graduate of Hiram College, she was for sixteen years Dean of Women at Milligan College, Tennessee. Her published works include *The Young People's Bible Teacher and Leader* and *Special Addresses.*

In the passing of Benjamin Dwight Phillips, the Restoration Movement has lost a vigorous advocate. His life was long and full, whether measured in terms of years or service. "He has gone —like the sun that drops behind the western hills on a quiet autumn evening when the light lingers, as if loath to go, and bathes with life-giving qualities the things of earth." He has gone —but being dead, he yet speaketh!

SALUTE TO B. D. PHILLIPS

Dean Everest Walker, *Chancellor of Milligan College*

"B. D." is a "Milligan Immortal."

Brusk and kind. Sharp and considerate both in tongue and in heart. Bold and cautious. Visionary and practical. Strategist and tactician. Impatient and meticulous. Proud and humble. Simple in intricacy. Fiercely competitive. Humanitarian.

He put great confidence in Milligan. He believed in our concept of Christian Education—the intelligent fusion of all data from all sources: revelatory, humane, scientific. He found a program to his liking. He supported it generously—but as an investment in young people, not as shim nor as self-monument. He was pleased with recognition but embarrassed by it. The work. The achievement. This was the important thing.

Shortly after coming to the College, I told him about our vision of educational support for the ideal of being Christian with no party ties or theological labels. Replying to his questions, I told him of the financial crisis which might very well force our clos-

240

ing. He said nothing. A few weeks later he made a gift. It bought recuperating time.

He watched keenly the long struggle to come to vital strength. And, encouraged us. He asked the penetrating central questions. Not only financial questions! How were we creating a service for our churches? What qualifications should distinguish the faculty of a Christian college? What makes a college Christian? Who would support such a college? How could a ministry be educated to serve churches free of ecclesiastical control but responsible in their stewardship of faith and fellowship? With scrupulous care I answered only in terms of Milligan. After a bit he did not invite me to compare our programs with those of others. Our "competition" was with sectionalism, particularism, secularism, indifferentism—all the "isms" and "ists."

Gradually ideals emerged toward realization. He was there to help. The P. H. Welshimer Memorial Library, an architectural and structural gem, arose from his generosity. More progress. Later, the Memorial Chapel—high spired simplicity in design and symbol of the New Testament Faith. He knew practicality and beauty could be one. . . .

Milligan recognizes both the honor and the trust of his inclusion of the College among his chief concerns—his family, his employees, his business, his city, his church, and the educational agencies of the churches: the T. W. Phillips Library, the many colleges, the rising Emmanuel School of Religion. No family has done more for Christian education in New Testament terms than the Phillips family. B. D. represented the long tradition. He asked no more than efficient and discerning advocacy, frankly stated, in behalf of the Church as revealed in the Word of God and delivered to us in the New Testament; Milligan can do no less than to accept in grateful humility the trust so given.

We extend our prayerful sympathy to his family, whom we deeply love—choice people in faith and life.

B. D. Phillips was a rare man. Among Milligan's immortals, perhaps singular. Yet, one of us all, in the Family of God in Christ.

241

B. D. PHILLIPS

Lewis A. Foster, *Dean, Graduate School Cincinnati Bible Seminary*

He was young in mind, with a firm step and a penetrating vision. The Lord seemed to save his finest hours for those years beyond the normally allotted three score and ten. Never was he more generous, never was he more determined in his stand for God's truth, never was he more anxious for the preservation of Restoration principles, never was he more abreast of the affairs of the nation, never was he more keen in the matters of business, and never was he more interested in the needs and potential of each individual—than he was even to that final evening, Wednesday, October 23, 1968, when the Lord called him home. Married to the daughter of his lifelong friend, P. H. Welshimer, he enjoyed contentment and genuine companionship in this period of life. This was the union of two famous names in the Restoration Movement when on July 11, 1963, B. D. Phillips married Mildred Welshimer. Here was a devoted couple who shared each other's interests and declined any extensive engagements which would keep them apart. They were together the evening of his death. He simply folded his newspaper and laid it aside, put down his glasses, and lay down on the couch for a nap; but the Lord had greater things in store. As in every stage of his life, he included careful, thoughtful planning, so B. D. Phillips had prepared for death. Not in a morose frame of mind, but with deep faith and trust in Jesus, he kept his life in tune and his affairs in order that when the time came, he would be ready. He had not expected this moment so soon, but if ever a man had made provision, putting the work of the Lord high on his list, it was B. D. Phillips.

To list his contributions to the cause of Christ and the Restoration Movement in particular, would be impossible. The majority of his gifts were not known to the public. Moreover, his contributions were far more than material grants. His advice, his challenge to all-out effort, his quick assessment of each situation, his insistence upon good planning, honest procedure and far-sightedness—all these were of inestimable value to the causes he supported. As long as there is a Restoration Movement, B. D. Phillips will be remembered as one of its greatest benefactors.

His heritage placed great demands upon his life. Born into a home where his father, T. W. Phillips, was outstanding as oil producer, congressman, religious writer, and philanthropist, this son, Benjamin Dwight, grew up in the shadow of greatness. His father in his seventieth year (1905) published one of the outstanding works of the Restoration Movement, *The Church of Christ*, printed in fifteen editions, translated into Hindi, Japanese, and Chinese. His brother, Thomas W. Phillips, Jr., followed the father in equally varied interests, but when much of his effort was engaged in politics, B. D. succeeded to the leadership in the industrial holdings of the family. To his death he was president of the Phillips Gas and Oil Company. His brother preceded him in death in 1956, but his sister, Mrs. Grace Phillips Johnson, still resides in the home city of New Castle, Pennsylvania. B. D. had just visited his sister the afternoon of his death. Family ties were exceedingly strong among the Phillipses. One did not need to converse long with B. D. Phillips before realizing the depth of admiration in which this son held his father and how he set him forth as example and challenge to the end of his days.

With like admiration his own family gathered along with many hundreds to give honor to the passing of this great man. The heart of Butler was jammed with traffic the eve before the funeral; over two hundred were graciously received at his home following the funeral. He leaves three daughters and three sons: Stella (Mrs. Rolland Ehrman) of Butler; Clarinda (Mrs. Joseph F. Sprankle, Jr.) and Undine (Mrs. Frank Weigand) of Pittsburgh; B. D. Phillips, Jr., Victor K. Phillips, and Donald C. Phillips, all of Butler. Acting as honorary pallbearers at the funeral were representatives of the Bible Colleges and institutions of learning associated with the Restoration Movement. This was a thoughtful reminder of the high esteem in which B. D. Phillips held faithful educational foundations. On the other hand, these institutions will be forever indebted to this one who has contributed so much to their cause.

The grandson, Phillips Weigand, speaking for the family, struck the note at the funeral which seemed closest to the heart of B. D. Phillips. His greatest concern, affirmed the grandson, was for the salvation of souls—of his family, of his loved ones, of men and women everywhere. In working for this goal, B. D. Phillips has

243

left his mark and will continue to witness as truly one of the great among God's people.

EMMANUEL SCHOOL OF RELIGION

Like his father before him (Mr. T. W. Phillips, Sr., author of *The Church of Christ*, By a Layman), B. D. Phillips loved the Church and was committed to the historic plea of "unity through restoration." He was not one to compromise this conviction and generously gave to those who he believed were seeking to be loyal to this historic plea. In this day when so many are seeking to gain the applause of the crowd, it was like a breath of fresh air to visit with this man who refused to alter his faith to fit each changing fancy.

When one visited Mr. Phillips, the subject sooner or later came around to Christ and His Church and those institutions seeking to advance the Kingdom of God. He was not one who wanted his own name perpetuated in stone or marble or brick, but he will live for years enshrined in the hearts of those of us who knew him and held him in the highest regard.

We of Emmanuel School of Religion wish to extend our deepest sympathy to his bereaved family. His wise counsel will be missed not only by them, but by each of us. We who have been the recipients of his generosity can best honor him by perpetuating in ourselves a depth of faith in the living God and a warm love for the Church of King Jesus our Lord.

JOHNSON BIBLE COLLEGE

Mr. Benjamin D. Phillips, Sr., passed to his eternal reward October 23. Wilbur Reid, Sr., his minister, had talked to him on the phone at about 7:30 P.M. He had read the evening paper, laid his glasses on the desk, hung his coat on the chair, and lain down on the couch. By 8:00 P.M. he was dead.

Mr. Phillips was a friend of Johnson Bible College. He had made contributions to the school from time to time. His largest contribution was made when the new library was erected. He was a strong advocate of the Restoration Movement, and he backed his beliefs with his personal energy and his financial resources.

244

Mr. Phillips was keenly interested in each member of his family. He had a wonderful relationship with Mildred Welshimer Phillips, his wife. Besides Mildred are his daughters, Mrs. Rolland (Stella) Ehrman, Mrs. Joseph (Clarinda) Sprankle, and Mrs. Frank (Undine) Weigand, and sons, B. D. Phillips, Jr., Victor, and Donald. He is also survived by a sister, Mrs. Grace Phillips Johnson, twenty-two grandchildren and eight great-grandchildren.

Mr. Phillips was a member of the North Street Christian Church in Butler, Pennsylvania, where he served as a trustee. Memorial services were from the church sanctuary on October 26 with the minister, Wilbur Reid, Sr., in charge. Sharing in the service were Dr. Wilfred Lown, President of Manhattan Bible College; Phillips Weigand, a grandson, and Dr. Perry Gresham, President of Bethany College. Burial was in North Cemetery in Butler.

KENTUCKY CHRISTIAN COLLEGE

"If any man seeks greatness," once said Horace Mann, "let him forget greatness and ask for the truth, and he will find both." With the recent passing of B. D. Phillips of Butler, Pennsylvania, we reason again that here was such a man.

His long years were joined to a glowing heritage of witnessing for Truth through the cause and venture of the Restoration Movement. Like his illustrious father, T. W. Phillips, he was diligent in his defense of the fundamental tenets of New Testament Christianity as upheld by Christian Churches and Churches of Christ. His continuing concern for the preaching of the Gospel was reflected in his generosity to colleges producing Christian leadership.

Death came to Mr. Phillips at his Elm Court home in Butler on Wednesday evening, October 23, after a sudden illness occurring earlier in the day. Memorial services were held in the North Street Christian Church, with the minister, Wilbur A. Reid, delivering the principal message.

Bible College representatives served as honorary pallbearers. Attending the memorial services from KCC were Lester E. Pifer, Jack M. Bliffen, and Trustee Art Poll. Our sincerest sympathy is extended to Mrs. Mildred Welshimer Phillips and the bereaved family.

LINCOLN CHRISTIAN COLLEGE

Mr. B. D. Phillips, beloved, honored, and admired by Christians of all walks of life, died suddenly Wednesday evening, October 23, 1968. Born 83 years ago the son of Mr. and Mrs. T. W. Phillips, Mr. B. D. Phillips carried on the business started by his father and continued to advance the faith his parents believed and lived. This faith is shown in the lives of his six children and, as was so vividly expressed by Mr. Phillips Weigand, his grandson, at the funeral, continues in his grandchildren.

Dignified yet simple funeral services in charge of Brother Wilbur Reid were held Saturday afternoon in the Butler church. Mr. Phillips leaves to mourn his passing Mrs. Mildred Welshimer Phillips, who made his later life very happy, his three daughters and three sons, his sister, his grandchildren, and a great multitude of friends.

God has blessed this family with great wealth. Yet, money has value only to the Phillips Family when it is used to honor God and His church. Mr. B. D. Phillips has given millions of dollars to advance the growth and development of New Testament Christianity.

Lincoln Christian College owes much of its strength to the help given by the Phillips family. Restoration Hall, which houses the graduate school, and the chapel soon to be built were made possible by the gifts of this family.

We have never known a man more interested in the advancement of the New Testament church, nor do we believe there is a person of this generation who has done more for the cause of Christ. He fought for the faith. He encouraged those who dared to obey God and he insisted men give their best to the Master. He placed his wealth in the hands of God and prayerfully used his money where he thought he could get the greatest return for God.

Fitting memorial services for Mr. B. D. Phillips were held during the chapel hour, November 12. Mr. James Emerson, who with President Hargrove attended the funeral, told our students about Mr. Phillips' death and funeral. President Hargrove told the students about his life, his faith, and his hopes for God's people. Dean Dowling prayed God's blessings upon his loved ones.

246

PACIFIC CHRISTIAN COLLEGE

B. D. Phillips impressed us as a man of humility. There was obviously strength there with incisiveness and deep conviction, but never did we sense arrogance, pride, or haughtiness.

His understanding of the plea of the Restoration Movement intrigued us, as did his continuing interest. And, he wanted this movement shared. We shall never forget his reaction to seeing framed quotations from Thomas and Alexander Campbell in the main hallway of the college. Two or three times he seemed drawn to return to them to re-read them. He liked their being where they could be seen. He loved this Movement. The reminiscences he shared with us in chapel were most meaningful because of obvious love and dedication.

His contributions of material wealth supported his profession. His vital concern for the Movement was backed by liberal benefactions—especially to our colleges. Who among us has given so much?

Friendliness, conviction, intelligent understanding of the Restoration Movement, and a positive demonstration that he took these things seriously—this is the heritage he left. Surely our people, and especially the colleges and institutions he assisted, can repay this man only by a faithful continuance in the way of the Christ he loved and served. We salute this gracious friend, Brother B. D. Phillips. We pray God's rich blessings upon his beloved companion and confidante of recent years, Mildred Welshimer Phillips, and others of his family.

PHILLIPS UNIVERSITY

B. D. Phillips, the last surviving son of Thomas W. Phillips, Sr., whose foresight and financial support made possible the founding of Phillips University, died in Butler, Pennsylvania, on October 23, 1968. A major benefactor of many Christian colleges and universities, Mr. Phillips made the initial gift of $325,000 to build the Zollars Memorial Library, the first capital project of Phase 1 of "Growth with Quality."

He was a brilliant businessman and a dedicated churchman. As president of the T. W. Phillips Gas and Oil Company, he saw the company achieve excellence in service and efficiency. In memory of his father, he and his family provided the Disciples of Christ Historical Society building in Nashville, Tennessee.

Mr. Phillips is survived by his widow, Mrs. Mildred Welshimer Phillips; three sons, B. D., Jr., Victor K., and Donald C.; three daughters, Mrs. Frank Weigand, Mrs. Rolland Ehrman, and Mrs. Joseph Sprankle; and a sister, Mrs. Grace Phillips Johnson.

LINCOLN CHRISTIAN COLLEGE
Benjamin Dwight Phillips

(A Citation presented to Mr. Phillips by Dean Charles E. Mills on the occasion of the dedication of Restoration Hall)

A child in a household aglow with the genial warmth of Christian faith and love, you have kept aflame in your own life the fires of Christian devotion. Scion of a distinguished family of Christian philanthropists, you have ever been sensitive and responsive to the needs of the Kingdom of God.

A son in a home that was alive to the need for Christian enterprise, where the needs of colleges, evangelists, and students were given sympathetic assistance, and, indeed, under the shelter of whose roof the *Christian Standard* magazine was set afoot, you have perpetuated and augmented this noble tradition of giving nurture to worthy Christian undertakings. Heir to a lineage of astuteness in business, you, like those before you, have brought the fruitage of that acumen to the service of the cause of Christ.

We pay tribute to your stature as a Christian parent. Heir to a notable heritage embracing many Christians of noble stature, you have reared six children, all of whom are active in Christian works.

We pay tribute to your faith, your love for faithful Biblical Preaching, and your concern for the progress of that preaching, all of which are evinced by your decisive gifts to institutions of Christian higher education.

We pay tribute to your passion for the restoration of New Testament order to the Church. Prompted by the noble example of your father, you have, by all the means at your disposal, made your own praiseworthy record of painstaking encouragement of an adequate and effective leadership for the movement which seeks the accomplishment of that objective.

We pay tribute to you for your encouragement of so many institutions of Christian higher education in a day when the winds of secularism have cooled the ardor of many philanthropic souls and turned their beneficence into temporal channels.

We pay tribute to your deep sense of Christian hospitality, the warmth of which has been enjoyed by a host of those who have been granted large portions of your time and genial courtesy of your household.

We pay tribute to your humility. Though your munificence may well have brought you laudatory acclaim, you have been prompted to remain in the background of your many notable deeds of beneficence without desire for plaudit and praise.

We pay tribute to you as a great Christian soul, dedicated, consecrated, and mightily used of God in His Kingdom's work.

On Behalf of the Trustees, Faculty,
and Friends of Lincoln Christian College

A Favorite Hymn of B. D. Phillips

IN THE HOUR OF TRIAL

In the hour of trial,
Jesus plead for me;
Lest by base denial
I depart from Thee;
When Thou see'st me waver,
With a look recall,
Nor, for fear or favor,
Suffer me to fall.

With forbidden pleasures
Should this vain world charm,
Or its sordid treasures
Spread to work me harm,
Bring to my remembrance
Sad Gethsemane,
Or in darker semblance,
Cross-crowned Calvary.

Should life's journey send me
Sorrow, toil and woe;
Or should pain attend me
On my path below;
Grant that I may never
Fail Thy hand to see;
Grant that I may ever
Cast my care on Thee

When my spirit yearneth
For relief from pain,
When my dust returneth
To the dust again;
On Thy truth relying
Thro' that mortal strife,
Jesus, take me, dying,
To eternal life.

—*James Montgomery*

251

INDEX

Acme Natural Gas Company, 54.

Adams, Hampton, 152.

Albert, Frank, 92.

Anderson Natural Gas Company, 53, 54.

Andover Theological Seminary, 3.

Anti-trust Legislation, 42.

Apostasy, 42.

Armco Steel Corporation, 53.

Athletic Club, Pittsburgh, 61, 74.

Atlanta Declaration, The, 171.

Banks, Robert E., 226.

Banowsky, William S., 92, 233, 238, 239, 240.

Barnes, Bill L., 137.

Baseball, 21, 59, 60, 61.

Basketball, 21, 59.

Bates, Miner Lee, 118.

Bethany College, 13, 97, 98, 102, 124-129, 219-222.

Bell, Robert M., 92, 171, 195.

Bible College Movement, 195, 196.

Bible, The Holy, 8, 9, 13, 14, 26, 27, 28, 82, 83, 98, 100, 193.

Black, Jeremiah S., 19.

Boatman, Don Earl, 91, 198.

Boatman, Gail (Mrs. Don Earl), 92.

Braun, George A., 228.

Brooks, Phillips, 4.

Brelos, Carl, 91.

British Columbia, 62-66.

Brown, Kenneth I., 118.

Brush Run Church, 104, 221.

Burns, Robert W., 171.

Butler County Memorial Hospital, 55.

Butler, Pennsylvania, 23, 47, 52, 53, 54, 55, 75, 78, 79, 82, 84, 89, 227.

Butler University, 136, 185.

Campbell, Alexander, 7, 9, 32, 97, 98, 100, 102, 103, 104, 106, 159, 160, 192.

Campbell Institute, 121, 122, 167.

Campbell, Thomas, 7, 32, 113, 184, 190, 192.

Camp Shiloh, 181.

Carpenter, Paul, 92.

Charitable Trusts, 55, 105, 133, 134, 178, 200.

Christian Churches/Churches of Christ, 173, 184, 189, 193, 199.

Christian Board of Publication, 135.

Christian Evangelist, 135, 164, 165.

Christian Publishing Association, 12.

Christian Standard, 12, 18, 42, 114, 115, 123, 173, 202, 227, 234, 235, 249.

Christian Theological Seminary, 136, 137.

Christian University, 13, 106.

Churches of Christ (non-instrumental), 91, 108, 145, 161, 173, 178-182.

Church of Christ, The, 13, 14, 32-39, 169, 216, 243.

Cincinnati Bible Seminary, 116, 197, 198, 242, 243.

Citizens National Bank, 202, 228, 229.

Cleveland, Grover, 20.

Coat-of-Arms, Phillips, 85.

Coban, William D., 229.

Coffman, Burton, 91, 179.

College of the Bible, 122, 123.

Committee for the Preservation of the Brotherhood, 168.

Compton, Kenneth R., 109, 112.

Conant, Anna Undine (Phillips), 78.

Cook, Gaines M., 164.

Cowden, William F., 16, 18, 140.

Crosby, Bing, 60.

Culver-Stockton College, 13, 106, 138, 139.

Dampier, Joseph, 92.

Davidson, Clinton, 91, 178-181.

Davis, Harold E., 168.

Declaration and Address, 190.

Derthick, Henry J., 184, 185.

Derthick, Lawrence G., 114.

Disciples of Christ Historical Society, 106-115, 173-178, 226, 227.

Dowdy, Barton A., 140-144.

Drake University, 13.

Duquesne Club, Pittsburgh, 74.

Ecumenicity, Modern, 162-164, 165, 171, 178.

Education, Higher Christian, 97-102, 184-187.

Ehrman, Rolland L., 54, 55, 58, 81, 89, 115, 168, 171, 202.

Ehrman, Stella (Phillips), 78, 81, 82, 89, 212, 239, 243, 245, 248.

Elm Court, 84-92.

253

254

Oil Industry, 9, 10, 22, 46.
Oklahoma Christian University, 39, 104.
Oliver, George T., 19.
Olympic Games, 21.
Open Membership, 122, 133, 139, 148, 152-155.
Osborn, Ronald E., 113, 137.
Ozark Bible College, 116, 198.
Owen, George Earle, 153, 154.

Pacific Christian College, 116, 199, 233, 247.
Panel of Scholars, 137, 158, 167.
Park Avenue Christian Church, 180.
Pennsylvania Christian Missionary Society, 155-158.
Pennsylvania Investment and Real Estate Corporation, 50, 51.
Pepperdine College, 199.
Perry, Woodrow, 91, 197.
Phillips, Anna Undine Conant, 78, 89.
Phillips, B. D., Addresses, 189, 190, 192; Administrator, 48, 49, 51, 54, 55; Athlete, 21, 22, 59; Banker, 202, 228; Bible Student, 26, 76, 95; Bibliophile, 72, 73; Birth, 15; Boyhood, 15-20; Builder, 84-88, 106-115; Business Career, 45-56; Business Philosophy, 32, 44, 45, 48, 49, 55, 56, 81, 93; Clubs, 74, 75; Collector, 70-72, 73; Community Concerns, 49, 50, 55; Competitor, 53, 54; Conversion, 17; Death, 203, 205-246; Defender of the Faith, 117-178; Dog Fancier, 80; Education, 16, 19, 20, 25-44; Family Gatherings, 83; Father, 25-44, 77-83, 92-94; Favorite Hymn, 251; Gentility, 43; Higher Education, Philosophy of, 39, 98-101, 146, 185, 188; Humility, 57, 101; Hunter, 61-70; Marriages, 77, 78, 90; Memorial Services, 209-222; Naturalist, 58, 72, 84, 87, 88; Patriotism, 58, 81, 93; Philanthropy, 43, 54, 55, 102, 103, 106-115, 133, 175, 179, 181, 188, 190, 197, 198, 199; Philatelist, 70-72; Politics, 18, 19; Social Philosophy, 32, 48, 49, 81; Sports, 59-61; Stewardship, 49, 55, 102-116, 200; Theological Views, 32-39, 93, 94, 116; Tributes to, 223-250; Versatility, 57-76.

Phillips, B. D., Jr., 55, 62-66, 78, 81, 82, 213, 240, 243, 245, 248.
Phillips Bible Institute, 40, 197.
Phillips Brothers, 9, 10.
Phillips, Clarinda Grace (Johnson), 7, 46.
Phillips, Clarinda (Sprankle), 78, 82.
Phillips, Donald, 78, 82, 213, 240, 243, 245, 248.
Phillips, Ephriam, 6, 7.
Phillips Exeter Academy, 3.
Phillips Gas Company, The, 46, 47.
Phillips, George, 2, 3.
Phillips, Greta (Mrs. T. W., Jr.), 55.
Phillips, Herbert C., 46.
Phillips, Mildred Welshimer, 90, 91, 173, 175, 196, 199, 201, 203, 212, 225, 235, 240, 243, 245, 247, 248.
Phillips, Pamphilia, 7, 17, 46, 105.
Phillips Petroleum Company, 46.
Phillips, Stella (Ehrman), 78, 81, 82, 89.
Phillips, Thomas W., Banker, 228; Bible Student, 8, 9, 13, 14, 26, 27, 32-39; Birth, 7; Business Career, 9, 10, 26, 46, 47; Congressional Years, 11, 12, 26-32; Conversion, 8; Church Relationships, 8, 12, 13, 17, 18; Death, 7; Education, 8; Family, 7, 25; Gentility, 43; Honesty, 42; Industrial Leadership, 11, 28, 29, 30, 41, 42; Labor Relations, 28, 29, 30, 31; Literary Attainments, 12, 13, 14, 32-39, 213; Marriages, 7; Memorials, 40, 102, 106-115, 221; Philanthropy, 13, 39, 40, 43; Political Career, 10, 11, 18, 19; Political Ideals, 27-32; Preacher, 8, 9, 13; Social Concerns, 13, 14, 30; Theological Views, 32-39; Youth, 8, 9.
Phillips, Thomas W., Jr., 1, 7, 14, 46, 47, 48, 50, 51, 54, 89, 102, 104, 105, 108, 115, 134, 161, 181, 243.
Phillips University, 13, 39, 104, 105, 106, 129-135, 163, 247.
Phillips, Undine (Weigand), 78, 82.
Phillips, Victor K. (I), 7, 46.
Phillips, Victor K. (II), 63, 64, 78, 79, 80, 81, 82, 213, 240, 243, 245, 248.
Phillips, Wendell, 4.
Pittsburgh Athletic Company, 60.
Pittsburgh Baseball Company, 60.

255

256

DUCIT AMOR PATRIÆ

Phillips